Waldemar Zacharasiewicz & Herta Nagl-Docekal (Eds.)

ÖSTERREICHISCHE AKADEMIE DER WISSENSCHAFTEN
PHILOSOPHISCH-HISTORISCHE KLASSE
SITZUNGSBERICHTE, 906. BAND

Waldemar Zacharasiewicz & Herta Nagl-Docekal (Eds.)

TRANSATLANTIC ELECTIVE AFFINITIES

Traveling Ideas and Their Mediators

VERLAG DER
ÖSTERREICHISCHEN
AKADEMIE DER
WISSENSCHAFTEN

This publication was subject to international and anonymous peer review. Peer review is an essential part of the Austrian Academy of Sciences Press evaluation process. Before any book can be accepted for publication, it is assessed by international specialists and ultimately must be approved by the Austrian Academy of Sciences Publication Committee.

The paper used in this publication is DIN EN ISO 9706 certified and meets the requirements for permanent archiving of written cultural property.

ISBN 978-3-7001-8504-8

Coverdesign: Bernd Ganser-Lion
Print: Prime Rate, Budapest
https://epub.oeaw.ac.at/8504-8
https://verlag.oeaw.ac.at
Made in Europe

Table of Contents

Acknowledgements

The present volume is primarily based on an international workshop on "Traveling Ideas and their Mediators" that was convened in June 2018 by "The North Atlantic Triangle" commission of the Austrian Academy of Sciences, in which scholars from several disciplines on both sides of the Atlantic participated. It continued the lively discussion on the exchange of ideas across the Atlantic, which in the nineteenth century was fostered by a growing sense, among scholars in the US and Canada, of elective affinity with Central European culture and of sharing scholarly and scientific interests and projects.

Joint efforts to meet major challenges in the modern world persisted in the twentieth century, despite major conflicts and dramatic confrontations resulting in estrangement from earlier affinities and leading to new alliances in the political sphere. Historians investigate how new conflicts gave rise to transatlantic social movements, which tried to prevent the nuclear build-up in the Cold War from resulting in an apocalypse. The twentieth century also saw the fertilization of philosophical thinking by the reciprocal adoption of key ideas from overseas, which was facilitated, for instance, by the establishment of international academic societies. Significantly, prominent American philosophers inspired new scholarly approaches in Austrian academic work such as film philosophy, while Ludwig Wittgenstein's thinking fostered the elaboration of sophisticated approaches by Canadian scholars in the same discipline. Analyses by experts from the field of philosophy of these influences which bring about a new elective affinity supplement the presentation of earlier interconnections discussed at the workshop.

The Austrian Academy of Sciences provided the necessary funds which permitted the invitation of scholars from abroad and the preparation of this publication.

The task of formatting and proofreading the manuscripts was undertaken by graduate students, especially by Anna Zalto and Theresa Flotz, which is here gratefully acknowledged. The index to this publication was also prepared by Anna Zalto.

WALDEMAR ZACHARASIEWICZ & HERTA NAGL-DOCEKAL

Introduction

The current collection is the latest contribution to a large-scale project in which the members of the interdisciplinary North Atlantic Triangle Commission of the Austrian Academy of Sciences have since its foundation in 2012 continued their scholarly engagement with the transatlantic exchange of people, ideas and commodities. They have initiated projects with the intention of jointly addressing the complex issues of these phenomena and have convened six international conferences and symposia. Together with other scholars from both sides of the Atlantic they have analyzed many aspects of the social and cultural exchange across the Atlantic in the nineteenth and twentieth centuries. The insights gained through individual research and interdisciplinary discussions were included in a number of collections of essays and a monograph published by the Austrian Academy of Sciences Press, which contain the fruits of these joint efforts and focus attention on aspects of the long-standing ties across the Atlantic previously insufficiently explored.

The demographic changes resulting from the movement of large numbers of people seeking a new home in the New World from the late eighteenth century onwards until the restrictions introduced in the 1920s in the number of immigrants to be admitted to the USA, and the flight of persecuted Jews and many members of opposition groups from Europe who tried to find shelter and a safe haven there in the 1930s and 1940s, offered abundant material for historians, sociologists and literary and cultural scholars in the commission. Together with their international colleagues who participated in the several conferences mentioned above they have analyzed the numerous encounters between individuals crossing borders on both sides of the Atlantic, and have considered the experiences of those immersing themselves in the societies they encountered in their transatlantic destinations (cf. *Riding/Writing Across Borders in North American Travelogues and Fiction*, published in the period of gestation of the commission in 2011, and *Narratives of Encounters in the North Atlantic Triangle*, published in 2015). The scholars also discussed the movement of many descendants of earlier immigrants to North America eager to return to the countries of origin of their ancestors, and thus considered the journeys of thousands of Americans who in the tradition of the 'grand tour' were keen to visit the shrines of culture in the Old World.

In collaboration with their peers from many countries the members of the commission also moved beyond the well-trodden paths taken by many experts in the field of exile studies, and seventy years after the end of Nazism and Fascism initiated a timely debate on the insufficiently researched return of a minority among the refugees to their countries of origin, where they were willing and ready to help rebuild science, scholarship, and the cultural scene after their destruction by the Nazis and Fascists (see *Return from Exile: Exiles, Returnees and their Impact in the Humanities and Social Sciences in Austria and Central Europe*, 2017). The pertinent investigations for this project, which considered the difficulties the returnees encountered in their former home countries, the bureaucratic hurdles they had to overcome, involved no fewer than twenty-eight experts from ten disciplines in the humanities and social sciences. Economists, political scientists, musicologists and art historians joined the core disciplines of the commission, namely literature and history, sociology and philosophy, in the inquiry into this still under-researched sphere, thus attempting to fill a significant gap in the knowledge of the impact of these returnees to Central Europe.

The preconditions for the – at least temporary – success of many refugees from Central Europe to achieve integration in the USA, despite the restrictions on the admission of immigrants adopted in the 1920s in the quota laws, were also investigated and presented in work conducted and published in the context of the commission. The extended networks which had come into being in Vienna and Austria in the interwar years, when many American authors visited the former capital of the Dual Monarchy and a dozen foreign correspondents working for US American newspapers and news agencies established close friendships with many members of Vienna's society, often with individuals of Jewish background, were later of singular importance for the refugees from Austria after the *Anschluss*. Austrian émigré writers and scholars, as well as many Viennese physicians, who despite major economic problems after the end of the Dual Monarchy had managed to continue and preserve the reputation of Vienna as a Mecca of medicine, were able to call upon their American friends and acquaintances from the preceding years. That literally hundreds of American doctors had every year attended special courses arranged for them by the American Medical Association of Vienna was of primary importance when the refugees urgently needed affidavits for admission to the USA and also had to secure suitable jobs there. A monograph representing these close relationships, entitled *Transatlantic Networks and the Perception and Representation of Vienna and Austria between the 1920s and the 1950s*, published in 2018, also benefitted from the interaction within the commission and the debates with the peers at its various conferences.

Apart from the movement of individuals and groups across the Atlantic the commission has also investigated the transfer of ideas. About thirty scholars, from literary and cultural disciplines, from the fields of philosophy and art history, law and sociology dealt at a conference in December 2016 with the reciprocal influences through the mediation of significant ideas, and demonstrated how in a number of cases such a transfer provided inspiration on the other side of the Atlantic in the twentieth century. The essays corroborated the hypothesis that the various stimuli absorbed by scholars and scientists were often dependent on the migration of their peers, whose journeys across the Atlantic were either prompted by individual desire or by the vicissitudes of life and the political developments in Europe. An awareness of this complex process led to a consideration of major mediators of ideas, who through their significant roles consolidated the ties between the two hemispheres. (Cf. *Ideas Crossing the Atlantic: Theories, Normative Conceptions, and Cultural Images*, published in 2019).

The current collection, which is based on an international symposium convened in June 2018, takes this investigation into the shared Atlantic history further, and opens with a scrutiny of the transfer of important ideas in the nineteenth century. It sketches several phases in the development of elective affinities between the academic cultures on both sides of the Atlantic. While several papers in this collection provide evidence for the keen interest of North American scholars and scientists in the nineteenth century in the progress made by their European counterparts in the humanities and natural sciences, and in the adoption of professional standards and procedures, the collection in its second part also delves deeper into complex twentieth-century phenomena in the political sphere which have not yet received sufficient attention as far as their significance for the transatlantic context is concerned. The interdisciplinary character of the commission's work warrants such a contribution to the necessary broader debate. The inquiry into the interconnections in the realm of shared ideas also accords space in the third part of this volume to an examination of the impact of European philosophers on their North American peers, a profitable endeavor as part of a wide-ranging discussion of the transatlantic ties and interconnections. The book thus includes also an analysis of the discourses in North America which the engagement and confrontation with European modes of philosophical thinking inspired.

The awareness of nineteenth-century American college graduates and their teachers of the pioneer role of European scholarship prompted a 'pilgrimage,' the 'grand tour' of North American graduates in many disciplines, especially the humanities and medicine, to continental Europe, in particular to the hitherto neglected regions of Central Europe. The systematic adoption of professional practices, for instance, in the reformed North German universities (Göttingen and Berlin) and the regular inclusion of residence there by young Americans eager to devote themselves to research and academic teaching, was accompanied by an awareness of deeper links to the scholars they encountered in those seats of learning, which permits the application of the concept of "elective affinities." This perception had first been expressed in early reports on the impressive achievements of German universities "north of the Mayne" round about 1830.[1]

This contact eventually prompted the imitation of the German seminar system, with the intimate involvement of graduates in the research work of their academic teachers.

The essay by *Waldemar Zacharasiewicz* sketches this process from its inception after the Napoleonic Wars and focuses on several of the chief mediators in the first generation in the aftermath of the wars, the so-called 'Literary Pioneers,' primarily from New England (George Ticknor, Joseph Green Cogswell and others), but also from the South, especially from South Carolina, until the Civil War. Many of them later served as influential university teachers, as college presidents and senior diplomats who cherished their memories of their transatlantic experience. The essay also considers the respect paid around the middle of the nineteenth century

[1] See Henry E. Dwight, *Travels in the North of Germany in the Years 1825 and 1826*, New York: Carvill, 1829, which includes the telling phrase: "The northern Germans resemble us much more than any other nation on the continent. Like us they are Protestants, and they show in their conversation that depth of feeling, which naturally arises from a religion addressed equally to the intellect and the heart." (170)

to the German 'gymnasium' and the German educational system generally (see reports by Horace Mann and others), and touches upon the decision of individuals and their families to benefit from the highly regarded schools there (see John Ross Browne) despite some angry criticisms by defenders of the American system against "outlandish innovations." Such conservative reservations also delayed the reform of the American college system until graduate education was introduced at Johns Hopkins in the 1870s. The essay also illustrates the role of college presidents as mediators, such as James Hampton Kirkland (originally from South Carolina) and G. Stanley Hall, who on the basis of their transatlantic experiences embraced the German academic model for tertiary education, which for more than a dozen years served as a blueprint for reformers. The article also shows how funds made available by philanthropic millionaires then boosted American institutions, providing a firm base for the enhancement of academic work, which through the new availability of Rhodes scholarships in England saw a reorientation towards universities in the former mother country. The deteriorating climate in political relations with the German Empire before and after 1900 undermined the formerly close academic ties until the outbreak of World War I with its fierce propaganda campaigns against the "Huns," and the following restrictions in academic freedom went hand in hand with the disappearance of the German educational model in American culture.

In the course of the nineteenth century the formerly neglected or even despised academic institutions in the south of German-speaking countries similarly gradually gained a better reputation: the medical institutions of Vienna had by about 1840 achieved a new status and won great respect, as is evident in the praise William Wilde, an Irish ophthalmologist (who was Oscar Wilde's father), expressed in his assessment of Vienna in 1843.[2] The strict organization of the General Hospital and the systematic dissection of corpses initiated there by Carl von Rokitansky and his collaboration with highly competent internists such as Josef Skoda had apparently significantly improved the diagnosis and the treatment of many illnesses. This appeared to Wilde and to later cohorts of American medical graduates to represent a true model for progressive medicine, which it seemed advisable to use as a blueprint for the re-organization of hospitals

[2] See his book *Austria. Its Literary, Scientific, and Medical Institutions*, Dublin, 1843.

in North America. As a result, as the essay by *Carmen Birkle* on the 'medical grand tour' documents, this conviction shifted the preferred destination of American medical students from Paris to Vienna and to Berlin. In Paris, Oliver Wendell Holmes had spent two years learning from leading French physicians, and he later passed on his knowledge of 'French therapeutics' (and his own use of dialogues in medical practice) to generations of his own students at Harvard.[3]

Long before the establishment of the American Medical Association of Vienna in 1904 regulated the admission and further training of American physicians, many members of this profession received special instruction in Vienna from the leading doctors: as the documentation for the preceding five decades is relatively sparse, several letters containing high praise for the Viennese medical school and its various special clinics – underlining the shift from Paris to Vienna – are considered in the essay by Carmen Birkle, which, while it includes some critical comments on certain practices in obstetrics, fills this gap in historical knowledge.[4]

The foundation of the AMA of Vienna formalized this practice and attracted hundreds of American physicians to Vienna annually – altogether 10,000 anglophone practitioners of medicine, mainly from the USA, registered with the AMA in Vienna between 1904 and 1938 – despite some criticism by advocates of medical training in the USA. The sojourners were primarily men but increasingly also pioneers of the medical education of women. Birkle's essay revisits the obstacles female doctors experienced in North America but also in Central Europe, though foreign women had a better chance to be admitted, and shows which hurdles they had to overcome until well into the twentieth century, despite the fact that some of them benefitted from the mentorship of the prominent Canadian physician and later Regius Professor of Medicine at Oxford, William Osler. His career and reminiscences in Birkle's essay provide further ample evidence for the greatly appreciated benefits of having access to advanced medical practice in Vienna and Berlin.

Another significant tie and major avenue of reciprocal influence across the Atlantic is explored by *Christoph Irmscher*, who brings his expertise

---

[3] There similar improvements had been made and Rudolf Virchow's important discoveries increased its reputation as a leading medical institution.

[4] Cf. the claim by Th. N. Bonner that in the second half of the nineteenth century no fewer than 10,000 graduates in medicine spent at least some time attending such courses in Vienna.

in the analysis of natural history writing in the eighteenth to twentieth centuries to bear on his article on the evolution of the thoughts and research experiences of a distinguished Viennese biologist: Franz Steindachner. This important mediator between the continents spent three years in close association with the prominent if controversial Swiss-born Harvard Professor of Natural History Louis Agassiz.[5] The devoted Viennese scientist, who was to serve for more than twenty years – until old age – as the director of the Natural History Museum in Vienna (1898-1919), after having worked for the institution for almost forty years before as an assistant and then curator, was recruited in 1870 for his remarkable skills and dedication as a connoisseur of fish and reptiles for Agassiz's museum in Cambridge, Massachusetts. He also joined Agassiz on expeditions to South America and to the Galapagos Islands. Irmscher's essay on Steindachner's transatlantic experiences as an associate of Agassiz for more than three years draws extensively on his correspondence with the latter, which is kept at the Houghton Library. It also capitalizes on the lively private letters sent by Steindachner to his sister Nettie and to friends in Vienna, which are held at the museum he later directed there. They reflect the lifelong bachelor's devotion and hard scientific work but also his sensitivity to the beauties of nature and his enthusiasm for the fish and reptiles he observed and collected. They also mirror his gradual disenchantment with his superior at Harvard, while the private impressions of Agassiz's second wife and fellow biologist reveal the evolution of respect and increasing sympathy for the quiet Viennese worker with his inquisitive mind. Her notes hint at the potential for an elective affinity between Steindachner and Elizabeth Cary Agassiz, but not with her ideologically conservative husband. He appreciated his Viennese associate rather as a "workhorse" to conserve the immense quantity of specimens retrieved from the expeditions and for his cataloguing skills, from which Steindachner was to benefit during his time as curator and later director at his museum in Vienna.

The close cooperation and interaction in scholarly and scientific matters and the adoption in North America of the Central European model and its methods in the second half of the nineteenth century declined as a result of the rapid professionalization of North American academic

[5] Irmscher has published a monograph on this opponent of Charles Darwin's evolution theory: *Louis Agassiz: Creator of American Science*, Boston: Houghton Mifflin Harcourt, 2013.

institutions and with the development of closer American ties to Britain through the Rhodes scholarship program. The outbreak of World War I then caused a dramatic rupture in the free exchange of ideas across the Atlantic.[6] The general suspicion towards hyphenated Americans, even when they were citizens born in the USA, radically diminished the appeal of any ideas crossing the Ocean and led to the dismissal of real or potential mediators from academic positions in America. Conversely, the development of modern trends in US society met with criticism in Europe, where "Americanism" emerged as a negatively connoted phenomenon soon after 1900. The erstwhile distinct readiness to stress the similarities across the North Atlantic and shared ideas was replaced by skepticism in American society, which was increasingly ready for isolationism following the disappointments in and after World War I. The emergence of the USA as a world power and its necessary support for Europe also inverted the primary direction of influence. It also led to new alignments and temporary alliances.[7]

One such link is analyzed by *Tibor Frank* in his assessment of the perception and representation of Soviet Russia by Ambassador Joseph Edward Davies, the second incumbent in this position after the establishment of diplomatic relations between the USA and the Soviet Union in the mid-1930s. That Hungary continued in the interwar years to be regarded – more than other successor states of the Dual Monarchy – as an important part of Central Europe, closely linked to its neighbor Austria, is apparent in the frequent coverage of Hungarian news by journalists stationed in Vienna. Its position as an integral part of the western transatlantic exchange merits the inclusion of this phase in Soviet - American relations in the study of transatlantic elective affinities. Frank tries to account for the seeming blindness and false perceptions of this close friend of President F. D. Roosevelt's, whose official reports,

---

[6] See W. Zacharasiewicz's volume *Images of Germany in American Literature*, Iowa City: U of Iowa P, 2007, esp. 77-89.

[7] The establishment of close links between the USA and Central Europe after World War II, which included the sponsorship of cultural and academic ties and the emergence of new "elective affinities," is a complex phenomenon which will be dealt with in a forthcoming collection of essays based on an international conference on "Cultural Politics and Propaganda: Mediated Narratives and Images in Austrian-American Relations." It was convened in Vienna in March 2019.

correspondence and bestselling book *Mission to Moscow* reflect his favorably biased view so different from the anti-communist attitude of his predecessor. His comments mirror an excessively naïve rendition of the 'successes' of the transformation of the Soviet economy and society, and reveal his egregious errors in commenting on Stalin's brutal measures and purges, including the liquidation of opponents and suspected 'traitors' in the party and the military. Frank's analysis of Davies' book and the large corpus of other documents shows how Davies' skewed assessment differed significantly from the rational judgement of his diplomatic associates, similarly observant of the effects of Stalin's paranoia. It poses the question for the deeper reasons for Davies' seeming (emotional) affinity to the Soviet dictator, which through his ties to Roosevelt strengthened the alliance between the USA and the Soviets in a crucial era of the War with Nazi Germany and even until the onset of the Cold War.

From the complex and diverse phenomena during the roughly forty years of this latter era mirrored in transatlantic exchanges this collection of essays has selected intellectual and political movements which tried to ensure that nuclear weapons, which had first been used to hasten the end of World War II in the Pacific, would not be employed.

In his essay *Philipp Gassert* surveys the development of opposition to the nuclear threat posed by the arms race during the decades of the Cold War. He sketches the contribution of individual politicians, scientists and scholars to the emergence and rise of transatlantic social movements from the early 1950s through the 1980s united by their fear of a nuclear Armageddon. The unwillingness of former Vice President Henry A. Wallace in the USA to accept a permanent rift in Soviet-American relations in the post-war era and the reluctance of the early advocates of a détente such as Walter Lippmann parallels the initial support of such stances by labor unions and Social Democrats in Western Europe. Gassert relates the initiatives of Bertrand Russell and the Pugwash Movement and describes the emergence of Peace and Conflict Studies as a scholarly discipline following Theodore Lentz's *Towards a Science of Peace* (1955) and their institutionalization both in the USA and in Europe (Britain, Norway). The essay stresses their increasing politicization (vide Johan Galtung) and deals with the treatment of the nuclear threat in popular culture in those decades. Tracing the "return of apocalypse" and the growth of mass movements linked to the controversial NATO Dual Track Decision in the 1980s, Gassert underlines the globalization of a transatlantic alliance in resistance to the overwhelming risk of a nuclear catastrophe resulting from the arms race.

Gertrude Postl emphasizes the crucial role of international academic societies as mediators of transatlantic intellectual exchanges. The case study she introduces is the International Association for Philosophy and Literature (IAPL), founded in 1976 by Hugh L. Silverman, philosophy professor at SUNY Stony Brook. Postl maintains that this society has contributed significantly to the evolvement of "continental postmodernisms in the USA and Canada." Explaining the initial concern of this innovative process, she cites the aim of challenging the dominance of analytic philosophy that had marked the Anglo-American philosophical discourse since World War II. IAPL participated, she argues, in "promoting an opening of what it means to do philosophy by 'importing' European thinkers and theories into the mainstream academic discourse of North America" – a transfer that first focused on phenomenology and hermeneutics. It is important to note, however, Postl adds, that "continental European philosophy underwent a transformation in the process of its transition from Europe to North America." Therefore, the term "continental philosophy" has come to commonly refer to "a distinctly US – and Canadian – enterprise." In this transformed version, "continental philosophy, a term virtually unknown within the European philosophical scene," was finally "(re)introduced to Europe as a typically North American way of responding to and working with the European tradition" – a process that IAPL sought to facilitate by the topics and speakers selected for its international conferences, and by holding these conferences in a number of European countries.

Explaining one outstanding feature of the transformation that took place on American soil, Postl discusses the impact of French "postmodernist" approaches. She highlights that "the term 'postmodernism' has never been limited to a strictly philosophical discourse," as authors such as Jacques Derrida, Michel Foucault, Jean-François Lyotard, Jean Baudrillard, Julia Kristeva, Luce Irigaray and Hélène Cixous "situated traditional philosophical questions within the context of […] literature, art, music, film, media, politics, or culture at large." American continental philosophy, Postl recounts, has engaged in transferring French postmodernisms across the Atlantic, and has embraced a mode of thinking that is based on interdisciplinary encounters ever since. Accordingly, "[o]ne of the founding premises of IAPL was that literature is philosophical and that, vice versa, philosophy always has literary qualities."[8]

Interdisciplinarity also constitutes a central feature in the essay by *Ludwig Nagl* on the connections between philosophy, psychoanalysis and film theory in the work of Stanley Cavell (1926-2018), Harvard's internationally renowned "Professor of Aesthetics and the General Theory of Value." Exploring the ways in which the Wittgenstein-inspired thinking of Stanley Cavell transgresses the received school boundaries of contemporary philosophical discourse, Nagl first provides some biographical annotations. He refers, in particular, to Cavell's numerous journeys to Vienna, Austria, where he lectured, *inter alia*, at the Department of Psychoanalysis of the University of Vienna, in the Wittgenstein House, in the Votiv Kino, and in the Theater Museum (where his topic was "Opera in [and as] film"). Nagl also elucidates the personal background of these frequent journeys to Austria, addressing the long-standing friendship between Cavell and Kurt Rudolf Fischer, who had – after his flight from the Nazis to Shanghai – studied philosophy in Berkeley, California, where he first met Cavell, and who later on returned to Austria to teach at the University of Vienna.[9]

The main segments of Nagl's essay introduce core ideas of Cavell's film philosophy, focusing on his reading of the cinematic genre, which he named "the Melodrama of the Unknown Woman." Intellectual relations between America and Austria are brought to light again here, since Cavell analyzes this genre with reference to Stefan Zweig's novella *Brief einer Unbekannten*, as well as to Max Ophüls's cinematic rendering of Zweig's text in his film *Letter from an Unknown Woman*. Nagl's essay provides an in-depth account of Cavell's approach, highlighting the way in which Wittgenstein's concept of "language games" is appropriated in connection

[8] Postl refers here to Silverman's in-depth analysis of this development in: Ludwig Nagl and Hugh L. Silverman (eds): *Textualität der Philosophie. Philosophie und Literatur*, Vienna: Oldenbourg, 1994.

[9] For a more detailed study of Kurt Rudolf Fischer's biography and academic importance see: Ludwig Nagl, "Some Reflections on how the Remigrant K. R. Fischer Influenced Vienna's Academic Discourses," in: Waldemar Zacharasiewicz and Manfred Prisching (eds.), *Return from Exile – Rückkehr aus dem Exil. Exiles, Returnees and their Impact in the Humanities and Social Sciences in Austria and Central Europe*, Vienna: Austrian Academy of Sciences P, 2017, 347-62.

with the claim to read Freud, differently from Freud himself, in a philosophical mode. Regarding the "melodramatic" genre, Nagl explains that Cavell presents it as the negative inversion of another genre that he extensively analyzes, the "Hollywood remarriage comedies." In both cases, he shows, "different ways of focusing on 'transcendence'" are emerging. The final part of the essay suggests, however, that "the 'robust secularism' of Cavell's film analyses" seems to be marked by limits, as it fails to take adequately into consideration "the long history of philosophical re-readings of religion after Hegel."

The following essay, written by the Canadian philosopher *Steven Burns,* also illustrates that the work of Ludwig Wittgenstein proved most relevant for intellectual innovations based on transatlantic encounters. Burns focuses on a British philosopher, born in the same year as Stanley Cavell: Peter Winch (1926-1997), who taught at the University of London, before moving to the University of Illinois at Urbana-Champaign in the US. Burns emphasizes the great influence Winch had on several generations of young philosophers from Canada, including the author of the essay and his Dalhousie colleague, Lynette Reid, co-editor of Winch's forthcoming *Nachlass* and of a collection of papers on Winch's continued legacy. Raising the question: "What were the ideas that Winch took from Europe to America and then back again?", Burns draws specific attention to a paper Winch wrote for the XIVth German Congress of Philosophy, held in Giessen in 1987. As Burns explains, Winch seeks to resolve the well-known problem "whether it is possible to derive value claims from a set of facts," elaborating his argument with references to seemingly diverse theories, such as Ludwig Wittgenstein's reflections, in *Philosophical Investigations*, on "the learning of pain-language," Simone Weil's concept of "that interval of hesitation, wherein lies all our consideration for our brothers in humanity," as presented in her essay "The Iliad or the Poem of Force," and Socrates' debate with Polus and Callicles in Plato's *Gorgias*.

Burns reads "the question of the ethical equivalence of the Good and the Evil" as providing the key to Winch's approach. Reconstructing Winch's mode of proceeding, he begins with "the 'firstness' of primitive reactions" that we consider as something similar in all human beings. However, he goes on to note, "Winch insists that common primitive reactions do not necessitate common value judgments," and suggests shifting attention to another element of our "natural history," namely to the fact that we "make moral demands on one another." Against this backdrop, Winch lays out his main point, which Burns summarizes as follows: That we impose moral demands on one another "is also a primitive reaction, and it makes the development of a moral form of life possible." The specific feature of this moral form of life is that it "supports both agreement and disagreement in judgments within it. But we agree in form of life." Thus, we find ourselves embedded in a moral unity that does, however, not "provide universality of moral judgments or principles." Based on this complex argument, Burns explains, Winch reaches his "closing insistence that we should not expect to find a 'scientific' foundation for ethics." As we consider this reconstruction provided by Burns, we see that Winch's essay presents a unique path of challenging any theories that claim to capture our understanding of morality exclusively by empirical means.

Moreover, we realize that this particular essay is representative of a methodical approach that shapes Winch's philosophy in general: to implement multi-faceted transatlantic elective affinities in search of an appropriate concept of human life. As Burns highlights, the ideas with which Winch was most concerned in his 1987 paper also had their independent trans-Atlantic lives: "Wittgenstein sailed to America, living with his former student, Norman Malcolm and his wife, for a few months (1949), holding frequent discussions with Malcolm and some of his colleagues. Simone Weil fled to New York from Nazi-occupied France, before returning to England (where she died in 1943) to write her final works. Her wonderful essay, 'The *Iliad* or the Poem of Force,' which Winch quotes in his Giessen paper, was translated by the American author, Mary McCarthy, and widely read in the USA."

As Burns claims, in more general terms, that the leading intent of Winch's entire work was to show that the methods of the natural sciences could be counter-productive in the human sciences, we find that the three philosophical essays in the present volume share one significant aspect that is of relevance for dealing with current issues: the contributions to a differentiated understanding of the human being and of human interaction that are discussed in these essays may prove important with regard to the ongoing international debates on the potential of Artificial Intelligence. As these debates explore the possible achievements of Artificial Intelligence as well as the limits of projects aiming to enhance humans by technical means, for instance in terms of "moral enhancement," or even at a recreation of the human being, careful philosophical analysis of the unwarranted claims of scientism is called for.[10]

[10] In October 2020 the "North Atlantic Triangle" Commission at the Austrian Academy of Sciences hosted the international conference "Artificial Intelligence and Human Enhancement. Affirmative and Critical Approaches in the Humanities from Both Sides of the Atlantic." The proceedings of this conference are due to be published by the Austrian Academy of Sciences Press.

PART I

The Medical "Grand Tour" to Europe and Nineteenth Century Cooperation in the Spheres of Education and Natural History

WALDEMAR ZACHARASIEWICZ

The Debate on Reforms in Education and Academic Institutions in Nineteenth-Century North America

Heated debates on the quality of education regularly erupt when the results of PISA tests are published and news of the unimpressive ranking of continental European universities in international polls conducted by experts (such as the Shanghai list) triggers controversies over the reasons why our own institutions are not a match for much better funded institutions in the USA, but also in Britain or some other continental countries which are very selective in their admission procedures. And quite a few are quick to argue that one should simply adopt the model and pattern of American institutions.[1]

It may be interesting to discover that international comparisons of this sort, though with very different preconditions and different conclusions, have a long history also in America; they certainly go back at least to the early nineteenth century. The focus in the following reflexions will be on debates on tertiary education, though there will also be references to discussions of desirable reforms in primary education and in teacher training institutions.

Considering the provenance of the majority of the settlers, it is not surprising that American Colonials regarded Oxbridge as the model, and the early foundations – some of the Ivy League schools – retain until today the architectural pattern of the English models. Affluent Americans who continued the tradition of the 'grand tour' in the eighteenth century included France and Italy in their itineraries, admiring the works of high culture there. Individual responses, such as those in Royall Tyler's *The*

[1] Some observers will, however, complain that the loss of some favorable characteristics of European academic practice are causally linked to the wholesale adoption and implementation of the credit system practiced in America. For the debate on the problems of the adoption and the bureaucratic implementation of the credit system in European universities see, for instance, Stefan Kühl, *Der Sudoku-Effekt: Hochschulen im Teufelskreis der Bürokratie. Eine Streitschrift,* Bielefeld: transcript Verlag, 2012.

Contrast,[2] and some statements by Thomas Jefferson, however, highlight attempts to avoid the corruption of European monarchical societies and to prefer the simplicity of American manners.[3] But at the same time the satires of the Connecticut Wits, e.g. John Trumbull's *The Progress of Dulness*, reveal an awareness of the frequent shortcomings of college education in America as presented by Trumbull in the vein of the Augustan satirists Alexander Pope and Jonathan Swift.[4] The prose satire *Modern Chivalry*, by the opponent of populism Hugh Henry Brackenridge, from 1792 onwards, exposes the foolishness and ignorance which permits the "bogtrotter" Teague O'Reagan to advance in society, and pokes fun at the American Philosophical Society and the universities, where gibberish can be offered as instruction in "Greek."[5]

That there was a sense of the need of improving education is not least reflected in the fact that Jefferson, a polymath, who had rejected the claims of French naturalists about the degeneration of all living beings when transferred to the New World, had himself planned the construction and many innovations at his own estate at Monticello and regarded the foundation of the University of Virginia as one of his major achievements.[6] Apparently it seemed more significant to him than his two terms of office as President of the USA. This can be gathered from the inscription on his tombstone, which omits this major political office but refers to his being

---

[2] His play juxtaposed an idealistic veteran of the War of Independence and an American traveler corrupted by his experiences of the cynical worldly wisdom of Europe, who is finally defeated in his intrigues.

[3] Some of Thomas Jefferson's letters from the 1780s and 1790s express the fear that young Americans might become attracted to "European luxury and dissipation," and they utter the wish for a true barrier, an "ocean of fire between us and the old world;" see Thomas Jefferson, *Writings*, ed. Merrill D. Peterson, New York: Library of America, 1984, 838 and 1044.

[4] In Trumbull's poem, published in 1772 and in an expanded form in 1773, the portraits of the stupid and slothtful parson Tom Brainless and of the foppish coxcomb Dick Hairbrain both appear as the products of an inadequate college education.

[5] In his comic narrative, expanded until 1805, Brackenridge exposes the gullibility of society, where Teague O'Reagan and other incompetent individuals can gain positions at universities or in quasi-scientific associations.

[6] See his *Notes on the State of Virginia* (1787), in which he refutes such claims of the Comte de Buffon and others echoing the latter's contention of the negative impact of the environment in America on all living beings transplanted there.

the "Father of the University of Virginia," stressing his active role in the design of the buildings and in the recruiting of academics.

After the temporary interruption of the 'grand tour,' which young affluent Americans had undertaken like their British counterparts in the eighteenth century, as a result of the Napoleonic Wars, however, a shift away from the dominant British model in culture, including the academic sphere, can be noted, though it took several decades before this transformed the system of education in the USA. The process seems to have had its origin both in the impressions gained by graduates from New England colleges during their residence in Germany after 1815, and in the very favorable reception Mme de Staël's book *De l'Allemagne* had in North America.[7]

The crucial importance of the residence of highly talented graduates from Harvard and Yale in the academic environments of Göttingen and Berlin was first documented by Orie William Long[8]. He related the enthusiasm with which individuals such as George Ticknor, Edward Everett, (within limitations also George Bancroft), and certainly Joseph Green Cogswell, described the high degree of academic specialization and the lively discussions characteristic of the universities of Göttingen and Berlin. It deeply impressed these future academic teachers, who sometimes became diplomats and politicians. On the basis of two years of studies in Göttingen, Ticknor, for instance, praised the advances of scholarship in Germany, and through his eulogy initiated a tradition which led to the decision of hundreds of American graduates to matriculate in

---

[7] After Napoleon had ordered the confiscation and destruction of all copies of the 1810 edition, the book appeared first in London in 1813. There was an American edition in 1814. The book extolled the large number and quality of universities in the north of Germany.

[8] His study *Literary Pioneers: Early American Explorers of European Culture* was published in 1935. On its significance and that of following studies of the reciprocal influences of German and American cultures, including the crossfertilization of university culture, see Zacharasiewicz, *Das Deutschlandbild in der amerikanischen Literatur*, Darmstadt, 1998, and *Images of Germany in American Literature*, 2007. On the early generation of American literary pioneers inspired by their visit to Germany, see *Das Deutschlandbild*, especially 27-37.

German universities and to benefit from the programs and the interaction with eminent scholars and scientists there.[9]

The findings in Long's study, which was, significantly, undertaken and published in the interwar years, one-and-a-half decades after the summary rejection of the German academic model in the last years of World War I and during its aftermath, were elaborated in the 1950s in investigations by Stanley Vogel (1955) and presented in a comprehensive account in Henry A. Pochmann, *German Culture in America: Philosophical and Literary Influences 1600-1900* (1957). This line of research was taken further by Kurt Mueller-Vollmer, whose essays[10] have confirmed the conviction that one may with confidence speak of networks of friends extending across the Atlantic in the first half of the nineteenth century.[11] Their experiences in Northern Germany prompted their demand for their own universities to be restructured on the model of German institutions. Through their accounts, first in their correspondence, and then in essays and autobiographical descriptions, they provided an impetus to be more ambitious and to transform American college/university education.

Among those early literary pioneers Cogswell was particularly articulate in praising the German model as more advanced than other

---

[9] On this topic see the studies by Orie W. Long, Henry Pochmann and Carl Diehl discussed or referred to below as well as my own treatment of the issue in *Das Deutschlandbild in der amerikanischen Literatur*, and on the popularity of this educational experience among the privileged sons of white Southerners see especially "Southern Alumni of German Universities: Fashioning a Tradition of Excellence" [2008], rptd. in my *Imagology Revisited*, Amsterdam, 2010, 271-85.

[10] See his essays, which were recently collected in *Transatlantic Crossings and Transformations: German-American Cultural Transfer from the 18th to the End of the 19th Century*, Frankfurt, 2015.

[11] There is ample evidence that American friends passed on essential information and provided recommendations regarding potential tutors in German university towns, and suggestions about where to find lodgings and suitable hosts. On the fruitfulness of network studies in American studies see the special issue of *Amerikastudien / American Studies* 60,1 (2015) ed. by Ulfried Reichardt, Heike Schaefer and Regina Schober. On the general theory see Christian Stegbauer, ed., *Netzwerkanalyse und Netzwerktheorie. Ein neues Paradigma in den Sozialwissenschaften*, Wiesbaden: Verlag f. Sozialwissenschaften, 2008. On specific networks of emigres see: Helga Schreckenberger, ed., *Networks of Refugees from Nazi Germany: Continuities, Reorientations, and Collaborations in Exile*, Leiden: Brill, 2016.

institutions. He founded Roundhill School, a reformed school in Northampton, following the model of the German *gymnasium*, which he initially managed jointly with Bancroft. His keen interest in the natural sciences later paved the way for his appointment as Professor of Mineralogy at Harvard, where he also advocated an expansion of the relatively modest library. He was also put in charge of reorganizing the book collections there and clearly exerted considerable influence on public opinion concerning the achievements of German science and its institutions in the following decades. In 1838 an essay of his in the *New York Review* on "National Education" encapsulates his great respect for German institutions. A phrase he uses illustrates his comparative evaluation of European models and patterns of education, "A single shelf of German literature is of more worth to the scholar than a whole French library."[12]

The inversion of traditional concepts familiar in the eighteenth century, according to which France was far superior to Germany in the intellectual and cultural spheres, was also implied in a book by Henry E. Dwight, a son of Timothy Dwight, the former president of Yale College. In his *Travels in the North of Germany, in the Years 1825 and 1826*, published in 1829, Dwight underlined the novelty of his self-imposed task of recording his experiences during his stay of several years in Europe. In his account he stressed the fact that Germany had been a *terra incognita* until recently and highlighted his impression that the country was "the most interesting nation on the continent." Initially, during his first encounters with Germans, he had still contrasted the proverbial agility and gracefulness of the French with the clumsiness of the Germans (5), but he was soon to revoke this judgment and reevaluate all the clichés. He later offers an American counterpart to Madame de Staël's appreciation of German culture when he maintains: "The prodigious fertility of the intellectual soil of Germany is unexampled in the history of literature" (332). He also expresses his high regard not only for Göttingen and Berlin, but also other educational institutions such as those in Halle, Leipzig, and Dresden in Saxony, and stresses the 'elective affinity' with Northern Germany, which is related to the shared Protestant faith: "The northern

---

[12] Quoted from Long (103f.), where he also cites Cogswell's claim that Germany was "the only country where the science of education [was] understood."

Germans resemble us much more than any other nation on the continent" (170).

He also lauds the *gymnasia*, the traditional European grammar schools, which he regards as being excellently equipped for work in the natural sciences and as providing a sound basis for university study. Admittedly, Dwight offers critical and even disparaging remarks on southern Germany and has only scorn and ridicule for Austria under Metternich. In this country, he claims, censorship and intimidation have cowed the people and restricted intellectual freedom, a view of Austria's universities that only the provisional adoption of "academic freedom" in 1849 and its confirmation through legislation in 1873 was to change.[13]

While Dwight had still had to struggle with the German language, the immediately following cohort of students was advised to acquire at least the rudiments of German before venturing abroad. Living, as was often the case, in the households of university professors, for instance in Göttingen, they were able to acquire the language more quickly. Its acquisition was then made easier for them by the appointment of instructors in German at American colleges. Such a position was held at Harvard, for instance, by Charles Follen, one of the early refugees from Germany, who had come to America as a political exile because of his advocacy of revolutionary republican ideas and had settled in Massachusetts in 1825. Follen compiled a popular anthology of German literature, familiarizing Americans with works by Herder, Goethe, Schiller, and the romantics.[14]

Considering the mediation of such information, it is no surprise that American educational reformers, such as Calvin Stowe and Horace Mann, were eager to assess the quality of the educational system in Germany, especially in the emerging political power of Prussia. They came to emphasize the model character of the German education. Calvin Stowe's *Report on Elementary Public Instruction in Europe* was published in 1837,

---

[13] Cf. Dwight's dismissal of the "ignorance and superstition of the Austrians" whom "the Germans of the north" scorn "as slaves both mentally and physically," and whom they are said to call "les autres chiens" (237).

[14] To facilitate his instruction he provided a *Deutsches Lesebuch für Anfänger* (1826), which included significant passages from major German authors. A 3rd ed., entitled *German Reader for Beginners,* appeared in Boston in 1836.

while Horace Mann's *Report of an Educational Tour in Germany, and Parts of Great Britain and Ireland* appeared in 1844.[15]

Before Calvin Stowe acknowledged the exemplary character of the German school organization late in 1837 in his report "to the ... General Assembly of the State of Ohio," the Parliament of Upper Canada across Lake Ontario had already received a report from Dr. Charles Duncombe.[16] Duncombe offered a rhetorical question underlining the lack of desirable initiatives for half a century in the universities of England and America, and referred to the Prussian system as being "unequaled in the records of time." His account was based not on autoptic impressions, but on a report composed by the prominent French educator and philosopher Victor Cousin for the French government, entitled in its English translation, dating from 1834, "On the State of Public Instruction in Prussia." Cousin had stressed the advantages of emulating the impressive quality of education in northern Germany. A few years later, Reverend Egerton Ryerson, who was to function as the Superintendent of Education for Upper Canada for thirty-five years, traveled to Europe with the task of studying the systems of education in several European countries. In his report, published in 1847, he provided comprehensive assessments of public elementary instruction, and again underlined the superior organization and management of this important sphere in Germany. He also included recommendations for the training of primary school teachers in so-called Normal Schools, again drawing on the report by Victor Cousin, and on Horace Mann's assessment published three years previously in Boston in 1844, thus illustrating the transnational consensus concerning educational models which had meanwhile developed.

---

[15] On the reports of these and other observers of primary and secondary schools in Germany, such as Alexander Dallas Bache and Henry Barnard, see Karl-Ernst Jeismann, "American Observations Concerning the Prussian Educational System in the Nineteenth Century," and on later reports by James Parsons and John Prince, see Gregory P. Wegner, "Prussian Volksschulen through American Eyes," *German Influences on Education in the United States to 1917*, ed. Henry Geitz, Jürgen Heideking and Jurgen Herbst, Cambridge, MA,1995, 21-41 and 57-67.

[16] In his *Report upon the Subject of Education* to the Parliament of Upper Canada, publ. in Toronto in 1836, 53. See Arndt A. Krüger, "The Image of Germany prior to World War I: Canadian Scholars and Germany," *Deutschkanadisches Jahrbuch* 14 (1995), 41-60, esp. 41-5.

The intensity of the interest in New England and beyond in the transatlantic educational model is apparent in the debates in the circle of the Transcendentalists, among whom Theodore Parker was perhaps the most outspoken admirer of German culture. He uses superlatives when assessing the value and importance of German culture.[17] The appreciation of German scholarship extended to biblical criticism as practiced by the theologian James Freeman Clarke, and the mediation of German high culture also occurred through the devoted study and translation of German literature and idealistic philosophy by Margaret Fuller in the 1830s and 40s.[18] Considering the dissemination of such positive views by college tutors and other mediators, it is not surprising that the immediately following cohort of New England graduates, including Henry Wadsworth Longfellow[19] and Charles Sumner,[20] was eager to attend German universities. The suggestions by their tutors, who had themselves been in Germany, eased the path of the younger generation into the German academic institutions and also paved the way to an effective use of their time abroad.[21]

The reform spirit the cultural pilgrims had imbibed overseas continued to be present in American academia, even though the attempts to reform the US colleges took much longer than the first generation of transatlantic visitors had hoped.

---

[17] See his statement "To our apprehension German literature is the fairest, the richest, the most original, fresh and religious literature of all modern times," quoted from John T. Krumpelmann, *Bayard Taylor and German Letters*, Hamburg 1959, 12.

[18] See her translations and then her contributions to *The Dial*, which she edited from 1840 to 1842.

[19] Longfellow paid several extended visits to Germany, residing there in 1829, 1835-36, and 1842. His *Hyperion* (1839) mirrors his intimate knowledge of German history and culture, and his *Poems* reflect his familiarity not only with German literature but also with several regions of the country.

[20] Charles Sumner, Longfellow's friend, benefitted from recommendations by Dr. Francis Lieber during his several years of study in Europe, where he contacted many scholars in Berlin and Heidelberg. During his convalescence, after the brutal attack on him in the Senate in 1856, he returned to Germany for treatment in various spas, and continued contacting German scholars in various places.

[21] Longfellow was given lessons by George Benecke in Göttingen, who had also taught and given board and lodging to Longfellow's older fellow countrymen.

That the admiration for German culture, including its institutions of tertiary education, did not please everybody, is indicated in a remark by the Germanophile Theodore Parker. His reference in *The Dial* suggests that there was increasing opposition to what intellectuals regarded as an excessive evaluation of this "new-fangled" thinking; he ironically echoes such resistance by alluding to "the immoral and irreligious writings, which it is supposed the Germans are engaged in writing, with the generous intention of corrupting the youth of the world." [22] That the German model in lifestyle and in academic matters was contested, can *inter alia* be inferred from the reception that a book, published in New York in 1853 with the title *Home Life in Germany,* met with in New England. Its author, Charles Loring Brace, a friend and travel companion of the Olmsted brothers, had in 1850 begun an extensive journey through Germany, which he wanted to finance by means of travel letters, at that time very popular components of many American journals and newspapers. His (amicable) contacts with German professors in Berlin and Göttingen[23] led to his offering a very favorable picture of the country, for which he felt in himself a particular affinity.

What antagonized some of the readers of Brace's book in New England was his favorable description of harmonious family life in Germany, "of sunny and friendly hospitalities, of quiet cultured tastes," manifest, for instance, in the way in which Sundays were spent in Germany. As a consequence, a letter to the editor of the relatively popular journal *Independent* insinuated that Brace could only be really happy, when "under the table with his boon companions, drunk."[24] And some illustrations contained in reports from Germany depicting the pleasures of easy living there may have supported such allegations. This bitter criticism was clearly related to the arrival in America of hundreds of thousands of immigrants from the German provinces, following the suppression of the revolutionary movements of 1848 and 1849. There was a fear that the beer

---

[22] *Dial* 1 (1841), quoted from Krumpelmann, *Bayard Taylor and German Letters*, 11.

[23] Among his contacts in Göttingen was also his fellow countryman Francis J. Child, who studied for a professorship and was later to become a prominent member of the Harvard faculty and the future editor of *English and Scottish Popular Ballads.*

[24] See his daughter's edition of *The Life of Charles Loring Brace, Chiefly Told in His Own Letters,* New York, 1894, 149-50.

gardens, imported by the immigrants and soon established in their own communities, might dramatically change the face of American society. The liberal spirit also apparent in academic disciplines, not least in Protestant theology, disconcerted not only a few. It led to occasionally heated debates and a summary dismissal of allegedly outlandish innovations in culture, including new academic structures.

The sympathy, which Brace showed for central aspects of German culture and which antagonized suspicious American critics, who rejected his alleged subversion of the Puritan lifestyle, found a counterpart in the early 1860s in an autobiographical narrative by John Ross Browne. He had grown up in Kentucky and took his family to Germany, where he chose Frankfurt as the place of residence in order to offer his children the advantages of German education, which had been widely praised since the 1820s. His book entitled *An American Family in Germany* appeared in 1866, after having already been published in installments in *Harper's Monthly Magazine* in 1862. It provided a vivid account of the *joie de vivre* prevalent in Browne's host country, illustrating it by humorous sketches of school life, which are meant to demonstrate that the schoolmasters in central Europe are no killjoys. Numerous anecdotes and illustrations enriched his narrative, which helped to consolidate the popular romantic image of Germany and the respect for its educational system.

While one stresses the impact of German ideas and academic practice on the intellectual life in New England, we need also to acknowledge the often ignored fact that it was not only from New England that talented graduates crossed the Atlantic but also from the American South. It is little known that the reform spirit also affected and fertilized colleges and universities in the South. Almost as many graduates as were sent overseas from Massachusetts came from the affluent state of South Carolina, at least until the destruction which occurred in the Civil War. They equally benefited from their sojourns on the other side of the Atlantic.

Among them were, for instance the prominent lawyer and classical scholar Hugh Swinton Legaré, and Thomas Reynolds and David Ramsay from Charleston, while figures like Jesse Burton Harrison arrived in Germany from Virginia. They followed in the footsteps of George Henry Calvert from Maryland, who had been one of the first to reap the full benefit of studies in the reformed German universities.[25] That the prominent German refugee Francis Lieber[26] taught for twenty years as a professor of international law in Columbia, South Carolina, helped to direct the attention of the sons of plantation owners and the landed aristocracy there to German universities. The famous expertise of professors of international law such as Johann Bluntschli in Heidelberg prompted the decision of scores of young Americans to spend some time there until the end of the nineteenth century. These facts have been demonstrated by the late Michael O'Brien in his massive monograph, the two volumes of *Conjectures of Order: Intellectual Life and the American South, 1810-1860,* after some earlier investigations by John T. Krumpelmann. And the links to Germany continued even after the catastrophe of the Civil War with its economic consequences for society in the South.

Yet a few years after the Civil War the political realities in central Europe were dramatically changed by Prussia's victory in the Franco-Prussian war. The methods used to bring about the French capitulation began to undermine the traditionally favorable picture of the idealistic German scholar as a model.[27] But the superior nature of German academic instruction, which had been recognized fifty years previously by American

[25] Though he preceded many graduates on their sojourn in Germany, the account of his experiences appeared only in the 1840s and even in the 1860s. See George Henry Calvert, *Scenes and Thoughts in Europe*, *First Series*, New York, 1846, and *First Years in Europe*, Boston, 1866.

[26] He had earlier adapted Brockhaus' *Real-Encyclopaedie* and transformed it into the *Encyclopaedia Americana.* Its thirteen volumes were published between 1829 and 1833.

[27] On the general importance of the inspiration by German scholars and institutions of higher learning for American educators and scientists, see Carl Diehl, *Americans and German Scholarship 1770-1870* (1978); specifically on the impact on the training of physicians, see Thomas Neville Bonner, *American Doctors and German Universities: A Chapter in International Intellectual Relations, 1870-1914*, Lincoln, 1963. An early appreciation of the quality of medicine in Austria, where universities did not at that time generally attract American graduates, was provided in the early 1840s in William R. Wilde, *Austria: Literary, Scientific, and Medical Institutions*. The father of Oscar Wilde did much to direct the attention of young American physicians to Vienna, which through its systematic dissection of corpses and the cooperation between various disciplines was regarded as very progressive and a suitable model for American medicine.

graduates, for the time being retained its formative influence and its impact on American academic life. In fact, it was only then that the delayed reform of the American college system was implemented. It was ushered in by the decision of the new president of the recently established Johns Hopkins University in Baltimore, Daniel Coit Gilman, to introduce the seminar system at his university.[28]

Gilman's action captured the attention and compelled other universities to follow suit. This initiative marks the beginning of a rapid development, which within a decade transformed American colleges and universities. This major change can be illustrated briefly by highlighting the evolution of a network which contributed importantly to the debate on reforms inspired by the German example.[29] The implementation of this model occurred after the Civil War at a new private university, which two decades later, in the early twentieth century, also exemplifies the fading of the influence of German academic models. It was at a small college in Spartanburg, Wofford College, in the foothills of western South Carolina, that the reform spirit was engendered in young academics who represent important nodes in the network of Germanophile scholars. It was there that the future Chancellor of Vanderbilt University, the newly established private institution in Nashville, Tennessee, James Hampton Kirkland (1859-1939)[30] received his first instruction and the advice to benefit from transatlantic study. He was inspired during his studies in Spartanburg by his fairly young mentor Charles Forster Smith, who was his professor of Latin and Greek at Wofford College, and who, as his first role-model, guided Kirkland towards his professional career. Smith had himself studied at Harvard, where Professor Fredrik D. Allen, the great classical

---

[28] Jurgen Herbst mentions other institutions which had slightly earlier included seminars in their programs. See Herbst, *The German Historical School in American Scholarship: A Study in the Transfer of Culture*, Ithaca, NY, 1995, 34-8. Yet the fact remains that it was Gilman's initiative which was followed by other academic institutions.

[29] I have dealt in more detail with the role of the American South in the reform process in American universities in my essay "Southern Alumni of German Universities: Fashioning a Tradition of Excellence" (2008), rptd. in *Imagology Revisited*, Amsterdam, 2010, 271-85.

[30] For the stages in his career and the significance of his studies in Germany see James Hampton Kirkland's Papers at Vanderbilt University, which include not only his essays on the German academic model but also many letters to his mother from abroad, mirroring his transatlantic impressions.

scholar, had advised him to go to Germany with the remark, "if you want to be a scholar you must go to Germany."[31] Smith had done so, had adopted the German methods of philology and had later returned there to complete his studies. After taking his doctorate, Smith taught Kirkland at Wofford College.

Together with a colleague of his, William Malone Baskerville, another prominent philologist, who had also been a student in Leipzig and who supported Smith's advice to the young Kirkland, Smith recommended an extended course of study there. Kirkland indeed then spent two and a half years in Leipzig and half a year in Berlin, and completed his PhD in 1885 with a critical and textual study of the Anglo-Saxon poem *The Harrowing of Hell*. His mentor in Leipzig had been Richard Wülker, an expert on Old English and the co-founder of the scholarly journal *Anglia*, who did much to initiate the publication of old texts and attracted quite a few students from abroad. Soon Kirkland's American mentors, who had themselves meanwhile transferred from the small college in South Carolina as professors to Vanderbilt University, which had been founded in 1873 and was endowed by the family of the railroad magnates, managed to get him invited to teach at Vanderbilt. There the three men, William Malone Baskerville, Charles Forster Smith and James Hampton Kirkland, together provided the foundations for the rapidly rising academic prestige and future development of Vanderbilt University. The energy and the acumen of Kirkland's was soon recognized, including his advocacy of reforms following the German model, and so he was appointed Chancellor of Vanderbilt University in 1893, a position he held until 1937.

Kirkland's enthusiastic approval of academic practices in German universities, different from the more familiar pattern of college structure in America, was expressed in a number of lectures in which he contrasted German and American universities and in essays based on these lectures, published between 1887 and 1890. The second article appeared under the title "The Influence of German Universities on the Thought of the World"[32] and acknowledged the superior status and impact of German

[31] See Charles Forster Smith, *Reminiscences and Sketches*, Nashville, 1909, 384 (at the beginning of his essay "From Harvard to Leipzig University").

[32] This essay appeared in July 1890 in the *Quarterly Review* of the Methodist Church, which originally had considerable influence on Vanderbilt University, an influence with which Kirkland had to struggle when he fought for academic freedom after the turn of the century.

universities, after having earlier juxtaposed the limited number of American graduates with the numerous advanced young scholars and scientists in Germany. As a result tertiary education was dramatically reformed under Kirkland's leadership at Vanderbilt. But it was only after a struggle with the Methodists, who had controlled the university and were skeptical about the transformation of the university, that Kirkland was able to assert academic freedom at his institution. It was not an easy victory for the Chancellor, as shown by the comparable situation in many institutions of tertiary education, both state and private universities, in those decades.

Among the influential mediators of the German approach to science and scholarship was also the experimental psychologist G. Stanley Hall (1844-1924), who had similarly profited from his studies in Germany. Like no fewer than fifteen other American graduates, he was indebted to Wilhelm Wundt, Professor of Psychology, also in Leipzig, who supervised no fewer than sixteen doctoral theses by Hall's compatriots. Hall himself served as president of Clark University from 1889 onwards, and on the basis of his experiences he demanded in 1891 "Educational Reforms," taking his cue from German educational institutions, which Hall wanted to emulate and match in effectiveness. The impact of the German model on American colleges in the late nineteenth century can thus also be related to the fact that many future college presidents had come to know it as graduate students.[33]

The lively debate over the German model and the advantages of its implementation had been complicated in the preceding decades by reservations articulated by the spokesmen of the traditional college system, who feared, like President Noah Porter of Yale, who had also been to Germany, that "the German trained professors would permeate all levels of higher education with their zeal for professionalism and academic freedom"[34] (Herbst 23). Traditionalists were afraid that the consciously

---

[33] Among the college and university presidents with experience of German tertiary education were James B. Angell (1829-1916) at the University of Michigan, Andrew White (1832-1918) at Cornell University, G. Stanley Hall (1844-1924) at Clark University, and Charles W. Dabney (1855-1945), who was consecutively University President in North Carolina, Tennessee and Cincinnati, Ohio.

[34] See his reflections in *The American Colleges and the American Public*, New York, 1878, summarized by Herbst in his thorough analysis of the impact of the "German Historical School" on "American Scholarship."

didactic purpose of a college education, in which the study of Latin and Greek was supposed to elevate and discipline the mind, would thus be lost. Colleges were still regarded as "a substitute … for *parental superintendence*," with "the professors acting *in loco parentis*" (Herbst 27). Hitherto colleges had served as places where adolescents could still be taken care of in a safe environment, but the German model suggested their transformation into an arena for the joint exploration of centrally important issues by young adults together with their professors. Defenders of the traditional colleges regretted the ostensible elimination of ethical and moral considerations in the humanities and feared that the ethical foundations of learning, especially in the humanistic disciplines, would be lost. It seemed as if the Germanic rigorous application of professional analysis was very close to the methods of the natural sciences. But by the late nineteenth century the new model was victorious, and the quest for truth, the emphasis on professional education and on the freedom of students and faculty had become prominent features of education in the major American universities.

While the rapid adoption of central elements of the German model transformed American academe, this process did not meet with unqualified approval in all quarters. There were quite a few who tried to stem the tide of what they regarded as "Teutonic innovation." Both tacit and overt opposition to this model was disseminated through other networks, and such reservations were also mediated by tutors to their disciples. At Cornell, for instance, some professors including deans expressed their irritation, among them E. A. Fuerts, who commented that he was "less and less reconciled with the teutonizing wave in educational matters."[35] That such contributions to the debate had an impact can be demonstrated by an example from the context of the same institution in the Upper South which has been chosen in this essay to illustrate the appeal of the German model: Edwin Mims (1872-1959), for many years chair of the Department of English at Vanderbilt University, and originally a disciple of the three main proponents of the German approach to scholarship there, expressed a similar concern, after having imbibed an antagonistic attitude to the new dominant model during his graduate studies at Cornell in 1896 and 1897. There he was under the tutelage of

[35] This remark by the dean of the College of Civil Engineering at Cornell University is quoted from Jörg Nagler, "From Culture to Kultur," *Transatlantic Images*, ed. Barclay et al., 142.

Hiram Corson, a Professor of English, who opposed this approach to scholarship, which was apparently also dominant at Cornell at that time. So vehement was Mims', as Corson's disciple, objection to the philological methods applied in the reading of poetic texts, that on one occasion, when referring to his former advisor Corson, he noted that "Germany has done incalculable harm: we lost the richness of English culture." [36]

It was under Kirkland's aegis and under Mims as chair of the Department of English[37] that Vanderbilt attracted a number of remarkable students and faculty. In the 1920s they formed the circle of the Fugitives, and by the early 1930s joined forces in an attempt to preserve what they felt was best in American culture, and in one of the former border states of the South opposed the spirit of the times with its materialistic, progressivist attitudes: they were known as the Agrarians.[38] Mims did not share their perspective and was increasingly isolated in the Department as he was associated with the reform spirit of the New South. His own concern was with moderate social progress in the region, which he defended against what he regarded as calumny by Northern liberals, acting as a mediator between the South and moderates in the North. His advocacy of the New South with initiatives tending to close the economic gap between the affluent North and the impoverished South made him skeptical of scholarship closely allied with the methods of the natural sciences, and a positivistic approach to literary texts.[39] But his opposition

[36] See Michael O'Brien's essay on the formative influence of some isolated academics at Cornell, such as Hiram Corson, on Edwin Mims, in *Rethinking the South: Essays in Intellectual History*, Baltimore, 1988, 131-56, especially 143.

[37] Mims worked at Vanderbilt from 1912 onwards, after teaching first at Trinity College, the future Duke University, and briefly at the University of North Carolina at Chapel Hill.

[38] In addition to John Crowe Ransom, Donald Davidson, Allen Tate, and Robert Penn Warren, were active there, and altogether a dozen intellectuals, tried to defend traditional values from a conservative position. See the Agrarian manifesto *I'll Take My Stand, The South and the Agrarian Tradition* (1930).

[39] Cf. Michael O. Brien's unpublished selection from the correspondence of Edwin Mims, which he generously made available to me. It offers abundant evidence for his distance from the rigorous investigations of the advocates of the apparently victorious reform movement in literary studies originating in Germany.

did not hamper the significant initiatives of his younger colleagues at Vanderbilt.

The debate on education had in the preceding decades moved in a different direction. Even Kirkland, who had presented the German system as a model during his first two decades as Chancellor of Vanderbilt University, modified his earlier statements of great respect by adopting a more confident stance regarding American universities. They had indeed undergone a rapid transformation, not least after having adopted the seminar system and having initiated graduate fellowships. The reception of generous donations from industrialists, railroad magnates or owners of steel corporations gave an enormous boost to academic institutions in the USA Large endowments by individuals such as Andrew Carnegie in Pittsburgh, later J. Pierpont Morgan, or owners of oil trusts, such as John D. Rockefeller, enabled the universities to expand their programs and to hire competent young scholars and scientists. They thus increased the autochthonous intellectual and academic productivity in the USA considerably. The Johns Hopkins University had an endowment of 3.5 million dollars from a Baltimore merchant of that name, Stanford received 24 million dollars from the estate of the California railroad king, who gave it its name, the University of Chicago 34 million dollars from the Rockefellers, and the son of Commodore Vanderbilt (a multimillionaire from the shipping business, who had earned millions from acquiring railroads), had given a similar grant to the university named after his father.[40]Another significant change occurred in England, where the new availability of Rhodes scholarships, awarded also to young promising American graduates from 1902 onwards, permitted them to stay within their own language community. Among the Vanderbilt graduates and future Fugitives and Agrarians John Crowe Ransom spent three years as a Rhodes Scholar in Oxford until the eve of World War I, which was to permanently change the perspective on the models for academic work and education.

These innovations reduced the need for young American scholars in the humanities and social sciences to go abroad for advanced work. The impetus received from transatlantic professional scholarship had also functioned as a catalyst for the foundation of scientific and scholarly

---

[40] See the informative study by Richard Hofstadter and Walter P. Metzger, *The Development of Academic Freedom in the United States*. NY, 1955, 413f, at the beginning of the chapter "Academic Freedom and Big Business."

associations. The founding of periodicals published by higher institutions or scholarly associations gave the scholars and scientists outlets in the USA for the publication of their work.

A number of prominent German scholars had still been hired in the 1890s, such as the constitutional historian Hermann von Holst at the University of Chicago – but there was already some skepticism and he encountered opposition, as some feared "he might become a representative of the German Reich" (1891),[41] or Hugo Münsterberg, the experimental psychologist, who held a chair at Harvard from 1892 until the early years of World War I.

What put an end to the lively exchange between Germany and the USA in the field of tertiary education and scholarship was the rapidly growing estrangement between the German Empire and the USA, who came into collision in their imperial goals. German scholarship was increasingly identified with authoritarianism and antidemocratic structures encapsulated in the Prussian state. The confrontation in various parts of the globe and several incidents before the entry of the USA into World War I led to a deterioration in the reputation of German science and scholarship. The numerous factors, which have been the subject of many investigations, cannot be listed here. But certain unfortunate actions by large numbers of German professors who defended the political position of the Empire – the war aims in 1915 and 1916 – had an extremely negative effect, which the concerted media offensive of the "Committee on Public Information," led by George Creel, took advantage of. The erstwhile highly respected German professors were blamed for the brutalities of the War, also associated with the use of poison gas on the Western Front.[42]

Briefly before the war American scholars had felt the need to defend academic freedom and protect academics against dismissal. They formed the American Association of University Professors, which formulated a

---

[41] Harry P. Judson, dean and later president of the University of Chicago, expressed his concern in this fashion. See Nagler, "From Culture to Kultur," *Transatlantic Images*, ed. Barclay et al., 141. See also Nagler's more extensive study of the German historian in the USA, "A Mediator between Two Historical Worlds: Hermann Eduard von Holst and the University of Chicago," *German Influences*, ed. Geitz et al., 257-72.

[42] See my more detailed description of the catastrophic consequences both for Americans of German heritage and for the reputation of German scholarship and science in *Images of Germany*, 77-89.

"Report on Academic Freedom and Academic Tenure" in the first year of the War, (Hofstadter and Metzger 407-12; 468-84), but it is a sad fact that the war hysteria soon afterwards led to the dismissal of professors despite the earlier report designed to maintain the ideal of academic freedom. It is also a fact that also former advocates of the German model, including the prerogative of academic freedom to think and advocate, for example pacifism, joined the chorus of those condemning such attitudes and demanded the resignation of those who clung to such opinions. This was also true at Vanderbilt University under J. H. Kirkland – though Hofstadter and Metzger lauded the restraint advocated in such debates by the president of Harvard, Abbott Lawrence Lowell, while the president of Columbia University, Nicholas Murray Butler, withdrew "the privilege of academic freedom for the entire duration of the war" (Hofstadter and Metzger 502-3 and 499).

The nadir in this development was reached when the "elective affinity," which Henry E. Dwight had asserted between the intellectuals in Northern Germany and in New England in 1829, was ninety years later not only denied but the fruits of that transatlantic region were branded as poison, with the slogan in Cleveland being "City to Burn Hun Poison," as bugs which had to be kept away from American minds. Bonfires of academic books produced by the enemy were lit. This was done in order to prevent the bacillus allegedly contained in these publications from infecting the healthy citizens of the USA, not only by fumigating them but by burning them, thus keeping them from infecting the major vehicle of thought, the books.[43] Thus World War I eventually led to the total abandonment of the reform spirit in American university inspired by the German model and the debates stimulated by a wealth of transatlantic encounters.

WORKS CITED

Barclay, David E. and Elisabeth Glaser-Schmidt, eds. *Transatlantic Images and Perceptions: Germany and America Since 1776.* Washington, D.C.: German Historical Institute and Cambridge UP, 1997.

[43] Cf. the pronouncements of Ohio Governor James Middleton Cox, a potential contender for the presidency. See Clifford Alfred Bernd, "World War I as a Shaping Force in American Germanics," *Teaching German in Twentieth-Century America*, ed. David P. Benseler et al., Madison, 2001, 58-68, esp. 62f.

Benseler, David P., Craig W. Nikisch, and Cora Lee Nollendorfs, eds. *Teaching German in Twentieth-Century America.* Madison: U of Wisconsin P, 2001.

Bonner, Thomas Neville. *American Doctors and German Universities: A Chapter in International Intellectual Relations, 1870-1914*. Lincoln: U of Nebraska P, 1963.

Brace, Charles Loring. *Home-Life in Germany*. New York: Scribner, 1853.

—. *The Life of Charles Loring Brace, Chiefly Told in His Own Letters.* Ed. Emma Brace. New York: Charles Scribner's Sons, 1894.

Browne, John Ross. "An American Family in Germany, Illustrated by the Author." *Harper's New Monthly Magazine* 27 (July 1863): 160-79, (August 1863): 306-20.

—. *An American Family in Germany, Illustrated by the Author*. New York: Harper & Brothers, 1866.

Calvert, George Henry. *Scenes and Thoughts in Europe.* First Series. New York: Wiley & Putnam, 1846.

—. *First Years in Europe*. Boston: Lee & Shepard, 1866.

Cogswell, Joseph Green. "National Education." *New York Review*, July 1838: 149-94.

Cousin, Victor. "On the State of Public Instruction in Prussia" (translated by Sarah Austin in 1834).

Diehl, Carl. *Americans and German Scholarship 1770-1870*. New Haven: Yale UP, 1978.

Duncombe, Charles. *Report Upon the Subject of Education*, made to the Parliament of Upper Canada, 25th February, 1836. Toronto: M. Reynolds, 1836.

Dwight, Henry E. *Travels in the North of Germany in the Years 1825 and 1826.* New York: Carvill, 1829.

Elliott, Stephen. "Education in Germany." *Southern Review* 4 (August 1829): 86-123.

Follen, Charles, ed. *Deutsches Lesebuch für Anfänger* (1826), 3rd ed. *German Reader for Beginners*, Boston: Hilliard, Gray and Company, 1836.

Geitz, Henry, Jürgen Heideking and Jurgen Herbst, eds. *German Influences on Education in the United States to 1917*. Cambridge, MA: Cambridge UP, 1995.

Herbst, Jurgen. *The German Historical School in American Scholarship: A Study in the Transfer of Culture*. Ithaca, NY: Cornell UP, 1995.

Hofstadter, Richard and Walter P. Metzger. *The Development of Academic Freedom in the United States.* NY: Columbia U, 1955.

Jefferson, Thomas. *Notes on the State of Virginia* (1787). Ed. William Peden. New York: Norton Library, 1972.

—. *Writings*. Ed. Merrill D. Peterson. New York: Library of America, 1984.

Kirkland, James Hampton. "The Influence of German Universities on the Thought of the World," *Quarterly Review*. Ed. W. P. Harrison (July 1890): 310-26.

Krüger, Arndt A. "The Image of Germany prior to World War I: Canadian Scholars and Germany," *Deutschkanadisches Jahrbuch* 14 (1995). 41-60.

Krumpelmann, John. T. *Bayard Taylor and German Letters*. Hamburg: Cram de Gruyter, 1959.

—. *Southern Scholars in Goethe's Germany*. Chapel Hill: U of North Carolina P, 1965.

Longfellow, Henry Wadsworth. *Hyperion* (1839). *Longfellow's Complete Works*, vol. 2. London: Riverside Edition, 1886.

Long, Orie William. *Literary Pioneers: Early American Explorers of European Culture*, Cambridge: Harvard UP, 1935.

Mann, Horace. *Report of an Educational Tour in Germany, and Parts of Great Britain and Ireland* (1844). London: Simpkin, Marshall, and Co., 1846.

Mueller-Vollmer, Kurt. *Transatlantic Crossings and Transformations: German-American Cultural Transfer from the 18th to the End of the 19th Century*. Frankfurt: Peter Lang, 2015.

Münsterberg, Hugo. *American Traits: From the Point of View of a German*. Boston: Houghton Mifflin, 1901.

O'Brien, Michael. *Conjectures of Order: Intellectual Life and the American South: 1810-1860*. 2 vols. Chapel Hill: U of North Carolina P, 2004.

—. *Rethinking the South: Essays in Intellectual History*. Baltimore: The Johns Hopkins UP, 1988.

Pochmann, Henry A. *German Culture in America: Philosophical and Literary Influences 1600-1900*. Madison: U of Wisconsin P, 1957.

Ryerson, Egerton. *Report on a System of Public Elementary Instruction for Upper Canada*. Montreal: Lovell and Gibson, 1847.

Smith, Charles Forster. *Reminiscences and Sketches*. Nashville: M.E. Church, South Smith & Lamar, 1909.

Staël-Holstein, Anne Germaine Necker, Baronne de. *De l'Allemagne*. London: John Murray, 1813.

Stowe, Calvin. *Report on Elementary Public Instruction in Europe, Made to the Thirty-Sixth General Assembly of the State of Ohio* (1837). Boston: Dutton and Wentworth, 1838.

Tyler, Royall. *The Contrast. A Comedy* (1787). Rptd. in *Anthology of American Literature*. Vol. 1. Ed. George McMichael. 2nd ed. New York: Macmillan, 1980. 440-82.

Vogel, Stanley. *German Literary Influences on the American Transcendentalists*. New Haven: Yale UP, 1955.

Wilde, William R. *Austria: Literary, Scientific, and Medical Institutions*. Dublin: William Curry, 1843.

Zacharasiewicz, Waldemar. *Das Deutschlandbild in der amerikanischen Literatur*. Darmstadt: Wissenschaftliche Buchgesellschaft, 1998.

—. *Images of Germany in American Literature*. Iowa City: U of Iowa P, 2007.

—. "Southern Alumni of German Universities: Fashioning a Tradition of Excellence." [2008] rptd. in *Imagology Revisited.* Amsterdam: Rodopi, 2010. 271-85.

CARMEN BIRKLE

The Medical Grand Tour: American Physicians In and Out of Europe

1 EASTWARD BOUND

Nineteenth-century North American medical students looked to European metropolises – such as Vienna, Berlin, Paris, Zurich, and London – as ideal locations for the perfection and completion of their medical studies. Men and – from the mid-1800s onward – women spent a few months or even a year or two at European universities to learn from the best in their fields of expertise. Except for Zurich, none of the institutions of higher learning officially admitted women, but arranged, for example, special courses, often taught in English, for their visitors. In both Berlin and Vienna, the local American Medical Associations would take over the organization of this opportunity of instruction from the early twentieth century onward. Apart from, for example, Susan Dimock (1847-75; United States) and Elizabeth Maude Abbott (1867-1940; Canada), Eliza Root (1846-1926), Elizabeth Mott, Mary E. Bates (1861-1954) as well as the surgeon Mary Dixon Jones (1828-1908) spent some time in Vienna in order to study and, in Dixon Jones's case, "toured European operating theaters" to "cement ... relationships ... with ... leaders in the profession ..." in 1886 (Morantz-Sanchez, *Conduct* 76). However, this medical grand tour was not a one-way street from the United States to Europe. No matter how dominant this direction was, the few medical women in the United States and Europe in many cases established a network of acquaintances and mutual support. The doctor Elizabeth Blackwell (1821-1910), born in England, but living most of her life in the United States, was the first woman to receive a medical degree in 1849 in the United States at Geneva Medical College, New York, and spent her final years touring and lecturing in England. She was, for example, strongly influenced by the British nurse Florence Nightingale (1820-1910) and the British doctor Elizabeth Garrett Anderson (1836-1917). As Thomas Bonner points out, the "ties between British and American women doctors were ... close, and all the pioneers – Blackwell, Zakrzewska, Preston, Putnam, Dimock, Garrett, Jex-Blake, Elizabeth Morgan – knew and supported one another" (*To the Ends* 26). However, the long nineteenth century was prominently shaped by two men in the United States and Canada respectively who paved the way for modern medicine: Oliver Wendell Holmes, Sr. (1809-94) and Sir William Osler (1849-1919). They, too, studied in Europe, Holmes in Paris and Osler mostly in Berlin and Vienna, and they will serve as a frame for their under-researched female colleagues. In my paper, I will offer a sketch of some of the networks, first in Paris and, beginning in the 1850s, in Vienna, among U.S.-American and Canadian medical women and men and their attitudes toward studying medicine in Europe. In the nineteenth century, these professionals crisscrossed the Atlantic in search of better and higher professional medical education because of the poor state of American medical instruction. After a brief look at the concept of what I will call the "medical grand tour," I will first outline Oliver Wendell Holmes's medical studies in Paris and then discuss some of the American medical practitioners coming to Vienna as early as the 1850s, initiating the shift from Paris to Vienna as the new Mecca of medicine. Letters by Henry K. Oliver, Jr. (1857), Hasket Derby (1860), Robert W. Johnson (1880), L. Harrison Mettler (1896), and Hugh Payne Greeley (1914) depict their authors' praise as well as occasionally critical impressions of Vienna as an emerging and developing capital of medicine. My subsequent analysis of medical women sojourning in Vienna toward the end of the nineteenth century shows both the obstacles women had to overcome on both sides of the Atlantic to pursue a medical education and the lack of extensive research on their Viennese medical apprenticeship. Sir William Osler's representation of his medical journeys to Vienna in 1874 and 1908 reveals the differences in – as well as development of – the Viennese and American medical institutions. The knowledge gained by these practitioners – whether men or women, doctors or medical students – not only shaped these individuals and their practices but also gradually began to take effect in the United States and ultimately caused the medical grand tour to shift direction and move from Europe, and Vienna in particular, to North America.

2 THE MEDICAL GRAND TOUR

Although the term of the "grand tour" was originally used to mark the "history of travelling in Europe … from the Restoration of the British monarchy in 1660 to the accession of Queen Victoria in 1837" (Buzard 38), and was, as James Buzard argues, "from start to finish, an ideological exercise" with "[i]ts leading purpose … to round out the education of young men of the ruling classes by exposing them to the treasured artifacts and ennobling society of the Continent" (38), it does, with some revision, also capture the nineteenth-century medical movements across the Atlantic. Originally, only English aristocratic upper-class families could send their sons to the Continent as "a social ritual intended to prepare these young men to assume the leadership positions preordained for them at home" (Buzard 38). With increasing technological progress in transportation, the crossing of the Atlantic became easier, so that Americans with enough money and interest in their European heritage began to visit European sites, above all in England, France, Germany, and Italy. These journeys can also be perceived as finishing schools for young Americans and, toward the end of the nineteenth century, turned into mass tourism.

In the medical field, a parallel development took place, with first young male American medical students studying with European experts, often in Paris, Berlin, Edinburgh, and Vienna. It was not until the second half of the nineteenth century that female medical students began to look for education across the Atlantic. Ideological factors continued to determine who was able to seek further instruction abroad. Young men from well-off American families were able to go to Europe. The first American to study in Vienna was probably the Maryland ophthalmologist George Frick as early as 1811, who worked with the eye specialist George Beer (Bonner, *American Doctors* 70). For women, this opportunity was not available at first because of gender barriers in the field: there were hardly any female medical students at medical universities and those that did enter medical studies in the United States, such as Elizabeth Blackwell and, later, Mary Putnam Jacobi and others, could not officially register at any European university because of their sex. In 1864, Zurich opened its doors for foreign women students, a move from which Susan Dimock profited, and Jacobi managed to fight her way toward a degree in Paris. Yet discrimination and sexism against women in the medical profession dominated in central European countries, and male scientists did their best to explain "scientifically" why women could not and should not receive higher education, study medicine, and become doctors.[1]

[1] For more information on these arguments, see my "Capitals of Medicine" and Mary Roth Walsh, *"Doctors Wanted, No Women Need Apply"* as well as Edward Hammond Clarke, *Sex in Education*, Arthur Kirchhoff, ed., *Die*

The medical students looked toward Europe for educational purposes because the American medical profession, its methods of diagnosis and treatment, as well as its research lagged far behind that of many European hospitals and research institutions. Whereas for most Americans the "European tour was – in theory, at least – an occasion for education, a chance to submit oneself to the influence of older civilizations, to round off one's sharp American edges, to polish up one's dull American surface, but not to relinquish one's proud American values" (Stowe 34), medical students sought further knowledge in a more humble mode, knowing about the professional superiority of European physicians.

As Thomas Neville Bonner emphasizes:

> Of all the medical schools of Europe, none had a more widespread and enduring attraction for Americans than Vienna. ... Here studied no fewer than ten thousand American physicians in the years of emigration from 1870 to 1914. Probably double this number knew Vienna from short visits and vacation tours. Small wonder that this city of romance and tradition was known as the medical capital of the United States. (*American Doctors* 69)

However, Bonner also points to the quite different pull factors with which Vienna attracted American physicians. On the one hand, it seemed to have been the place mostly for those who had little time, or for "the practitioner who wished to specialize. The more scientifically oriented Americans tended to avoid Vienna and its hordes of practitioners in favor of the smaller German universities" (69). The American physician, pathologist, bacteriologist, and school administrator William Henry Welch (1850-1934) from Johns Hopkins School of Medicine, who had sought further education from 1876 to 1878 in Leipzig and the then German cities of Strassburg (now Strasbourg) and Breslau (now Wrocław), from where he moved on to Vienna, also complained about the focus on practical subjects (Bonner, *American Doctors* 69). For him, Vienna was a disappointment although he did enjoy the city's cultural attractions. For others, on the other hand, Vienna offered exactly what they needed because of the medical school's wide range of courses specifically geared toward these visitors. Viennese professors were quick to recognize the advantages American doctors brought – above all financially – and adjusted their teaching to their visitors' needs. They arranged private courses for shorter

akademische Frau, S. Weir Mitchell, *Wear and Tear*, and Dr. Paul Julius Möbius, *Über den physiologischen Schwachsinn des Weibes*.

periods with a limited number of students. Clinics, wards, autopsy rooms, and lecture halls were in close proximity and did not require an official matriculation to attend those classes. The clinics of Theodor Billroth, Heinrich Bamberger, Carl Braun, and Carl Ferdinand von Arlt did get a number of interested Americans as participants. Eventually, beginning in 1879 with the ophthalmologist Ernst Fuchs, classes were also offered in English (Bonner, *American Doctors* 74). The increasing demand for such special courses required some form of organization so that – after one failed attempt in 1889 – the American Medical Association of Vienna was founded in 1903-04 (cf. Birkle, "Vienna as Medical Contact Zone"; Lackner). As Bonner points out, "[s]ince the Americans in Vienna represented an important source of income to the university, the faculty was disposed from the first to cooperate with the association" (79) and eventually also issued diplomas (*Zeugnisse*) that were, however, strongly criticized by some because they by no means meant that the recipient was really an expert in the field indicated.[2] With the social upheavals in Vienna in the 1930s and the turbulence of World War II, the heydays of the American presence in medical Vienna was over (Birkle, "Vienna as Medical Contact Zone"). Nevertheless, even if American interest in Vienna was more practically oriented and not focused on research, Bonner maintains that "it would be a mistake to underestimate the influence which Vienna exerted on American medicine" (70). No matter how long American doctors stayed in Vienna, they returned as experts with a new and fuller understanding of their own field and communicated their insight to an American audience in medical journals such as the *Boston Medical and Surgical Journal*. However, it was not until after the American Civil War (1861-65) that the focus gradually turned from Paris to Vienna.

3 OLIVER WENDELL HOLMES, SR. (1809-94): AN AMERICAN IN PARIS

Both American and Canadian female and male practitioners staying in Europe in the later nineteenth and early twentieth centuries had one significant predecessor and role model each: the American from New England Oliver Wendell Holmes, Sr. (1809-94), and the Canadian from

---

[2] "More affluent Americans simply hired the underpaid Austrian instructors or adjunct professors to give them tutorial instruction" because the "Austrian teachers" were generally "poorly paid" (Bonner, *American Doctors* 76).

Montreal Sir William Osler (1849-1919). Since they not only represent two significant steps in American-European medical relations but also served as role models for men and women in their fields and prominently shaped the American and Canadian medical profession, they could be considered pioneers in the development of modern North American medicine. As I suggest, it is in their wake that the medical sojourn in Europe in search of knowledge and expertise gradually leads to the twentieth- and twenty-first century European recognition that some North American medical institutions have become leading facilities in the field in their own right.

One of the best-known early American medical students who studied in Europe was Oliver Wendell Holmes, Sr. (1809-94), who spent two years in Paris (1833-35), profited from the large number of hospitals (about thirty-six altogether [cf. O'Brien 119-20]) and patients – in particular after the cholera epidemic of 1832 (cf. McCullough 105) – and registered at the École de Médicine and the Sorbonne, where lectures were free for American students (McCullough 106). What Holmes and three American medical colleagues – James Jackson, Mason Warren, and Henry Bowditch – gained in knowledge shaped American medicine for decades after their return to the United States. For thirty-five years, Holmes later taught anatomy and physiology at Harvard University until 1882, as he himself outlines in this travelogue *Our Hundred Days in Europe* (1887, 7-8). Holmes not only became a famous teacher and practitioner of medicine but also a man of letters because he published a number of essays and novels, in which he experimented with unusual cases that were hard to diagnose and treat effectively. In his novels, he often combined the spiritual, psychological, and physical aspects of a human being in order to consider his patients as a whole (cf. Birkle, "Narrative Praxis" 87).

Holmes wrote essays on homeopathy and puerperal fever and gave practical advice to young practitioners on how to deal with patients. Since he moved in between old beliefs in bloodletting and vomiting to purge the body of whatever wanted to destroy it and the developing scientific approach to focus solely on the symptoms and forget the patient as a human being, he emphasized a dialogical interaction between doctor and patient. Thus, for him, the doctor became a participant in the patient's illness and not just an observer (Davis 125). However, the doctor still had to remain distant and apply reason and rationality rather than emotions.

This was a technique that Holmes had learned when receiving instruction from the internal pathologist Pierre Charles Alexandre Louis in the hospital of La Pitié, from Auguste Chomel at the clinic Hôtel Dieu, and from lectures by Gabriel Andral at the École de Médicine (cf. Dowling 29). Holmes, in contrast to many American physicians later attending short-term classes at Vienna, perfected his command of the French language and easily followed the most complex lectures. What his teachers shared and what Holmes brought back to the United States and published in his Boylston Prize essay (1836-37) is considered to be a form of "skeptical empiricism" (Dowling 49), that is, a skepticism toward the strong French reliance on empirical investigation; "ruthlessly and systematically jettisoning anything that did not meet the same exacting standards" (Dowling 50). Holmes furthermore battled for most of his life against any form of medical quackery that was common in the United States in the first half of the nineteenth century and that he had not seen in Paris. Quackery bloomed because of a serious lack of organized and structured medical education, and because medication was considered a commodity which the more affluent could afford to buy. Holmes fought "the dominance of market forces," which some claimed to be "the purest expression of American democracy" (Dowling 80).

After his return from Paris, Holmes's way of proclaiming his new insights was to turn into a major author. He revolutionized obstetrics with his essay on puerperal fever in 1843 "The Contagiousness of Puerperal Fever" (1843) – long before Nightingale's ideas about hygiene, Ignaz Semmelweis's[3] theory of cadaverous poisoning, and Pasteur's germ theory – claiming that it was the doctor himself who would spread the disease by moving from one bed to the next in a birth clinic (Dowling 91). The "highly esteemed physician" William Osler later praised Holmes for his understanding of puerperal fever and called him "'the most successful combination the world has ever seen of the physician and man of letters'" (qtd. in Kass 57). As mentioned before, Holmes had brought back from

[3] "It was Ignaz Semmelweis, an assistant physician in the maternity wards at the Vienna General Hospital, who provided definite empirical evidence of the contagiousness of puerperal fever and of affective preventive medical practices. In 1847, Semmelweis ordered the medical students who had performed autopsies of puerperal fever patients to wash their hands with chloride of lime before examining women in labor. Within a month, maternal fatalities were reduced from more than 10 percent to less than 2 percent" (Kass 52).

Europa a critical view of the traditional practice of medicine that included a shift from a generalized view of illness with one treatment for all ailments toward a more "localized pathology, focusing closely on particular diseases and particular parts of the body" (Gibian 73). His solution was "conversation … to promote the freedom of discussion that might open up a healthy questioning of old systems and remedies and perhaps also pave the way for the emergence of the new" (Gibian 75). He urged "physicians to talk, and to think, before they act" (75). This, at the time, provocative attitude disrupted the traditional course of medicine and questioned the authority of experienced physicians. Holmes could only do so because he had learned in Europe that to adopt a new perspective and to critically question established practices could result in new insights and improvements in treating patients. With his idea of the relevance of dialogue in medicine, Holmes also influenced the eminent psychologist William James who turned "Holmes's theories of the self as a conversation between multiple personalities" into his own ideas of the "'social self'" and new conceptions of the unconscious (Gibian 91). Holmes thus had an impact on subsequent thinkers such as Sigmund Freud, Alfred Adler, Carl Jung, and Otto Rank in their development of what Freud later called the "talking cure" and of the field of depth psychology (Weinstein 93). Holmes remained attached to French medicine throughout his medical career, strongly embracing these elective affinities, and returned to France in the early 1890s to revisit, with fond memories, the locations of his earlier training. He was followed throughout the nineteenth century by many men and later women of medicine whose location of higher learning gradually shifted from Paris to Vienna.

4 THE MEDICAL MECCA MOVING FROM PARIS TO VIENNA

It was a common belief among American physicians that therapeutics in particular had to be adjusted to the needs of the specific patient in specific and highly different contexts (Warner 217), and therefore French therapeutics could not simply be applied in the United States since it would even be "professionally irresponsible" (219) and destructive to the American patients (219). Americans saw as the core of the French therapeutic practice a "skepticism expressed at the bedside as the expectant method" (219), thus a "passivity" that might run counter to what, to Americans, it meant to be a physician, namely curing patients. As some

American physicians also thought, "French physicians were not simply passively uninterested in treatment, but actively placed science above healing" (220), which caused in the Americans the fear "that excessive scientific zeal could unfit a man for practice, replacing his responsibility to his patients with an allegiance to science" (222). Moral issues were very much at the center of interest of American physicians, as my analysis of some of their letters home from Vienna will also show in the following. However, what physicians did take home from Paris – as they did from Vienna later – was a belief in Parisian "therapeutic epistemology," that is, an "active denunciation of rationalism and an allegiance to clinical empiricism in the tradition of Condillac and Cabanis"[4] (224) and an endorsement of "empirical observation" (224). While they embraced knowledge as a universal category applicable anywhere, they considered therapeutics as following "the principle of specificity" (225) and, therefore, in need of adjustment to context. Americans did take over "empirical clinical observation" (229) and applied it to the American bedside although this practice, too, in the form of "Pierre Louis's numerical method" was not unanimously praised in the United States Warner finally concludes: "The transmission of French therapeutics to America suggests a model of active and selective transference" (230). A study like Warner's seems to be – as far as I can tell – still missing for Vienna. Unfortunately, in spite of Bonner's claims about numbers, it is not only hard to find out how many Americans did study in Vienna in any given year before the foundation of the American Medical Association of Vienna, but also what, where, and with whom they did so: "Almost none of them registered with the university and the archives there carry only fragmentary records of the numbers of American 'auditors' in medical courses" (Bonner, *American Doctors* 73).

The gradual shift from Paris as the main destination for medical visitors to Berlin and Vienna is an issue in a letter written in 1857 by the American physician Henry K. Oliver, Jr., of Boston, to Dr. Jonathan Mason Warren (1811-67), a graduate of Harvard Medical School, who passed the letter

---

[4] Étienne Bonnot de Condillac (1740-80) was a French philosopher and epistemologist who studied psychology and the philosophy of the mind. He promoted "sensationism," which argues that all knowledge comes from the senses (see Falkenstein and Grandi). Pierre-Jean-Georges Cabanis (1757-1808) was a French physician and physiologist noted for his *Rapports du physique et du moral de l'homme* (1802) (see Editors of the Encyclopaedia Britannica).

on to the editors of *The Boston Medical and Surgical Journal.*[5] Warren recommends the letter for publication by praising the Vienna institutions: "The superior advantages of the Vienna hospitals, for students, over those of Paris, have of late years attracted much attention. The great facilities afforded for both medical and surgical study and observation, have quite turned the tide in favor of the German institutions" (49). Henry K. Oliver, who had received his M.D. from Harvard in 1855, depicts the Vienna General Hospital in highly appreciative terms and comments on the building's simple architecture but also its perfect arrangement for teaching and learning. He praises the clinics of Oppolzer and Skoda and their way of lecturing. Oliver considers Oppolzer a clinical lecturer superior to all those in Paris (51) and concludes: "… what a treat Oppolzer's clinic is; everything that he touches upon, he has a happy faculty of making interesting" (52). In contrast, "Prof. Skoda's clinic is also an exceedingly valuable one"; his own manner, however, of speaking is slow and void of any "pleasantry which would serve to relieve the monotony of his style …" (52). Oliver continues to praise "Prof. Hebra, the teacher of diseases of the skin" (53) at great length and seems to have enjoyed Ferdinand von Hebra's "good humor," "[a]necdotes," and his "humorous style of relation" (53). Prof. [Carl Ludwig] Sigmund receives similar praise, also because "his material is much richer than that at Paris …" (55).

Oliver concludes by depicting the advantages of the midwifery department and the extensive practical experiences medical students can profit from. Oliver himself was present at 200 births, forty of which he himself delivered, and some women, as he, ironically, delights in, "were kind enough to offer abnormal presentations" (57) so that he could enhance his knowledge. He mentions the most interesting, however questionable, phenomenon at the end, something he calls "a romantic part of the story connected with the women who give birth at the Hospital, and

---

[5] As early as 1840, Dr. William Robert Willis Wilde (1815-76), an ophthalmologist from Dublin, father of the later well-known writer Oscar Wilde, spent sufficient time in Vienna to offer a detailed depiction of its medical institutions, the General Hospital, the Museum of Anatomy, the New Vienna Medical School, the schools of Pathology and Anatomy, maternity wards, and many other phenomena in his *Austria: Its Literary, Scientific, and Medical Institutions. With Notes upon the Present State of Science, and a Guide to the Hospitals and Sanatory Establishments of Vienna* (1843). He may have initiated a development that took on speed in the 1850s (see Blodi; Montjoye).

that is … that they are all unmarried" (57). As he points out, "[m]arried women and widows who apply … are sent to another hospital" (57).[6] He hastens to say that the women who are treated at the General Hospital are by no means "prostitutes" but simply "unmarried" (57) and unable to afford marriage and a house. Their children are then placed in the adjacent "foundling-house," and the women who cannot pay for their hospital stay are made to work at this house for a specified amount of time. The brutal irony, however, is that the Hospital itself furnishes the cadaver of a woman and the foundling-house those of children – five or six daily – for the students to operate on in a class with Dr. Braun so that they can later perform actual operations in the delivery room (58).

This is where the article ends. Although Oliver seems to have intended a sequel to this letter, it does not seem to have been published. Nevertheless, the advantages of Vienna over Paris have all been pointed out: the perfectly practical arrangement of the hospital buildings, the rich amount of material to be analyzed and dissected, and, above all, the great expertise of the teachers, whose knowledge, effective way of lecturing, and bedside treatment Oliver considers to be far superior to what is done in Paris. Yet, to a present-day reader, some phenomena would be questionable, not only the separation of married and unmarried women or the use of the bodies of the deceased foundlings (in spite of their having a mother known to the Hospital), but also the lack of privacy of the women, the exposition of their naked bodies to all students, and the subsequent external and internal examination of their bodies in front of all students present. Yet, as Oliver and most probably all physicians at the time viewed it, this was done for the sake of medical teaching, learning, and research. There is no word about the individual women and their possible reactions or his own thoughts about seeing women exposed to him or the corpses of children offered as operational material.

Two further letters from American medical men pick up Oliver's letter, one directly, one indirectly, both published in *The Boston Medical and Surgical Journal*, one in 1860 and one in 1880. The first letter by Dr. Hasket Derby, published on 2 August 1860, directly refers to Oliver's "very full description of the different courses and their advantages" (51) and, therefore, suggests to add a more detailed praise of one field, namely,

---

[6] Charles Carroll Fulton similarly points out in 1874 that of the ten thousand children actually born in the General Hospital "only two hundred of them [are] legitimate" (59).

"the study of the eye" (52) with Carl Ferdinand von Arlt (1812-87) and Christoph Friedrich Jäger von Jaxtthal (1784-1871), and proceeds to explain a day of study with these experts and their assistants. Apart from their expertise, he particularly enjoys the "private operation course to physicians only" (52) with Arlt,[7] where, "participants are principally foreign physicians" (52) and, every day, they have "a fresh head and a sufficient quantity of eyes from the slaughter-houses" (52). Derby also admits that he is unable to compare Vienna practices with those in the United States because he had not paid any attention to them prior to his departure, which might imply that he is or at least was not an eye specialist before his time in Vienna.

The second letter by the American physician Robert W. Johnson from Baltimore dates from 4 December 1880, and gives advice to those who prepare for a medical stay in Vienna and also comments critically on some of the practices he encounters, particularly in obstetrics. Praise is omnipresent in the first deliberations, in which Johnson informs future visitors that they will need about one month to get adjusted, both to the language and the ways in which the institutions work. Proficiency in the German language is of advantage, as he points out, although some "instructors speak English fluently" (130) and not much German is needed for the practical courses, also because many medical terms are the same in German- and English-speaking countries (probably because they are in Latin or Greek). Johnson then lets his fellow Americans know that there are two types of classes: first, "the lectures, theoretical and clinical, which are given by the professors, more especially to men seeking a degree from the University"; second, clinics and courses "more patronized by our fellow-countrymen" (130). The division indicates what later on was highly common, namely the organization of classes for English-speaking physicians for which they had to pay extra and which were, as Johnson also mentions, mostly conducted by the professors' assistants and frequently also organized privately in advance and only known to those who were part of such a group (133). He subsequently lists the schedule of lectures for the winter semester 1879-80. This schedule is a very valuable source of names of teachers and professors of the time, such as von Braun (gynecology), Chiari (pathology), Sigmund (syphilis), Politzer

[7] Von Arlt was "renowned all over Europe as the greatest oculist living, and has accumulated an immense fortune from his practice" (Fulton 59), also because he took in a large number of private patients at his house.

(diseases of children), Hebra (skin), Jaeger (eyes), and Schauta (obstetrics). His first point of criticism concerns the easy availability of bodies for dissections and operations that, for him, "breeds among some men a careless hacking propensity that does not result in that knowledge acquired where subjects are harder to obtain and more expensive" (134). What others praise without limitations for him provokes ethical questions. This perspective and critical approach is also at work in his view of obstetrical practices in Vienna. Not only are child delivery and pregnant women's examinations a mass phenomenon at the General Hospital, but also ethically questionable with regard to the babies' identities that cannot be fully accounted for because of their large numbers (136) as well as to the treatment of the mothers. Not only do students and instructors "leave the dead house for the lying-in-room to make examinations with hands imbrued with the blood of the dead, and it may be consciences dyed with the blood of the living" (136). Johnson immediately evokes the specter of puerperal fever – into which both Holmes and Semmelweis had already gained significant insights – and calls it "criminality" (136) if practitioners wash their hands – if at all – in "carbolized water" (136) only. He labels this practice "something near homicide" and "impending calamity" (136) and concludes: "The profession here and elsewhere will not do its whole duty to its neighbor until obstetricians refuse contagious cases which may endanger mother and child" (136). His most severe criticism is hurled at the practice of exposing women infected with syphilis naked and treated with absolute disrespect when "compelled to hurry off the little covering to their nakedness, and reveal, as a text to a serio-comic lecture, parts that even in the most debased women deserve the respect that nature entails on animals. I do not say that this is the universal procedure, but in one of the courses I was much tempted to instruct the instructor on points of ethics by a more forcible and striking way than mere precept" (137). He even suggests to American students withdrawing their subscriptions when they encounter such behavior. His final criticism goes to his fellow countrymen who, upon their return, seem frequently to boast of "an intimate friendship with a great gun, and [I] know by experience how little notice is taken of students by their superiors" (137).

Johnson's strongly critical words are unusual in the general praise of Vienna. However, while his ethical concerns are serious in nature, he does not belittle the great knowledge of the Viennese medical teachers and the advantages of the facilities that allow much more practical work than is possible in the United States. He does conclude on a more light-hearted note and praises the frequent sunshine in Vienna, the health of the city, "a delightful water-supply" (137), the cheaper living, and even the presence of an English church where Americans are welcome; but he also indicates "the temptations that ruin young Americans abroad" (138) – unless accompanied by a wife who serves as protection.[8]

Russell M. Jones points to this ultimate shift in focus from Paris to Vienna: "After the Civil War, especially in the 1870s and 1880s, still another and by far the most numerous wave of medical argonauts studied in Vienna and at universities in Germany and Switzerland" (40), while the decades roughly between "1820 to 1861 have been called the 'French' or 'Paris period'" (40). Gradually, the label "medical mecca" (Jones 41) shifted from Paris to Vienna. Jones's study is not only significant as a source of the names of the many American physicians who studied in Paris, but as proof of these physicians' influence on American medical practice upon their return to the United States. As he shows, "sixty-seven of the doctors who studied in Paris taught in American medical schools either before or after they went abroad" (46) and "introduced their students to French medicine" (47). Some of the doctors, such as Charles Alexander Pope from St. Louis, studied in both Paris and Vienna; he did so for two years after his graduation from the University of Pennsylvania Medical School in 1839 (47). Paris attracted them via the many reports published by practitioners in American medical journals, reports that Russell M. Jones calls "a genre of travel literature" (52). Paris's pull factors were "breadth of learning and clinical experience" (56), no quackery, the state and not the students paying the professors, many and large hospitals with "numerous cases of various diseases as well as surgical operations" (57), the availability of private lessons, "facilities and material for human dissecting" (62), and a "flourishing Parisian medical press" (63). Overall, as John Harley Warner maintains, "the knowledge and technique they

[8] Being distracted by the city's cultural offerings was not a rare phenomenon for anyone – no matter of which nationality – who studied in Vienna, as Charles Carroll Fulton proclaims in 1874 in his *Europe Viewed through American Spectacles*: "They [the students at the General Hospital] were of all nationalities, including a dozen or more Americans, and we were pleased to learn that the latter are the most studious and attentive to the lectures of any who attend. The professors all admit this, and hold them up as examples to the German students, most of whom come here merely to enjoy Vienna life" (58-9).

[American doctors] brought back [from Paris] were leading components in the transformation of American medicine" (213); yet, "American physicians were highly selective about which aspects of Parisian medicine they transmitted to America and which ones they eschewed" (214).

To understand the social changes in the medical profession between the late nineteenth century and the early years of the twentieth century, when the shift from Paris to Vienna had firmly been established, it helps to look at further medical responses to Vienna. In 1896, L. Harrison Mettler, an American physician from Chicago, communicates his view on Vienna and Heidelberg by taking the reader through his own experiences in those two very different university cities. Mettler arrives with high expectations and is immediately disappointed by the "very muddy canal and a very much muddier creek" (1056) in Vienna, that is, the Wien river. However, as soon as he reaches the heart of Vienna, he notices a "touch of orientalism" (1056) and, with the exception of Paris, depicts Vienna as "probably the most beautiful city in Europe" (1056).

Mettler focuses on the achievements and the reputation of Viennese medical institutions and physicians. "The reasons for the preëminence of Vienna," for him, "are many. One is the cosmopolitan character, size and wealth of her population. The generous support and favor of the government in educational matters is another. Above all, however, is the unusual concentration of learning in the capital and its matchless University" (1057). In contrast, he blames his own country for the gap in education and learning between central Europe and the United States. He names "our numerous ill-prepared colleges, our low standards of medical education, our senseless desire for cheap notoriety, our tolerance of 'isms and 'pathies, our ofttimes badly-concealed efforts to maintain a professional air with a trade-and-barter method of conduct, and especially our too frequent attacks of professional jealousy and absence of laudable *esprit de corps*" (1057) as main reasons but also takes comfort in more recent improvements in the medical profession in the United States. While architecturally the Viennese hospitals for Mettler have nothing to boast of, they, in all other respects, can still rightfully be considered supreme. Mettler's self-critical and historically aware comparison between American and Viennese institutions reflects a time when the medical grand tour is about to become medical mass tourism.

In spite of all the advantages Vienna offered American doctors and the high reputation of the city as the new Mecca of medicine, some critical voices pointed to the "shallowness, commercialism, or pretensions engendered by the practical courses. These voices became louder as American facilities improved and abuses of the brief training programs in Europe became more evident" (Bonner, *American Doctors* 103). If you add to this the low reputation of some of the assistants who mostly conducted these courses for financial reasons, their impreciseness in the use of English, and the disregard for and often inhuman treatment of the patients and their sufferings, one can understand the sharp criticism that was voiced in the *Journal of the American Medical Association*: at Vienna, as Hugh Payne Greeley complains in 1914, a time when the AMA of Vienna was still functioning, "[s]ome are there for one month and they gorge themselves, eating much and digesting little. Others are there for the side shows and the beer and take only food enough to get their certificate, which the University of Vienna issues to any one who can pay the price of a course whether he attends or not" (Greeley 2150). This criticism obscured the fact that Vienna offered expertise and information not available to the same extent in the United States and, above all, not available to female students of medicine, who were in dire need of practical hospital experience. While some male members of the field may have considered some of their own colleagues not serious enough about their training in Vienna, their female contemporaries soaked in all the practical education they could get.

A closer look at Hugh Payne Greeley's account of American physicians studying in Berlin and Vienna reveals some of the potential but, to some extent, hidden reasons for his generally harsh criticism of both the motives of those who sought medical education abroad and the universities that seem to have easily granted certificates and, thus, "encourage[d] the quick-lunch variety of study" (Greeley 2150).[9] He not only points out that classes taught in German were too difficult to understand in their full depth and those taught in English were "generally botched" (2150) by the instructors, but also establishes an opposition between "us" and the "average American physicians in Vienna" (2150), which seems to imply that most serious physicians would not spend time and money to go abroad. As a

[9] Greeley himself spent a year (1911-12) abroad, not, however, in Europe but in Newfoundland in the small and isolated fishing community of Pilley's Island. His autobiographical narrative *Work and Play in the Grenfell Mission* (1920) describes in detail this experience. For more information on Greeley, see the Hugh Payne Greeley Papers in Yale University's Archives.

graduate of Harvard Medical School, Greeley certainly includes himself in the former group. Furthermore, he writes during the initial stages of World War I (in December 1914) and suggests the concomitant closing of foreign markets as an opportunity for the United States to finally and efficiently organize American postgraduate studies. Europe would, as he argues, eventually send its medical students to the United States just as it did its laborers. He concludes by evoking the all too well-known "America First" sentiment: "Let us at once set to work and organize ourselves for this task and give to American physicians practical postgraduate work in *our own* language and with our own *trade-mark*" (2151, emphasis in original). Although Greeley's American patriotism as well as criticism of medical studies abroad in 1914 certainly contained grains of truth, he seems to forget or ignore the fact that foreign studies had undergone significant changes in the wake of the grand tour's development toward mass tourism. The easier European sojourns became, the more people joined the travelers, and more European markets adjusted their offerings to the new customers because students, teachers, professors, and researchers in Europe were not among the most affluent.

In spite of Greeley's and Mettler's opposing points of view, neither doubts that Vienna in 1896 and in 1914 had a historical and contemporary reputation and that it was rather the commercialization of its offerings – often triggered by existential need – and the onset of World War I that lowered the city's attractiveness for more research-oriented American physicians. Thus, the medical grand tour was strongly contingent on the cultural grand-tour-turned-mass-tourism at the turn of the nineteenth to the twentieth century, from which, ultimately, women physicians profited in spite of the fact that, on both sides of the Atlantic, women were often not taken seriously in their desire to study and practice medicine. Even the prominent William Osler made such a remark, as Lilian Welsh reveals in her autobiographical sketch: "In those days it was occasionally borne in upon us that we belonged to a class apart. Dr. Osler jocularly said: 'Human kind might be divided into three groups – men, women and women physicians'" (44).

5 MEDICAL WOMEN AS SOJOURNERS IN VIENNA

Women in the nineteenth century began to look for further medical education in Europe. As discussed elsewhere (Birkle, "Capitals of

Medicine" 93-4), Elizabeth Blackwell, who "felt … keenly in need of much wider opportunities to study than were open to women in America" (Blackwell, *Pioneer* 133), left for Paris in 1849, but had to realize that she was only allowed to register as a nursing student in gynecology at La Maternité. Yet, these studies proved to be indispensable for her later foundation of a hospital for female patients and a women's college to train female medical students in gynecology and obstetrics in New York City. The British nurse Florence Nightingale and the British female doctor Elizabeth Garrett strongly influenced Blackwell's views on hygiene and the need for institutional reforms in the education of future doctors.

Similarly, Mary Putnam Jacobi (1842-1906) went to Paris in 1868 already with a degree from the Female Medical College of Pennsylvania (1864), registered at the École de Médecine, and received a degree in 1871 as the first female foreigner. She, too, focused on the diseases of women and children, fought against the idea of "female individualism" (Bittel, "MPG" 31), and kept close academic affiliations. She later worked at the Women's Medical College of the New York Infirmary from 1871 until 1889 (Bittel, *MPG* 5) together with Elizabeth and Emily Blackwell (1826-1910) and closely interacted with Marie Zakrzewska (1829-1902) and Mary Dixon Jones. Others, like Susan Dimock and the Canadian Elizabeth Maude Abbott, went to Zurich and Vienna, as discussed elsewhere (Birkle, "Capitals of Medicine" 95-100). Thomas Neville Bonner points to an astonishing number of women physicians who managed to go on the medical grand tour to Europe:

> Of the sixty-eight prominent nineteenth- and early-twentieth-century women physicians listed in the *Dictionary of American Medical Biography*, thirty-two, or nearly half, spent some time in postgraduate study abroad. In all, according to an earlier estimate by the author, between six and eight hundred American women studied abroad, chiefly in postgraduate clinics and hospitals, between 1870 and 1914. (*To the Ends* 27)

Apart from the very well-known women doctors staying in Europe, such as Blackwell, Jacobi, and Dimock, many others, as Bonner indicates, crossed the Atlantic, among them Eliza Root (1846-June 12, 1926), Elizabeth Mott, Mary Dixon Jones (1828-1908), and Mary E. Bates (1861-Sept. 17, 1954). While they, too, were prominent physicians of their time, more research still needs to be done on their motives for traveling, their choices of doctors to study with, and their reasons for staying in Vienna in particular. Dr. Eliza H. Root[10] – affiliated with the Woman's Medical College of Chicago (which became part of Northwestern University in 1891) until 1902, when the women's section was closed because of decreasing registration rates – worked in gynecology and obstetrics and, as a practitioner and researcher, published articles on women and childbirth in the *Woman's Medical Journal.* Root had graduated from the Woman's Medical College in Chicago in 1882, had taught at Chicago since then, and decided to spend some time in Vienna in 1891. She was then Dean of the Woman's Medical College, editor-in-chief of the *Woman's Medical Journal*, secretary of the alumnae association (Lovejoy 97; *Woman's Medical School* 37, 103-4), and wrote the entry on "The Woman's Medical School" for the four-volume companion to the history of Northwestern University (cf. Root 365-89).

Whereas her female colleagues on the Chicago medical faculty, Dr. Sarah Hackett Stevenson (grad. 1874) and Dr. Marie Josepha Mergler (grad. 1879) went to France and England and to Zurich respectively, Dr. Root, who by 1891 had already worked as an obstetrician, went "to Vienna for special study in obstetrics" (Lovejoy 92; cf. *Woman's Medical School* 104), just as did Dr. Mary E. Bates (grad. 1881; born in Manitowoc County, Wisconsin, 25 February 1861 – died in Denver, Colorado, 18 September 1954) of Denver, Colorado, had done before her in 1883 and 1884 (*Woman's Medical School* 102). Bates had also gone to Heidelberg, then returned to Chicago to become "professor of anatomy" and lecturer in minor surgery from 1885 to 1890 and subsequently practiced medicine in Denver (Lovejoy 93). In Vienna, she had done advanced work in surgery and anatomy.

Elizabeth Mott, whose dates of birth and death I have been unable to locate, was a very different kind of female practitioner, one that was at the time called a "quack" but had a strong influence on Harriot Kezia Hunt (1805-75), who was the first woman in the United States who practiced medicine professionally but without a degree. Hunt applied for admission to the Harvard Medical School (1847) but was denied access once[11] and refrained from entering Harvard the second time – in spite of her

[10] Root's father had moved to the United States from Scotland in 1842, six years prior to her birth in Illinois.

[11] Although, at the time, Oliver Wendell Holmes, Sr., was Dean of the Medical School and did consider Hunt's admission, she had to be rejected because of immense pressure by the student body to do so.

subsequent admission (1850) – because of the demonstrations against her and three African American students (Martin Robison Delaney, Daniel Laing, Jr., and Isaac Humphrey Snowden) by male students. Harriot Hunt met Elizabeth Mott and her husband Richard Dixon Mott, who had both immigrated from England in 1832 ("First Woman") and opened a joint practice in Boston with Elizabeth Mott treating women and children, while her husband treated male patients, when Hunt's sister Sarah became seriously ill and no doctor was able to cure her. Elizabeth Mott claimed that she was applying "'European vegetable medicine'" ("First Woman"). The Motts were able to cure Sarah, and, as a consequence, both sisters decided to study medicine with them. When Elizabeth Mott left for Europe in 1835 – the same year Holmes returned from Europe –, the Hunts agreed to take over her patients. Elizabeth Mott returned a few months later to New York City. Harriot Hunt, although she had never been in Europe, was influenced by Mott's European experiences. Harriot Hunt subsequently became an abolitionist and advocate of women's rights and was granted an honorary degree from the Female Medical College of Philadelphia in 1853. In 1856, she published her autobiography *Glances and Glimpses; Or, Fifty Years' Social, Including Twenty Years Professional Life*.

While foreign women "were gladly received at the famous clinics, and appeared in increasing numbers during the last years of the nineteenth century," "the medical education of Austro-Hungarian women was another matter" (Lovejoy 194). It was not until 1900 that the doors of the medical faculty were opened to local women (Lovejoy 195). Several Austrian women had meanwhile received medical degrees in Zurich (Dr. Gabrielle Possauner-Ehrental (1893), Dr. Hilda Petrovic-Stevenow, Dr. Frederika Lubringer) and then took advantage of the new law that allowed women "with medical degrees from foreign universities … to register for practice, and the medical schools of Austria-Hungary were opened to women students" (Lovejoy 195).

Medical Europe offered similar attractions to Canadian physicians. As shown in my essay "Capitals of Medicine," Maude Elizabeth Abbott (1867-1940) from Montreal visited Europe several times, studied in Heidelberg, Berne, Zurich, and finally also in Vienna from 1895-97. She did work at (Friedrich) Schauta's (1849-1919) Clinic and attended many of the classes offered in English, but also experienced sexism because male American students occasionally rejected their female colleagues ("Autobiographical Sketch" 137) and prevented them from being admitted to classes where admission was "hereditary." Abbott returned to Vienna in later years and kept in touch with her European colleagues because she wanted to communicate and put into practice the idea of an International Association of Medical Museums, an idea that her admired teacher Sir William Osler had instilled in her.

6 SIR WILLIAM OSLER (1849-1919): A CANADIAN IN VIENNA

Sir William Osler (1849-1919) could be considered Oliver Wendell Holmes's Canadian counterpart. Osler admired Holmes and "clearly used [him] as a role model in some respects," as Charles Bryan maintains (16). Osler and Holmes met on various occasions (1877, 1883, 1888-89). While Holmes has kept his place in the American collective memory as a man of letters rather than a physician, for example through the bestselling *The Autocrat of the Breakfast-Table* (1858) (Bryan 17), Osler is today much better known for his medical work such as *Principles and Practice of Medicine* (1892). In many ways, such as in bedside training, psychological ideas, the introduction of the idea of sepsis, and their opposition to old medical traditions such as bloodletting, Holmes preceded Osler, but Osler introduced these practices more broadly, enhanced, and spread them. Osler pays tribute to his colleague and concludes that Holmes "has permanently enriched the literature of the race" ("Oliver Wendell Holmes" in *An Alabama Student* 67).

In Osler's brief professional autobiographical sketch, *Vienna after Thirty-Four Years*, published in 1908 and looking back to the year 1874 when he studied "pediatrics with Hermann Wiederhoffer, skin disease with Ferdinand Hebra … general medicine with Heinrich von Bamberger … and ear disease with Adam Politzer …" (Bliss 77), he expressed his deep admiration for some of the achievements of the Vienna Medical School and its experts; however, he was critical of Vienna's "general medicine and pathology" (Bliss 78) after having studied pathologic anatomy with Virchow in Berlin. He seems to have been unable to get into the small select classes that Carl Rokitansky taught but was at least able to view the ceremonies held on the occasion of the doctor's seventieth birthday (Bliss 78; cf. Grant). Overall, he spent two years in London, Berlin, and Vienna (to return briefly to Berlin in 1884 [Rodin 892]) and to North America in 1874. Superlatives have been used to describe his achievements such as "The Father of Modern Medicine." Like Oliver

Wendell Holmes, Sr., he was not just a physician, but also an author and historian and quite well-known for his jokes during speeches and presentations. He studied at the Toronto School of Medicine (1868), only to leave for McGill University's Faculty of Medicine in Montreal, where he received his medical degree in 1872. After about two years in Europe, he returned to McGill in 1874, was appointed Chair of Clinical Medicine at the University of Pennsylvania in 1884, co-founded the Association of American Physicians, and left for the Johns Hopkins Hospital in Baltimore, MD, in 1889, where he was one of the four founding professors of Johns Hopkins Hospital. Finally, in 1905, he was appointed to the Regius Chair of Medicine at Oxford.[12]

Osler's time in Vienna is depicted in retrospect in his essay *Vienna after Thirty-Four Years* (1908). Arriving in Vienna in January 1874 from Berlin and staying until April, Osler found time to stroll around the city, as he then also does in 1908 when visiting Vienna again and reminiscing about the earlier trip. In 1908, he walks around the *General Hospital*, up and down *Alserstrasse* next to it, revisits the *Riedhof*, a prominent beer garden for doctors, military officers, and civil servants in the 1860s and 1870s, where he used to have dinner, meets old friends from Boston, and is surprised by the changes on the *Ringstrasse* with the new university buildings, the new *Rathaus*, and the *Burgtheater*. He then dives into the details of the *Congress für Innere Medizin* (2), which he attends together with his old friend and former student Dr. Joseph H. Pratt of Boston. One little comment he offers should be noted because any conference organizer can learn from it. Apart from the fact that the university hall was unsuitable for lectures because of its poor acoustics, Osler adds the following: "It is a miserable mistake in introducing a discussion on any subject to speak for more than half an hour, but to continue for an hour and a quarter is too much for human endurance …" (2).[13]

---

[12] McGill named its medical library Osler Library in his honor, where Osler's and his wife's ashes are also buried.

[13] He continues to present the different lectures on gynecology, syphilis, the pancreas and thyroid, etc. and names the respective speakers, most of whom were either speakers of German or from the United States and England. Interestingly enough, this meeting was not yet considered an international congress since the participants, too, discuss the timeliness of the foundation of "an International Congress for Internal Medicine" (5), which other fields in medicine already seemed to have established.

In 1908, Max Neuburger, known as the editor of the *Handbuch der Geschichte der Medizin*, shows Osler the Vienna libraries, among them that of the *Wiener medizinische Gesellschaft*, "built under the presidency of Billroth" (7), with its large library and lecture hall, and the, as Osler writes, "excellent" university library with a separate room for "a collection illustrating the evolution of the history of the medical department of the university" (7), which found an imitator at the University of Pennsylvania in William Pepper III (8). Osler goes on to describe the *Hofbibliothek* (the Court Library), comments on specific copies of rare books, but also finds mildly critical words for the unchanged situation in the old medical clinic with the wards still looking as they had been in 1874.[14]

Osler concludes his essay by emphasizing once more Vienna's importance in the medical world and its influence on North American medicine in particular. He refers to Van Swieten of the so-called first Vienna school in the eighteenth century, the new Vienna school with Rokitansky and Skoda, who, as Osler maintains, "really made Vienna the successor of the great Paris school" (15). But he attributes Vienna's fame even more to specialists, such as Hebra, Arlt, Schnitzler, Politzer, and others (Sigmund, Neumann, Jaeger, von Schrötter, Gruber), who, for Osler, "have been more than others responsible for the successful development of these specialties in the United States" (15-16). Yet for him, the reputation has moved from the Danube to the Spree; this, for him, is the law of history. "Minerva Medica," as he maintains, "has never had her chief temples in any one country for more than one generation or two" (16). He points to Johannes Müller and Rudolph Virchow in Germany but even more metaphorically he imagines a conversation between himself and Minerva Medica, in which he "boldly suggested that it was perhaps time to think of crossing the Atlantic and setting up her temple in the new

---

[14] He refers to the disease "'Morbus Bamberger'" (11) and later to Prof. Brauer, who was to arrive from Marburg for the session of the American Medical Association (11). New clinics are being erected in 1908, of which he praises "the organization and the completeness of the arrangements for teaching and for the scientific study of disease" (12). Osler reveals the effects of the American Medical Association of Vienna, founded in 1903-04, when he refers to American doctors (Dr. George Cheyne Shattuck III of Boston, Dr. Fischel of St. Louis) working with Professor Schlesinger on "acute infectious diseases" (13) at the Franz Josef Hospital. This hospital's children's department then becomes, as Osler puts it, "an admirable model for the new Harriet Lane Johnston's children's department at the Johns Hopkins Hospital" (14).

world for a generation or two" (17). In this imagined conversation Osler attempts to persuade Minerva Medica to move to the United States by enumerating the advantages of such a shift: "the absence of tradition" — a tradition which he also calls "poison" —, "the greater freedom, the enthusiasm," and the possibility for "missionary work" (17). These words are highly revealing because they show the obstacles for innovation and progress.[15] Medicine as a goddess that moves by "the eternal law" (18) reveals that the field is more than a natural science; it is rather worshipped like a religion; it is a belief system that embraces researchers and practitioners as well as patients. It can unfold best in an atmosphere of acceptance and belief rather than doubt and criticism. And it is the last sentence that fully and clearly states Osler's understanding of American and Canadian medicine: "Doubtless she [Minerva Medica] will come, but not till the present crude organization of our medical clinics is changed, not until there is a fuller realization of internal medicine as a science as well as an art" (18). The ideas of medicine as science and art, medicine as a religion (even if only metaphorically so) reveal the tension that had grown already in the late nineteenth century between a positivist and scientifically solid understanding of illness as a physical-biological phenomenon that can be cured with the knowledge gained in the natural sciences, and on the other hand, medicine as an art as a more aesthetic notion that implies empathy, intuition, knowledge of the human being in its entirety, that is, the treatment of a human being as human and not (just) as a biological phenomenon. Medicine as religion adds the spiritual dimension, the idea that the soul has as much to do with human health as the mind and the body. Osler situates himself in a tradition to which Oliver Wendell Holmes also adhered. The Canadian was philosophically inspired by Sir Thomas Browne's (1605-82) *Religio Medici* (1642) that had already discussed the relationship between science and religion. Osler emphasizes the discrepancy between the American and Viennese, or central European, medical systems, which, however, gradually begin to change on both sides of the Atlantic.

---

[15] While tradition is usually positively connoted as offering stability and opportunity for solid work, it also implies fixity, unchangeability, an oppressive atmosphere in which creativity can hardly unfold.

7 REVISING THE DISCIPLINE

Ultimately, as the sequence of reports from Vienna from 1857, 1860, 1874, 1889, 1896, 1908, and 1914 shows, Vienna begins to attract medical visitors in the 1850s – if not earlier, as the Irishman Dr. Wilde's publication proves – and continues to do so into the twentieth century until World War II (cf. Birkle, "Vienna as Medical Contact Zone"). While the expertise of the professors, the ready availability of material to dissect or operate on,[16] the arrangement and organization of the medical facilities, and the practical and comfortable living conditions in Vienna as well as the city's cultural offerings are almost unanimously praised by all visitors and letter writers, some at least voice their ethical concerns and show an awareness of the significance of the power of money and, thus, the power of the American visitors to influence ethical practices. The reports respectively indicate that American medical studies in Vienna are highly commercialized and that money – in addition to the professional and scientific interest – plays a significant role in the mediation of medical knowledge. Furthermore, because of their absence in the correspondence of American physicians with American medical journals, women seem to have been a negligible factor in the profession. In spite of the strong resistance to women in the field by men of science, the few American women do not provoke any comments from their colleagues, at least not from those to whose correspondence I have had access. This fact, perhaps due to the limited accessibility of letters, makes it necessary to dig further for those women's testimonies who actually had the opportunity to participate in the medical grand tour.

---

[16] One of the reasons why so much dissection material was available was that "all who die within its [the General Hospital's] walls must be subjected to a post-mortem examination" (Fulton 59), so that there were about "thirty to fifty deaths daily" (Fulton 59). Even more gruesome is the following explanation stated rather matter-of-factly: If the dead "are friendless, as is generally the case, they are cut up and quartered off among the students, one taking a leg, another an arm, another a head, as the case may be" (59). The recently dead were kept for twelve hours in a separate room just in case they would wake up again (59). The "upwards of fifty American physicians" present in Vienna in the winter before the report's completion, mostly from New York and Massachusetts, thoroughly enjoyed themselves mixing among the locals and thus significantly perfecting their German through intimate contact.

As the selected sketches show, male physicians' stays in Europe have been researched and documented extensively. The American Oliver Wendell Holmes, Sr., and the Canadian William Osler, traveling to Europe some forty years later, demonstrate that talented male medical students and doctors had no trouble rising through the ranks of the profession, however, never without postgraduate training in Europe – either in Paris in the earlier nineteenth century or in Vienna and Berlin in the later nineteenth and early twentieth century. Women, at the same time, could legally study medicine neither in the first half nor – to a large extent or with obstacles to overcome – in the second half of the nineteenth century, as the examples of Harriot Kezia Hunt and Elizabeth Blackwell show. Subsequently, through the foundation of medical colleges in the United States for women, the next generation, such as Susan Dimock, Ann Preston, Mary Putnam Jacobi, or Emily Blackwell, were able to get medical degrees in the United States. Elizabeth Mott was considered a quack and had no medical training in spite of her journey to Europe.

In the wake of the Blackwell sisters, Jacobi, Dimock, and others, Eliza Root, Mary Dixon Jones, Mary E. Bates, and Maude E. Abbott did become certified doctors and sought further training and knowledge in Europe, in their cases most prominently in Vienna. However, with the gradual closing of many of the women's medical schools in the United States toward the end of the nineteenth century and with only very few medical schools with a good reputation becoming co-educational – Harvard did so only in 1945 – women again often faced insurmountable obstacles in their pursuit of medical education. However, all of the men and women discussed here sought medical training in Europe – in cities such as London, Edinburgh, Berlin, Paris, Zurich, and Vienna, with the last becoming one of the most attractive places for the profession because of its teachers, its willingness to accommodate the needs of its foreign visitors, and, of course, because of its cultural attractions.

Networks were established, also among the American and English women doctors because they largely faced the same gender-based obstacles but were at least allowed to study abroad and could communicate easily with one another. Links with women doctors from other countries were rare but existed, mostly because some European universities did open their doors for women from abroad but not for their own native women. Many North American male and female sojourners –not least among them Holmes and Osler – were impressed by the organization of medical education in Europe, in Germany and Austria in particular, in spite of some criticism by others. In the wake of their return, they began to create a new medical system in the United States and Canada in imitation of what they had seen in Europe. However, they often mistook their research-oriented studies with experts for what they believed to be general medical education in Europe and, as a result, established such a system for all students of medicine (cf. Bonner, "The German Model of Training Physicians").

The career that I have not looked at in my paper is that of Marie Zakrzewska (1829-1902), who was born in Berlin, Germany, trained as a midwife before she finally moved to the United States to study medicine at Cleveland Medical College in 1856 in order then to work at the New York Infirmary for Women and Children and finally at the New England Female Medical College from 1859 onward. In 1862 she founded the New England Hospital for Women and Children. Zakrzewska's journey from Berlin to New York City and then to Cleveland and back to New York City, and finally to Boston makes her one of the central figures in the late nineteenth-century American medical profession. She is one of the main connecting links in the networks of European and North American women in the medical profession, although she never visited Vienna.

BIBLIOGRAPHY

Abbott, Maude Elizabeth Seymour. "Autobiographical Sketch." *McGill Medical Journal* 28.3 (Oct. 1959): 127-52.

Birkle, Carmen. "Narrative Praxis und diagnostische Interpretation: Literatur und Medizin in Amerika." *Literatur und Medizin: Interdisziplinäre Beiträge zu den* Medical Humanities. Ed. Pascal Fischer and Mariacarla Gadebusch Bondio. Heidelberg: Winter, 2016. 79-100.

—. "Capitals of Medicine: North American Women and Their Encounters with Europe (1850s-1930s)." *Narratives of Encounters in the North Atlantic Triangle*. Ed. Waldemar Zacharasiewicz and David Staines. Vienna: Verlag der Österreichischen Akademie der Wissenschaften, 2015. 85-105.

—. "Vienna as Medical Contact Zone: American Doctors in the Austrian Capital in the Late 1930s." *"Anschluss" March 1938: Aftermath on Medicine and Society*. Ed. Wolfgang Schütz et al. Special Issue of *Wiener*

Klinische Wochenschrift 130.5 (2018): S295-S300. https:// doi.org/ 10.1007/ s00508- 018-1366-4.

Bittel, Carla. *Mary Putnam Jacobi and the Politics of Medicine in Nineteenth-Century America*. Chapel Hill: U of North Carolina P, 2009.

—. "Mary Putnam Jacobi and the Nineteenth-Century Politics of Women's Health Research." *Women Physicians and the Cultures of Medicine*. Ed. Ellen S. More, Elizabeth Fee, and Manon Parry. Baltimore: Johns Hopkins UP, 2009. 23-51.

—. "A Literary Physician? The Paris Writings of Mary Putnam Jacobi." *Communicating Disease: Cultural Representations of American Medicine*. Ed. Carmen Birkle and Johanna Heil. Heidelberg: Winter, 2013. 95-117.

Blackwell, Elizabeth. *Pioneer Work in Opening the Medical Profession to Women*. 1895. Introd. Amy Sue Bix. Amherst: Humanity, 2005.

Bliss, Michael. *William Osler: A Life in Medicine*. New York: Oxford UP, 1999.

Blodi, Frederick C. "William R. Wilde (1815-76) in Vienna." *Documenta Ophthalmologica* 81 (1992): 59-73.

Bonner, Thomas Neville. *American Doctors and German Universities: A Chapter in International Relations, 1870-1914*. Lincoln: U of Nebraska P, 1963.

—. *To the Ends of the Earth: Women's Search for Education in Medicine*. Cambridge: Harvard UP, 1992.

—. "The German Model of Training Physicians in the United States, 1870-1914: How Closely Was It Followed?" *Sickness and Health in America: Readings in the History of Medicine and Public Health*. Ed. Judith Walzer Leavitt and Ronald L. Numbers. 1978. Madison: U of Wisconsin P, 1997. 189-99.

Bryan, Charles S. "'The Greatest Brahmin among them': William Osler's (1849-1919) Perspective on Oliver Wendell Holmes (1809-94)." *Journal of Medical Biography* 18 (2010): 15-18. DOI: 10.1258/jmb.2009.009059.

Buzard, James. "The Grand Tour and after (1660-1840)." *The Cambridge Companion to Travel Writing*. Ed. Peter Hulme and Tim Youngs. Cambridge: Cambridge UP, 2002. 37-52.

Clarke, Edward Hammond. *Sex in Education, Or, A Fair Chance for Girls*. 1872. N.p.: General Books, 2009.

Davis, Cynthia J. *Bodily and Narrative Forms: The Influence of Medicine on American Literature, 1845-1915*. Stanford: Stanford UP, 2000.

Derby, Haskell. "Medical Advantages of Vienna for American Students." *The Boston Medical and Surgical Journal* 63.3 (2 Aug. 1860): 51-3. *Internet Archive*. Access 30 Dec. 2018.

Dixon-Jones, Mary. "Reminiscences of Travels in Europe in 1886, Nos. 1, 2, 3." *Woman's Medical Journal* 4 (Dec. 1895): 299-304; 332-37; 5 (Jan. 1896): 11-14. Web. Access 28 Febr. 2019.

Dowling William C. *Oliver Wendell Holmes in Paris: Medicine, Theology, and the Autocrat of the Breakfast Table*. Hanover: UP of New England, 2006.

Editors of the Encyclopaedia Britannica. "Pierre-Jean-Georges Cabanis: French Philosopher and Physiologist." *Encyclopaedia Britannica*. June 2019. https://www.britannica.com/biography/Pierre-Jean-Georges-Cabanis. Access 3 Nov. 2019.

Falkenstein, Lorne, and Giovanni Grandi. "Étienne Bonnot de Condillac." *The Stanford Encyclopedia of Philosophy*. Ed. Edward N. Zalta. Stanford: Stanford UP, 2017. https://plato.stanford.edu/archives/win2017/entries/condillac/. Access 3 Nov. 2019.

"First Woman to Apply to Harvard Medical School: Harriot Kezia Hunt." *History of American Women: 19th Century Women*. Web. Access 28 Feb. 2019.

Fulton, Charles Carroll. *Europe Viewed through American Spectacles*. Philadelphia: J. B. Lippincott & Co., 1874. Particularly "The Vienna General Hospital" (58-59); "The Dissecting-Rooms" (59); "The Jolly Students" (59).

Gibian, Peter. "Doctor Holmes: The Life in Conversation." *Oliver Wendell Holmes: Physician and Man of Letters*. Ed. Scott H. Podolsky and Charles S. Bryan. Sagamore Beach: Watson, 2009. 71-92.

Grant, Ted. *This Is Our Work: The Legacy of Sir William Osler*. New York: Nature, 1955.

Greeley, Hugh Payne. "Postgraduate Study: Foreign Realities versus American Realities." *JAMA* 63.24 (12 Dec. 1914): 2150-51. University of California. Digitzed by Google. Access 26 Dec. 2018.

Holmes, Oliver Wendell. *Our Hundred Days in Europe*. Boston: Houghton Mifflin; Cambridge: Riverside P, 1891.

Johnson, Robert W. "Impressions of Vienna as a Medical School." *Philadelphia Medical Times* 11 (4 Dec. 1880): 129-38. *Google* U of Michigan. Access 30 Dec. 2018.

Jones, Russell M. "American Doctors and the Parisian Medical World, 1830-1840." *Bulletin of the History of Medicine* 47.1 (1 Jan. 1973): 40-65. *ProQuest* Johns Hopkins University, 2003. Access 27 Jan. 2019.

Kass, Amalie M. "A Private Pestilence: Holmes and Puerperal Fever." *Oliver Wendell Holmes: Physician and Man of Letters*. Ed. Scott H. Podolsky and Charles S. Bryan. Sagamore Beach: Watson, 2009. 39-58.

Kirchhoff, Arthur, ed. *Die akademische Frau: Gutachten hervorragender Universitätsprofessoren, Frauenlehrer und Schriftsteller über die Befähigung der Frau zum wissenschaftlichen Studium und Berufe*. Berlin: Hugo Steinitz, 1897.

—. Vorwort. *Die akademische Frau: Gutachten hervorragender Universitätsprofessoren, Frauenlehrer und Schriftsteller über die Befähigung der Frau zum wissenschaftlichen Studium und Berufe*. Berlin: Hugo Steinitz, 1897. vii-xvi.

Lackner, Franz X. "Exploring Vienna between the two World Wars: Doctors of the American Medical Association and Their Families." *Narratives of Encounters in the North Atlantic Triangle*. Ed. Waldemar Zacharasiewicz and David Staines. Vienna: Verlag der Österreichischen Akademie der Wissenschaften, 2015. 107-25.

Lovejoy, Esther Pohl. *Women Doctors of the World*. New York: Macmillan, 1957.

McCullough, David. *The Greater Journey: Americans in Paris*. New York: Simon & Schuster, 2011.

Mettler, L. Harrison. "Medical Vienna and Heidelberg: Notes from My Sketchbook." *JAMA* 27 (14 Nov. 1896): 1056-61. *Google* University of California. Access 26 Dec. 2018.

Mitchell, S. Weir. *Wear and Tear, Or, Hints to the Overworked*. 1871. Walnut Creek, CA: Altamira, 2004.

Möbius, Paul Julius. *Über den physiologischen Schwachsinn des Weibes*. 1900. Munich: Matthes & Seitz, 1977.

Montjoye, Irene. *Oscar Wildes Vater über Metternichs Österreich*. Frankfurt: Lang, 1989.

Morantz-Sanchez, Regina. *Sympathy and Science: Women Physicians in American Medicine*. 1985. Chapel Hill: U of North Carolina P, 2000.

—. *Conduct Unbecoming a Woman: Medicine on Trial in Turn-of-the-Century Brooklyn*. New York: Oxford UP, 1999.

O'Brien, Michael. "European Attachments." *Conjectures of Order: Intellectual Life and the American South, 1810-1860*. 2 vols. Chapel Hill: U of North Carolina P, 2004. Vol. 1: 90-161.

Oliver, Henry K. "The Vienna Hospitals." *The Boston Medical and Surgical Journal* 57.3 (20 Aug. 1857): 49-58. *Internet Archive.* Access 28 Dec. 2018.

Osler, William, M.D. *Vienna after Thirty-Four Years*. Charleston, SC: Nabu P, 2013. Rpt. from: *JAMA* 50.19 (1908): 1523-5. DOI: 10.1001/jama.1908.25310450033003.

—. "Oliver Wendell Holmes." *Celebrating the Contributions of William Osler: Selection of Writing.* www.medicalarchives.jhmi.edu/osler/alabacontents.htm. Access 25 Dec. 2018. 55-66. Rpt. *From an Alabama Student and Other Biographical Essays*. New York: Oxford UP, 1909.

Podolsky, Scott H., and Charles S. Bryan, eds. *Oliver Wendell Holmes: Physician and Man of Letters*. Sagamore Beach: Watson, 2009.

Rethford, Wayne. "Dr. Eliza H. Root." *Scots Great and Small, People and Places*. Web. Access 26 Dec. 2018.

Rodin, A. E. "Canada's Foremost Pathologist of the Nineteenth Century – William Osler." *C. M. A. Journal* 107 (4 Nov. 1972): 890-6.

Root, Eliza Hannah. "The Woman's Medical School." *Northwestern University: A History, 1855-1905*. Ed. Arthur Herbert Wilde. New York: University Publishing Society, 1905. 4 vols. Vol. 4: 365-89. *Northwestern University Archive*.

Singer, Sandra L. *Adventures Abroad: North American Women at German-Speaking Universities, 1868-1915*. Westport, CT: Praeger, 2003.

Stowe, William W. *Going Abroad: European Travel in Nineteenth-Century American Culture*. Princeton: Princeton UP, 1994.

Tappan, Lucy M. "The Study of Obstetrics in Vienna." Read before the Alumnae Society, Philadelphia, 10. Sept. 1892.

Walsh, Mary Roth. *"Doctors Wanted, No Women Need Apply": Sexual Barriers in the Medical Profession, 1835-1975*. New Haven, CT: Yale UP, 1977.

Warner, John Harley. "The Selective Transport of Medical Knowledge: Antebellum American Physicians and Parisian Medical Therapeutics." *Bulletin of the History of Medicine* 59.2 (Summer 1985): 213-31. *ProQuest* Johns Hopkins UP, 2003.

Welsh, Lilian. *Reminiscences of Thirty Years in Baltimore*. Baltimore: Norman, Remington, 1925. *Internet Archive*. Access 26 Dec. 2018.

Weinstein, Michael A. "Oliver Wendell Holmes's Depth Psychology: A Reconstruction." *Oliver Wendell Holmes: Physician and Man of Letters*. Ed. Scott H. Podolsky and Charles S. Bryan. Sagamore Beach: Watson, 2009. 93-103.

Wilde, William R. *Austria: Its Literary, Scientific, and Medical Institutions. With Notes upon the Present State of Science, and a Guide to the Hospitals and Sanatory Establishments of Vienna.* Dublin: William Curry, Jun. and Comp., 1843.

Woman's Medical School Northwestern University (Woman's Medical College of Chicago): The Institution and Its Founders. Class Histories 1870-1896. Chicago: H. G. Cutler, 1896. *Harvard University Archive.*

CHRISTOPH IRMSCHER

"In Gedanken in Amerika": The Evolution of Franz Steindachner[1]

Franz Steindachner (1834-1919) was the curator of the fish, amphibian, and reptile collections at the Natural History Museum in Vienna when his work came to the attention of the world's most famous scientist, Louis Agassiz (1807-1883), the Swiss-born Professor of Natural History at Harvard University. In 1869, Agassiz invited Steindachner to come work for him. Worlds collided that day.

Ill. 1: Franz Steindachner at the time of the *Hassler* trip. From J. H. Blake, Scrapbook of Clippings, Photographs, Cartes-de-Visite Studio Portraits, Manuscripts and Other Materials. Spec. Coll. Archives sMu 326.43.1. Ernst Mayr Library, Museum of Comparative Zoology, Harvard University.

[1] Thanks to Professor Christa Riedl-Dorn, Mario Dominik-Riedl, and their staff at the Naturhistorisches Museum for making this correspondence accessible to me during my visit in March 2019. Dr. Verena Stagl, former Curator of the Myriapod Collection at the Museum, and Dr. Ernst Mikschi, Department Head, Zoological Department I of the Naturgeschichtliches Museum Wien, kindly read and commented on drafts of this essay.

It is indeed hard to think of a man more unlike Agassiz than Dr. Steindachner. Photographs from around that time show a thin, spare man with a scraggly beard and rimless glasses, a science "nerd," so to speak, the polar opposite of the hedonistic Agassiz, who loved good wine, big meals, and cigars (ill.1). Married twice, Agassiz, a protégé of the famous Alexander von Humboldt, had left his native Switzerland for the United States in 1846, originally just for a lecture tour. He took Harvard by storm and soon found himself at the center of a new scientific school at the university.[2] Steindachner, by contrast, was a lifelong bachelor, living, for a large part of his career, in an apartment provided by the museum, with his unmarried sister Anna or "Netti" cooking meals for him and doing his laundry for him.

In the literature about Agassiz, Steindachner is frequently mentioned. But he is mostly portrayed as something of a "weirdo." That is an unfortunate misreading. It minimizes Steindachner's own importance in the history of science: he published more than 200 ichthyological and 52 herpetological articles and described over 1,000 new recent or fossil species of fish as well as more than 150 new species of reptiles and amphibians.[3] In terms of the purposes of this essay, Steindachner's response to the kind of science Agassiz practiced sheds new light on the history of Austrian-American relations during a crucial period in the development of biological science. Moreover, while many of Steindachner's publications sag under the weight of piled-up taxonomic detail, he is often a good, vibrant, and entertaining writer and would deserve to be remembered only for that reason.

***

Franz Steindachner had come to his elevated position at the Naturhistorisches Museum the old-fashioned way, by dint of hard work and patience, rising, over the course of a long career, from volunteer helper to, eventually, museum director or "Intendant." Born on 11 November 1834, to a physician originally from Melk in Lower Austria and a Viennese mother, Steindachner attended the Schottengymnasium and then the

---

[2] For more, see my biography *Louis Agassiz: Creator of American Science*.

[3] See Riedl-Dorn, "Steindachner, Franz."

University of Vienna, studying first law and then natural history. Among his teachers was the geologist Eduard Suess, the inventor of the term "biosphere."[4]

Even as a student, Steindachner was magically drawn to the fish in the "k.k. Hof-Naturalien Kabinett" on the Josefsplatz in Vienna, the Imperial-Royal Natural History Cabinet, as the Naturhistorisches Museum was then known. In 1860, the new Director of the cabinet, Dr. Ludwig Redtenbacher (1814-1876), put young Steindachner—who had by then, one may safely assume, made himself essential to the cabinet's operations—in charge of the museum's ichthyological collection, at first only as a salaried helper. A year later, he was promoted to curatorial assistant. Steindachner immediately began to put his personal stamp on the museum, embarking on ambitious collecting trips to Dalmatia, Switzerland, France, Spain, Portugal and the Canary Islands, from which he returned laden with new specimens. In 1868, he expanded the radius of his activities to Africa, traveling to the Senegambia region. It was in December 1868 in Saint-Louis, right where the Senegal River meets the Atlantic Ocean, that Steindachner received the letter from Louis Agassiz that would, in many ways, change his life. In April 1870, after getting the Viennese court to approve his leave of absence, Steindachner, who had just been appointed curator, sailed for the United States. He did not come back until January 1874. He had been gone for forty-five months.

After Steindachner's return, he was elected to full membership in the Austrian Academy of Sciences (he had been a corresponding member since 1869). He also finally became the director of the "Zoological Cabinet" he had done so much to transform. Thanks to the thousands of specimens he had brought back with him, the rooms containing his ichthyological and herpetological collections were bursting at the seams, and one imagines that, in 1886, he greeted with both elation and relief the opportunity to move them into the monumental new museum building at the Burgring. Now a "Hofrat" (court counselor), a title bestowed by the

[4] On Steindachner's life and career, see Paul Kähsbauer, "Intendant Dr. Franz Steindachner," which includes a list of species first described by Steindachner as well as his publications in the fields of ichthyology and herpetology; Stagl, "Steindachner Franz"; Riedl-Dorn, "Steindachner, Franz." For an instructive account, based on the holdings of the Naturhistorisches Museum Wien, of Steindachner's later expedition to Brazil, see Böhme, "Briefe Franz Steindachners."

Austrian emperor on deserving civil servants and academics, Steindachner commanded respect and enjoyed high visibility, even internationally. More ambitious government-sponsored expeditions followed, especially to the Mediterranean and twice to the Red Sea (the so-called Pola Red Sea expeditions).[5] Although he did return to Brazil in 1903 to collect more fish, he never made it back to the United States.

In 1898, Steindachner ascended to the directorship of the entire museum, a position he held until his retirement at the age of 84 in 1919. On 10 December, within a few weeks of stepping down, still living in his apartment at the museum, he died from complications of pneumonia. The real cause of death was perhaps heartbreak over no longer being officially involved in his museum; it would be hard to imagine Steindachner as a part-time volunteer at the Naturhistorisches Museum. The "Allzeit-Chef" (the Forever Boss) or "Fisch-Hofrat" (Fish Counselor), as Steindachner is still remembered by museum employees today, was famously frugal in his personal habits: summoned for an audience with Emperor Franz-Joseph, he inked a pair of his underwear black so no one would see the hole in the seat of his black suit pants and, in another celebrated instance, when he was *en route* back from Brazil via Madrid and Monaco, he traveled hundreds of miles back to Monaco to retrieve an umbrella he had left behind.[6]

Fish were constantly on Steindachner's mind; he is said to have thought nothing of keeping visitors, including his own sister, waiting for hours when he was preoccupied with his specimens.[7] Whatever personal funds he had Steindachner lavished on his beloved fish. He had spent his life not only living *in* the museum but *for* the museum. One of his obituaries blamed Steindachner's quick and undignified end—he had, after all, lived through worse medical calamities during his travels abroad, including a severe bout of malaria in Brazil when he was already in his late sixties—

---

[5] See Stagl, Sattmann, and Dworschak, "The Material of the 'Pola' Red Sea Expeditions."

[6] Kähsbauer 12, 8.

[7] Personal communication, Dr. Ernst Mikschi, Department Head, Zoological Department I, Naturhistorisches Museum Wien, 18 June 2019.

on the catastrophic heating situation at the museum.[8] No wonder that some believe that his ghost still haunts the premises today.[9]

***

In December 1868, when Steindachner opened Agassiz's letter in Saint-Louis, what seemed like a famous scientist's gratuitously generous offer to a little-known curator was not really a bolt out of the blue. The tentacles of Louis Agassiz's collecting instinct had reached Vienna long ago. In 1854, the zoological cabinet had obliged him with a collection of fish (160 pieces, to be exact). In March 1863 Agassiz, late as always, finally promised, in a letter addressed to Professor Rudolf Kner,[10] that he would return the favor and send a collection of echinoderms. A disappointed Steindachner—he wanted fish, not invertebrates!—wrote back to tell Agassiz that Professor Kner, though he was a worthy gentleman and indeed had a collection of his own ("a small museum, with some precious things"), was not working at the museum but teaching at the university. Of course, Steindachner's purpose was not just to clarify who the proper recipient of those undesirable echinoderms should be, but to open up an avenue for a regular "Tauschverkehr" (a traffic of specimen exchanges) between his museum and the United States.[11] Little did he know that, just few years later, he himself would become one of those specimens caught in Agassiz's net.

Arguably, when the famous American Professor asked Steindachner if he would come to work for him, his intention was less to provide this humble Austrian curator with a nice study abroad experience than benefit directly, and at minimal cost to himself, from Steindachner's

8 Written by Steindachner's former assistant, Viktor Pietschmann; see Pietschmann, "Franz Steindachner."

9 Personal communication, Dr. Ernst Mikschi, Department Head, Zoological Department I, Naturhistorisches Museum Wien, 18 June 2019.

10 Formerly associated with the museum's ichthyological collections, Rudolf Kner (1810-1869) was appointed professor of zoology at the University of Vienna in 1849.

11 Steindachner to Louis Agassiz, 2 March 1863, Louis Agassiz, Correspondence and Other Papers, Ms Am 1410, Houghton Library, Harvard University (hereafter abbreviated LAC). All the translations of Steindachner's German are mine.

meticulousness, of which he had gotten a taste in the earlier exchange. To his credit, Steindachner was not entirely oblivious to Agassiz's motives and fought valiantly to get himself a fair deal. Even as he tentatively accepted Agassiz's offer, he was quick to reiterate those parts of the proposed deal that were to *his* benefit, such as ownership of the results of all his own work, even when carried out under the auspices of Agassiz's museum, as well as the promise that he would be able to send home any duplicate specimens he had gathered (i.e. duplicates of specimens Agassiz's museum already owned).[12]

But the next few letters make for excruciating reading as we watch Steindachner trying to get Agassiz to hold up his end of the deal. After initially expressing confidence that Agassiz would not take advantage of him, since he knew best what yearly income was needed to live an "anständiges" (civilized) life in Cambridge, Steindachner lost heart and named his own price tag ($2,000 per year)—a sum he subsequently, disconcerted by Agassiz's silence, reduced to $1,500. In the end, Steindachner found himself diminished to begging that Agassiz send him some money to help pay for his travel or that, given his connections, he might secure for him free passage on one of the steamers out Hamburg. (Rather humiliatingly, Dr. Steindachner's mother ended up paying for most of her son's expenses).[13]

When things finally seemed all set and he was getting ready to say farewell to his family ("eine Qual," torture, as Steindachner admitted), his sister Betti suddenly fell ill with typhoid fever. And when that situation was under control again, a new shipment of fish from Siam, India, and Japan, the spoils of the Austrian-Hungarian expedition to East Asia, arrived at the museum, and Dr. Redtenbacher demanded that Steindachner stay and get some order into them (which he did, working from 8 in the morning to after 6 pm at night).[14]

Over and over again, Steindachner reminded Agassiz that he was not out to enrich himself, that whatever money he had been able to save had always gone toward the museum, for books bought to supplement the library—irresponsibly depleted by his predecessor Leopold Fitzinger—or

---

[12] Steindachner to Louis Agassiz, 9 December 1868, LAC.

[13] Steindachner to Louis Agassiz, 9 December 1868; 29 July 1869; 27 November 1869; 31 March 1870; LAC.

[14] Steindachner to Louis Agassiz, 15 February 1870; 31 March 1870; LAC.

for the collections themselves.[15] Each Wednesday, he would scour the fish markets of Vienna for specimens that he thought would interest Agassiz—salmon, trout, you name it—which he would then dispatch to Cambridge, sometimes adding interesting things from his personal collection as a bonus, such as a small gathering of fish from Trieste, immersed in copious amounts of liquor for safekeeping.[16]

Impressed by Steindachner's obvious generosity and pertinacity, Agassiz apparently relented and sent some money. A grateful Steindachner quickly assured him that he had used the funds for more fish shipments, not on himself, and that he would arrive bearing even more gifts: seven boxes of books from his personal library, more crates of freshwater and ocean fish, and even a small collection of Microlepidoptera from Austria.[17] In an earlier letter, he had mentioned some of the books he had set aside for Agassiz, among them gems like Temminck and Schlegel's *Fauna Japonica* and—was Steindachner really unaware of Agassiz's problems with Darwin?—the zoological volumes of the *Voyage of the Beagle*.[18]

The annoying delays and the constant fretting about money and family notwithstanding, Dr. Steindachner was genuinely excited about his American adventure. There are even subtle indications in his letters that he was fervently hoping that his Cambridge sojourn might turn into more than just that. Repeatedly he laments Agassiz's insistence that he only stay for "einige Jahre" (a few years), which will, he fears, not give him enough time to save any money and also severely restrict his ability to do the serious research he has in mind (the projects he mentions are a study of the fish of the Mississippi and a comparative analysis of fish collected from the Amazon, the Orinoco, and Magdalena Rivers).[19] Once, when apologizing for having postponed his departure so many times, Steindachner even fantasizes how "in a few years" Agassiz will be as sad to see him go as Vienna now seems sad to see him depart (a subtle hint that perhaps Agassiz might not want to see him depart at all).[20]

---

[15] Steindachner to Louis Agassiz, 5 January 1869; 29 July 1869, LAC.
[16] Steindachner to Louis Agassiz, 5 January 1869; 27 November 1869, LAC.
[17] Steindachner to Louis Agassiz, 31 March 1869, LAC.
[18] Steindachner to Louis Agassiz, 27 November 1869, LAC.
[19] Steindachner to Louis Agassiz, 31 March 1870; 29 July 1869; LAC.
[20] Steindachner to Louis Agassiz, 31 March 1870; LAC.

All in all, it is clear that Steindachner could hardly wait for the day he would find himself traveling across the Atlantic with, in his own words, the fresh breezes from Agassiz's "land of freedom" wafting around him—or were these winds, as he adds with a scientist's penchant for irony, coming from the North Pole? "In Gedanken bin ich jetzt schon mehr als in Amerika als in Wien" (In my thoughts I am already more in America than in Vienna).[21]

***

Steindachner's arrival in Boston on 11 May 1870 was not auspicious.[22] Getting off the train from New York, he found that Agassiz had forgotten to meet him. Poor Steindachner was standing on the platform in Boston in the pouring rain, with all his bags, and did not have enough money to hire a cab to Cambridge. A coachman finally relented and dropped him off at the 10-cents Cambridge omnibus, the horse-drawn ancestor of the "T," which took him to the Harvard campus. Once there, no one could tell him where the Museum of Comparative Zoology was. Or perhaps no one was able to understand his Austrian version of English. While Steindachner was looking for the museum, he ran into one of Agassiz's assistants, fortunately a German, who helped him get situated and, even more importantly, saw that he got a cup of coffee.[23]

Agassiz's museum proved to be a major disappointment. The fish collection was a mess, jars and barrels everywhere, in no discernible order. Staff implored him not to tell anyone back home. When he finally met Agassiz, the great scientist asked him not to start working right away but to enjoy Boston and Cambridge first.[24] Now one needs to remember that

---

[21] Steindachner to Louis Agassiz, 31 March 1870; LAC.

[22] While he was in the United States, he sent nearly 200 letters to his family, his sisters Netti and Betti, as well as his brother-in-law, Anton Gerstner, a maker of fine pastries. Most of these letters are now in the Archive of the Naturhistorisches Museum Wien (hereafter abbreviated NHMW). Except for a handful of letters written during his Brazilian trip in 1903, they have never been published. Hans Rebel (who became director of the Natural History Museum in 1925) transcribed a few of them for his privately printed *Reisebriefe Franz Steindachners*. Where original letters could not be located at the NHMW, I have relied on Rebel's transcriptions. Translations are my own.

[23] Steindachner, *Reisebriefe* 7-8.

[24] Steindachner, *Reisebriefe* 8-9.

Harvard had a little over 1,100 students at the time,[25] and Cambridge was a far cry from the tourist attraction it is today. There were trees everywhere, which Steindachner liked. The landscape was beautiful—gardens and meadows and lakes with beautiful turtles and fish swimming in them were in walking distance. At night, the frogs sounded as if they were playing the Jew’s harp.[26] He was less impressed by the wooden houses—they seemed so flimsy to him that the slightest gust of wind could blow them away. Set them on fire, and nothing will be left. Because they were so cheaply made, you could simply move them like you would your bedroom closet. What Steindachner found particularly amusing were the many bay windows, as if residents wanted to be able to survey the street from all angles. And then, inside, there were all these small rooms, each one for a different purpose, for sleeping, writing, eating, and socializing. Four rooms in Cambridge or Boston were like two regular rooms in Vienna.

The eternal bachelor Steindachner did appreciate the way American women looked—they were as thin and graceful as the limbs of sycamore trees, he wrote, a remark specifically intended for his niece Milli, who, he had heard, had developed quite an appetite. And he liked the way the women dressed—even the older ones were invariably elegant and appealing. But the men could be mistaken for manservants.[27] And everything cost an arm and a leg—he couldn’t believe how much he had to pay for a water pitcher he needed.[28]

Agassiz had put him up at Zoological Hall, his faculty dorm, where Steindachner wasted no time to make himself comfortable, exchanging his bed for a divan, adding bookshelves, and a photograph of his sister Betti, which was much admired by visitors (because, as Steindachner remarked unkindly, writing to that same sister, the photographer had liberally retouched the image). One rather striking feature of Steindachner’s living quarters: there were exotic plants everywhere, which he had obtained from the Harvard greenhouse: a *Passiflora*, a pomegranate tree, two bromeliads,

---

[25] Information provided by John Bethell, former editor of *Harvard Magazine*, personal communication, 2 June 2019.

[26] Steindachner to Mil[l]i Gerstner, page 4 of letter to Anton and Betti Gerstner, 24 November 1870. NHMW.

[27] To Mil[l]i Gerstner, page 4 of letter to Anton and Betti Gerstner, 24 November 1870. NHMW.

[28] Steindachner, undated letter fragment, NHMW.

and an Australian acacia tree (he had obtained them from Harvard's botanical garden). A bit more predictably, he also put up plaster busts of Schiller, Goethe, and Dante, and he draped some ivy around his bedroom mirror. His American colleagues had never seen anything quite like it. Once, when he had a few guests over for Rhine wine, a lady teasingly asked Steindachner how many times he had been married—judging from how nice his quarters looked, she expected him to be already on his third wife.[29]

Socially Steindachner felt out of place. Americans were speaking too fast, swallowed the syllables of half of what they said and mumbled the other half.[30] They were also offish, but that was the least problem (Steindachner said he adjusted by becoming somewhat offish himself). When he went to a reception at the house of the Harvard physicist Professor Joseph Lovering, he found 150 people squeezed into the house and no chairs (remember the small rooms!). He was bored out of his mind.[31]

It seemed that there was nothing else to do for him but to work. Cambridge had no coffeehouses, and the theatre performances, done by overpaid artists, were usually terrible, except when there were guest stars from abroad.[32] The worst thing by far was the dismal weather, milder than in Vienna but infinitely more annoying. When snow fell that there was usually so much of it that one would sink in up to one's knees. Then it would melt, of course, and a veritable lake would appear right in front of your door. In Steindachner's apartment, the windows did not close properly, so that at night he would lie in his bed with the wind howling

---

[29] Steindachner to Anton and Betti Gerstner, 24 November 1870, NHMW. Fortunately, as he soon found out, everybody of note with whom he worked at the museum—the entomologist Dr. Hermann Hagen, the paleontologist Dr. Georg Augustus Maack; Agassiz's Swiss disciple, Louis François de Pourtalès, and Agassiz himself—spoke excellent German. "I only speak enough English as is required for my daily bread," reported Steindachner to Netti closer towards the end of his stay, dampening her hopes that he might be able to teach her English someday; Steindachner to Anna ("Netti") Steindachner, 5 March 1873, NHMW.

[30] Steindachner to Anton Gerstner, 14 February 1871, NHMW. Joseph Lovering (1813-1892) served as the Hollis Professor of Mathematics and Natural Science from 1838-1888.

[31] Steindachner to Anna (Netti) Steindachner, 5 February 1871, NHMW.

[32] Steindachner, *Reisebriefe* 19.

around his freezing ears.[33] No wonder that Steindachner was getting depressed: "The dreary weather of the last few days dampens my spirit," he wrote to Louis Agassiz, who was away in Deerfield, Massachusetts. "I feel at times lonely and abandoned, though I am still hopeful that sufficient intellectual stimulation will help me regain my formerly cheerful disposition."[34]

***

Yet, as Steindachner would soon realize, the intellectual stimulation was a problem, too. Agassiz's star, once so brilliant that it had seemed to illuminate all known areas of science, was on the wane. People had watched him implode in embarrassing public debates about Darwinism, where his antagonist, the modest but keen-witted Harvard botanist Asa Gray, made mincemeat out of the unprepared Agassiz. Even worse, Agassiz's grandly named Museum of Comparative Zoology, in reality a hodgepodge of leaking barrels of specimens, began to drain all Steindachner's energy. He had worked hard in Vienna; now he was working even harder in America. Much of his efforts were focused on the thousands of fish that had come back from Agassiz's much-publicized trip to Brazil in 1865, the Thayer Expedition, on which William James had served as an increasingly disenchanted volunteer.[35] Predictably, there was no time for Steindachner's own research. He did mention his desire to work on a collection of fish from the Society Islands (which had to come to the Cambridge Museum via the self-taught scientist-explorer Andrew Garrett) and half-heartedly asked for Agassiz's permission to publish an article about one of those species in an American journal ("mein Erstlingswerk in englischer Sprache"; my apprentice work in the English language), but Agassiz's earlier guarantee that Steindachner would be entitled to the results of his own research had apparently been forgotten.[36] And Steindachner's hope that he might be allowed to participate in the

[33] Steindachner, *Reisebriefe* 21.
[34] Steindachner to Louis Agassiz, 23 May 1870, LAC.
[35] For more on this, see my *Agassiz: Creator of American Science*, chapter 8. James's involvement in the Thayer Expedition is detailed in my *Poetics of Natural History*.
[36] Steindachner to Agassiz, 20 June 1870, LAC.

Darien (Isthmus of Panama) Expedition of 1870 was similarly thwarted.[37] He was, first and foremost, Agassiz's workhorse.

Fortunately, it turned out that there was an expedition Agassiz did want him on. Agassiz's long-standing feud with Darwin had not, as he had hoped, been resolved by the frantic specimen-collecting of the Thayer Expedition. Agassiz wanted a do-over, a new trip, this time one that would include much of the South American continent, and he knew that Steindachner's proven adeptness at packing and unpacking fish would be crucial to the success of such an undertaking. More specimens, more truth: Agassiz was certain that fish especially, limited to the river habitats, would confirm his sense that all created beings stayed where God had first put them and had better things to do than to evolve into something different.[38]

ll. 2: The *Hassler* party. From left to right: Louis Agassiz; Thomas Hill, Elizabeth Agassiz, Franz Steindachner (hidden behind Elizabeth; only the hat is visible); Commander Philip C. Johnson; Lt. Commander C. Kennedy; Elvira Lindsay Johnson; William White; James Henry Blake; Louis de Pourtalès. Spec. Coll. Archives sMU 1329.70.1-37. Ernst Mayr Library, Museum of Comparative Zoology.

---

[37] Steindachner to Agassiz, 14 October 1870, LAC.

[38] Agassiz's profoundly conservative worldview—at odds with his progressive scientific methods, which emphasized fieldwork rather than book learning—is summarized in my introduction to Agassiz, *Introduction to the Study of Natural History* 1-22.

The U.S. Coast Guard provided the ship, the 151 feet, 350-ton steamer *Hassler*. Agassiz's party left Boston's Navy Yard in December 1871. It was a motley crew Agassiz had put together, including a former Harvard president and physicist, Dr. Thomas Hill; Elizabeth Cary Agassiz, Agassiz's wife; the naturalist Louis-Francois de Pourtalès; the artist James Henry Blake, and so forth. Philip Johnson, a brother of the painter Eastman Johnson, was the ship's captain, and he was accompanied by his half-Chilean wife, Elvira Lindsay, a source of endless fascination, especially to Mrs. Agassiz (ill. 2).

The Hassler would travel along the eastern coast of the continent, through the Straits of Magellan, up to the Galapagos Islands and then back to the U.S. west coast, where the party would then spend some time in San Francisco. Agassiz, who was convinced that the key to his refutation of evolution lay at the bottom of the sea, was especially excited about the *Hassler's* modern deep-sea dredging equipment. Agassiz's default mode when talking about his science was hyperbole; even by that standard, his expectations for this expedition were extremely high: "the results of this voyage will be as important for the increase of our knowledge of the characteristics of the sea, as the voyages of Capt. Cook were, a century ago, for the improvement of navigation and geography."[39]

***

After their return from their last Brazilian junket, the Agassizes rushed a big book about the trip into print, *A Journey in Brazil* (1866). More a travelogue than a scientific account, the chatty volume was mostly written by Elizabeth, with scientific notes contributed by Louis (the one on race would later become infamous). The *Hassler* trip did not generate a similar volume nor did it lead to other publications of note, with the exception perhaps of a series of taxonomic accounts of Brazilian fish published a few years later by Steindachner, which did, however, cast a much wider net—if the metaphor, given the subject, is permissible—drawing on specimens from the Thayer collection and Steindachner's own holdings at the museum in Vienna. The truth is that while the *Hassler* expedition yielded barrels of specimens, more than anyone this side of the asylum could

[39] Agassiz to Hon. Thomas Russell, 16 August 1871, Archives of the Ernst Mayr Library of the Museum of Comparative Zoology, Harvard University.

reasonably process,[40] it did not produce much in the way of new scientific insights. Yet Elizabeth Agassiz's extensive letters home, sent to her sisters as well as her mother, along with Steindachner's letters to his family, provide us with a rather intimate view of what happened during that voyage.[41]

The *Hassler* expedition was no pleasure cruise, to be sure, but it does seem that Steindachner flourished during the trip. As always, he worked incessantly, getting up early in the morning, fishing, dredging, taking trips to the coast when the *Hassler* stopped, procuring and preparing and packing specimens. His hands were lacerated by the spines of fish and sore from digging endlessly in saltwater.[42] Agassiz had taken Steindachner along to pack up specimens, and he rarely forgot to remind him that this was precisely what he was supposed to do. He had to share a cabin with the ex-Harvard president Thomas Hill, a weird fellow who wore cardigans as if he were back in his office, and the coffee was execrable. But the experience of South American nature compensated Steindachner for everything, including recurring bouts with seasickness and the rivers of sweat that were running down his body with every movement he made.[43] Steindachner's letters are full of glowing descriptions of South American nature, the morning glories the banks of St. Thomas (ill. 2), the Euphorbia or spurges in Barbados, the palm, breadfruit and clove trees of Rio. "Here grows in abundance what is a rarity in our greenhouses."[44]

Under the deep blue Brazilian sky, trees looked like giant flower bouquets, and their scent was intoxicating: "many trees were covered with blossoms in the fieriest colors so that they resembled a single, grand avenue of flowers in colors ranging from rose-red, yellow, coral-red, or

[40] The sheer plethora of material they had gathered ironically prevented the researchers from identifying the new species they had collected. See the work of Judith E. Winston, Leandro M. Vieira, and Robert Woollacott, who, more than 140 years later, found dozens of new species among the bryozoans (invertebrate marine animals) brought back by the *Hassler* team. See Winston, Vieira, Woollacott "Scientific Results of the Hassler Expedition. Bryozoa. No. 1"; "Scientific Results of the Hassler Expedition. Bryozoa. No. 2,"

[41] Elizabeth Cary Agassiz, The *Hassler* Letters (1871-72), now part of the Elizabeth Cary Agassiz Papers at Schlesinger Library, Harvard University.

[42] Steindachner to Anton Gerstner, 23 February 1872, NHMW.

[43] Steindachner to Anton Gerstner, 23 February 1872, NHMW.

[44] Steindachner to Anna ("Netti") Steindachner, 22 February 1872, NHMW.

purple."[45] When they stopped in Rio, Steindachner went for a ride through the most luxuriant rainforest he had ever seen, underneath trees festooned with lianas, while hummingbirds and butterflies whirred around his head. Months later, in Glacier Bay in the Straits of Magellan, as his party was making its way to the world's most magnificent glacier, walking across the soft, moss-covered ground became a sensual experience for him.[46] Even when the landscape seemed bare, as was the case in Patagonia, he still found some beautiful amaryllis amidst all the grass that warmed his heart.

Although his job was to collect and pack, random killings bothered Steindachner. On Magdalena Island, he watched in disgust as Agassiz's men clobbered birds to death by the hundreds, which pained him "deep in his heart," so much so that he went to a different part of the island. He was particularly distraught by the fate of the penguins harvested by the sailors, "those poor, helpless things, to be caught and knocked dead by everyone who comes along" ("Die armen, unbeholfenen Dinger, die Jedermann fangen u. erschlagen kann").[47]

Remarkably, Steindachner's descriptions of the people he met are free of the racism that contaminates the writings of Louis and Elizabeth Agassiz. During their stop in St. Thomas, for example, he received an invitation to a dance and, although he had expected a very different kind of entertainment ("a nice dance"), he spent part of the evening polkaing with black washerwomen, whose flower-adorned hair he noted.[48] His description of the indigenous people they meet in Tierra del Fuego shows none of the prejudice that creeps even into Darwin's account in *Voyage of the Beagle*. While Darwin, four decades earlier, was so shocked when he saw the Fuegians that he could not believe that these people were "fellow-creatures, and inhabitants of the same world" (he would later, arriving in civilized Sydney, explicitly "congratulate myself that I was born an Englishman"),[49] Steindachner merely reports that the men and women he met were charmingly attired in their sealskin costumes, seemed well-

[45] Steindachner to Anton Gerstner, 23 February 1872, NHMW.

[46] Steindachner to Anna ("Netti") Steindachner, 28 March 1872, NHMW.

[47] Steindachner to Anna ("Netti") Steindachner, 9 March 1872; Steindachner to Anton Gerstner, 6 April 1872, NHMW.

[48] Steindachner to Anna ("Netti") Steindachner, 20 December 1871.

[49] Darwin, *Voyage of the Beagle* 178, 318.

nourished, and were exceedingly friendly.[50] No grandstanding about how lucky he was to be an Austrian.

Later, when Agassiz's party arrived in San Francisco, Steindachner felt magically drawn to Chinatown, where he loved the Chinese theatre, "all so new to me," as he said in one of his letters: the gorgeous costumes, the sudden changes in volume when they sang, the unusual accompaniment. As Agassiz was hobnobbing with the city's intellectual elite and had his portrait taken "in all sizes," Steindachner kept going back to the theatre.[51]

***

While Elizabeth Agassiz is barely mentioned in Steindachner's letters, he is a larger than-life-presence in hers. She writes about him with a warmth that makes one suspect that there was more at play: "I grow more & more attached to Steindachner and I think every one on board likes him!," she notes, close to the beginning of the trip. "He is a general favorite," she adds. "So simple hearted, kind and unobtrusive, —as obliging as he is modest & unassuming." But she also admires him for his impressive stamina: "Every body respects his devotion & his work;—nothing daunts him—heat or rain or sun any discomfort & exposure of any kind—It makes no difference to him; he works through every thing—up early & to bed late and always busy."[52] It helped that Steindachner devoted some of his precious time to tutoring Elizabeth in German, with mixed results. (He later remarked, somewhat uncharitably, that since Elizabeth was already fifty, her mind had slowed down).[53] Whenever they went on shore, Steindachner was always around to lend a helping hand, readily agreeing to accompany her on walks. Once he even saved her from a deadly snake ("I immediately consented to postpone a farther investigation of the scenery," joked Elizabeth in letter to her mother).[54]

---

[50] Steindachner to Anton Gerstner, 6 April 1872, NHMW.

[51] Steindachner, *Reisebriefe* 60-1.

[52] Elizabeth Agassiz to Sarah Gray Cary (sister), 10 February 1872, *Hassler* letters, Schlesinger.

[53] Elizabeth Agassiz to Mary ("Mollie") Cary Felton (sister), 26 February 1872 ("If I do not learn, it's my fault"); Elizabeth Agassiz to Sarah Gray Cary, 2 June 1872, *Hassler* letters, Schlesinger; Steindachner to Anna ("Netti") Steindachner, 5 March 1873, NHMW.

[54] Elizabeth Agassiz to Mary Perkins Cary (mother), 6 March 1873, NHMW.

When Elizabeth and her husband left the *Hassler* to travel overland to Santiago de Chile, Steindachner was on hand to assist them again, since he was the only one in the party (apart from the captain's wife) capable of conversing in Spanish. "Steindachner is a great comfort to me as a travelling companion." He shared Elizabeth's keen interest in how people lived: "He's just like a woman in some respects,—enjoys going prowling about in strange places,—into the churches or into the private gardens." Elizabeth Agassiz memorably describes one of these scenes:

> We see a house door standing open (they all do stand open here) giving a fascinating view into a "patio" within planted with flowers & trees, sometimes with grape trellises—We walk in—the Senhora appears,—*Steindachner* –"Pardon Senhorita, but we are strangers walking and your garden looks so charming, so inviting, we ventured in" & c. &c. Of course the Senhora asks us to come in, often gives flowers and is full of amiable curiosity as to who we are and the strange countries we have come from.[55]

Perhaps the funniest episode recounted by Elizabeth involves an obstinate parrot Steindachner had procured in Peru as a present for Agassiz's German assistant Dr. Hagen. Steindachner's famous persistence was lost on that bird. Although he spent an inordinate amount of time trying to teach the parrot the phrase, "Guten Morgen Mr. Hagen," the bird was unimpressed:

> It's melancholy & interesting as showing how human industry may be thrown away to hear Steindachner say in loud & distinct tones about 20 times "Gu-ten-Mor-gen-Mis-ser–Hag-en." during which the parrot puts his head one side, rolls his beady eyes at him, seems to listen assiduously and then opens his oracular mouth and utters the most awful squall you can conceive.

Steindachner despaired: "The Doctor then looks sad and says 'I fear me that he is a stupid bird.'" But then he would nevertheless resume his lessons. It is not reported what happened to the parrot. But if Elizabeth had initially had friendly feelings toward Steindachner, she was now clearly in love: "There never was any body so good & kind as Steindachner." He was, she sighed, "a truly good man."[56]

---

[55] Elizabeth Agassiz to Mary Perkins Cary (mother), 4 May 1872, *Hassler* Letters, Schlesinger.

[56] Elizabeth Agassiz to Mary Cary Felton, 26 May 1872, *Hassler* letters, Schlesinger; Elizabeth Agassiz to Mary Perkins Gray, 12 July 1872, *Hassler* Letters, Schlesinger.

***

As "good" as Steindachner was, he knew how to keep his counsel. For all the gratitude he professed, he maintained a healthy skepticism towards his mentor Agassiz's skewed ideological principles. That is nowhere clearer than in his response to the Galapagos Islands. In his *Schlangen und Eidechsen der Galapagos-Inseln* (Snakes and Lizards of the Galapagos Islands, published in 1876), instead of engaging in the demonization of Darwin his mentor Agassiz would have required, Steindachner quietly agreed with most of Darwin's observations, praising both the *Voyage of the Beagle* and the "celebrated naturalist" himself. [57]

Particularly fascinating is a passing comment in his description of *Dromicus chamissionis [Pseudalsophis dorsalis*], the "Galápagos snake," where Steindachner actually scoffs at the idea that these snakes, whose closest relatives are found on the coasts of Peru or Chile, must have been brought over by the first humans to visit the islands, one of the many refutations of Darwin used by Agassiz. Indeed, Steindachner points out that the insular species differs from its mainland relatives in the number of its ventral scales—an indication that a separate evolutionary process must have taken place.

And he directly engages with Darwin in his comments on *Amblyrhynchus cristatus*, a species of marine iguana endemic to the Galapagos. Much of this description is vintage Steindachner, an exact accounting of how many scales one finds on the head and where, of the position of the nostrils, and of the pigments on their skin. Even the lips, used to scrape seaweed of the rocks, are described with absolute precision: they consist of twelve to thirteen small square scales, growing in size and breadth towards the ninth or tenth infralabial plate (the scale bordering on the lower jaw), whereas the median plate, the *scutum mentale*, is smaller and has a blunt tip. And so forth. The marine iguana, in Steindachner's hands, becomes a work of art. Whereas Darwin's notes show stupid these lizards were, Steindachner watches them disappear when humans approach, retreating into the water. He also devotes several pages to the non-swimming variant of the Galapagos lizards, the land iguana, where,

---

[57] Steindachner, *Die Schlangen und Eidechsen der Galapagos-Inseln.* A full text facsimile is available from the Biodiversity Heritage Library in https://doi.org/10.5962/bhl.title.61015.

again after extensive notes about skin, coloring, and skeleton of these species, he allows himself only a slight demurral from Darwin, pointing out that that lizard is not always smaller than its sea-going brother—several of the individuals he caught on Albemarle Island (now Isabela) weighed 22 pounds.

Ill. 3: Eduard Konopicky, artist, *Conolophus subcristatus* (male), plate IV from Steindachner, *Die Schlangen und Eidechsen der Galapagos-Inseln* (1876).

The illustrations Eduard Konopicky, the taxidermist of the Vienna museum, had produced for Steindachner's publication serve to put the reader right on the scene. Konopicky had shown up in Cambridge on 18 April 1871, almost a year after Steindachner's arrival, and had also begun working for Agassiz.[58] While he did not travel on the *Hassler* (in Steindachner's absence, he had taken possession of the latter's apartment in Zoological Hall), he clearly had paid close attention to Steindachner's

[58] See Steindachner to Anna ("Netti") Steindachner, 27 April 1871, NHMW.

account of the trip. And while Steindachner, in his letters home, missed no opportunity to complain about Konopicky's laziness,[59] the artistry of these pictures is impeccable. In pages taken from a fragmentary letter written to a Viennese colleague (perhaps Eduard Suess?) during the Galapagos portion of the trip, Steindachner mentioned how he would pull these clumsy, good-natured lizards by their tails (imitating what Darwin did to them as well),[60] and it is such a moment of discovery that Konopicky's engraving captures, as he represents the animal's head turning in our direction (ill. 3).

Another impressive illustration features the male as well as the female of *Amblyrhynchus cristatus*, emphasizing the contrast between the extravagant forms of these animals and the stark, volcanic landscape, so bare that it had once reminded Darwin of the desolate landscapes of Staffordshire dotted with iron-foundries (ill. 4).[61]

[59] "Whenever I visit him, he is *not* at work"; Steindachner to Anna ("Netti") Steindachner, 10 December 1872, NHMW.

[60] Darwin, *Voyage of the Beagle*: "I then walked up and pulled it by the tail; at this it was greatly astonished … and then stared me in the face, as much as to say, 'What made you pull my tail?'" (283).

[61] *Voyage of the Beagle* 270.

Ill. 4: Eduard Konopicky, artist, *Amblyrhynchus cristatus* (male and female), plate III from Steindachner, *Die Schlangen und Eidechsen der Galapagos-Inseln* (1876)

The pleasure Steindachner's derives from the natural world does not manifest itself in predictable ways. Mary Winsor has called his descriptions ordinary,[62] when in fact they are not. Delight, for Steindachner, resides precisely in the distance between a fish's dorsal and caudal fins or in the size of the plates that encase its body. Fish of all kinds are beautiful to him, as he is not ashamed to admit. Consider his detailed description of a suckermouth catfish with circular eyes, which animates the fish's body as Steindachner's eye travels around it, assessing the distance between the eyes and its mouth, the shape of its mouth, the patterns that make each part and particle distinct—assessing, as it were, the inner logic of this particular fish's structure, the exact reasons for its beauty. The fish becomes a small, undulating landscape, to be traversed with patience, attention, and love.

> The shape of this beautiful species is stout. The top of its head and the sides of its torso are arched; its body appears to be compressed only where the caudal fin begins. The

[62] Winsor, *Reading the Shape of Nature* 76.

> upper part of the fish's snout, leading from the nostrils to the tip, is covered with small plates; the lateral margin of the snout is raised all the way back to the interopercle and less boldly striated and grooved than the other upper and lateral areas of the head. The temple plate, however, appears more insistently striated that the preceding plates of the head. Since, beginning with the area of the eyes, the fish's head gradually decreases in breadth, the opening of the mouth, situated far away the front of the head, can only be moderate in terms of its breadth.[63]

Steindachner's fish was *Rhinelepis agassizi*,[64] a new species collected in the Manacapuru Lake System in Brazil during the Thayer Expedition. He had decided to name it after his former mentor, ostensibly because two of the specimens now owned by the Vienna museum had come from Agassiz (ill. 5). But was it just a coincidence that he named an armored or spiked catfish (now often misleadingly referred to as "Pineapple Pleco") after him?

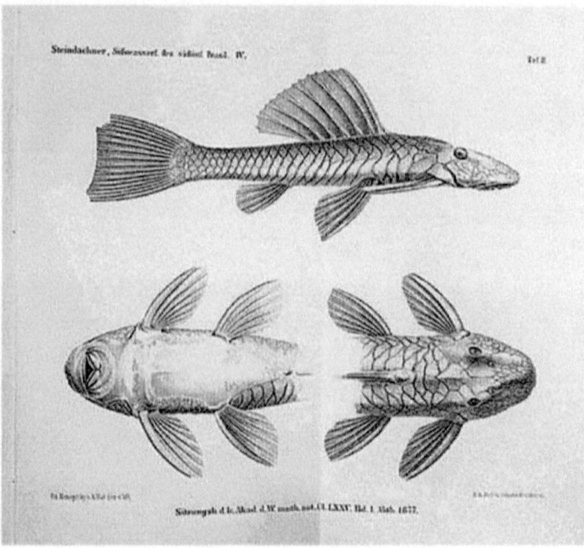

Ill. 5: Eduard Konopicky, artist, *Rhinelepis agassizi* (or *Parahybae*), from Steindachner, "Süsswasserfische des südöstlichen Brasilien, IV," plate II (1878). Now *Pseudorinelepis genibarbis.*

[63] Franz Steindachner, "Die Süsswasserfische des südöstlichen Brasilien, IV" 229.
[64] Now known as *Pseudorinelepis genibarbis*.

***

The journey back to Boston from San Francisco, by train, was disappointing. Steindachner found himself longing for the rich vegetation of the jungles he had seen, and the onset of winter disconcerted him. He did like the fact that the Mississippi, when they finally got there, reminded him of the Danube. When he was back in Cambridge on 18 October, Steindachner realized how little he had missed it. Konopicky was out every night till the wee hours, guzzling beer. He had no desire for better things, noted Steindachner, and, unlike him, was not at all interested in returning home.[65] Steindachner was bored, though not for lack of work. “I have unpacked 250 crates of fish since November,” he told his brother-in-law in March 1873. Every day he reported for duty at the museum at 7:30 a.m. and toiled till 5:30 in the evening, with only a half-hour break for lunch, which was the reason he had barely had any time left for letter-writing.[66]

The great fire of Boston in November 1872, which confirmed Steindachner’s suspicions about all these rickety wooden houses, provided some distraction, though not of the good kind—it went on for nine days, and Steindachner watched the spectacle standing on the bridge to Boston.[67] When Christmas rolled around, the Agassizes gave him a collection of Longfellow’s poems, a box for keeping matches, and a wallet made of straw, insignificant gifts that were easily surpassed by what he had brought: golden cuff links with inlays of amethyst, Chinese pendants, lots of books, and bouquets of violets for everyone.[68] Yes, he had gone back to work for Agassiz’s museum, but the work had become more of a chore than before. Agassiz to him was now distinctly an emperor without any clothes. When Agassiz neglected to invite Steindachner to join the teaching staff for his new summer school of natural history on Penikese Island, Steindachner shrugged off what others would have considered an affront. Agassiz’s activities were “viel Lärm um nichts,” much ado about nothing, and his public lectures, though they attracted large crowds, were mediocre and made no real contribution to the progress of science.[69]

---

[65] Steindachner to Anna (“Netti”) Steindachner, 5 January 1873, NHMW.

[66] Steindachner to Anton Gerstner, 24 March 1873, NHMW.

[67] Steindachner to Anna (“Netti”) Steindachner, 19 November 1872, NHMW.

[68] Steindachner to Anna (“Netti”) Steindachner, 5 January 1873, NHMW.

[69] Steindachner to Anna (“Netti”) Steindachner, 23 March 1873, NHMW.

In July 1873, Steindachner, having successfully applied for an extension of his leave, embarked for a grand tour of the U.S. during which he collected more specimens for the museum in Vienna. He hated the Fourth of July celebrations in New York—the worst day for a peace-loving man, he said. Other stops included Philadelphia, Baltimore, Washington, Niagara Falls, Detroit, then St. Paul, where he loved the falls that Longfellow had described so well (it seems he had derived some benefit from the volume Agassiz had given him). Then on to Denver and Salt Lake City, where he went to inspect the Mormons. He departed for Europe from San Francisco, without seeing Agassiz again.

In an attempt to retain his services for the museum, Agassiz, in marked contrast to his earlier reluctance to do anything for him, had suddenly offered Steindachner an annual salary of $2,500, as well as the chance to go on expeditions to the former Russian North America (Alaska), the Aleutian Islands, and China. Steindachner politely ignored Agassiz's advances.[70] When he left Cambridge, he avoided saying good-bye to his boss.[71] He was sad and knew he would miss him, but the truth is that he was done with a science that uneasily mixed fieldwork and theology. If Agassiz's science consisted in counting the scales on a snake's back to prove that the location where he had found the animal was the very same one where God had put it, or rather its ancestors, Steindachner was content to count just the scales, and, because he wasn't distracted by thoughts of God, to do a better job of counting them than anybody else.

Agassiz must have been aware of Steindachner's mounting disdain, too. When they were in San Francisco at the end of the *Hassler* trip, Steindachner could not help but notice that Agassiz did not introduce him to anyone, as if he were afraid that people would second-guess his achievements and find out that, as Steindachner put it with fine irony, Agassiz's Austrian assistant had done "the bigger half of the work." [72]

Counting scales was Dr. Steindachner's way of staving off chaos and arbitrary speculation. In practical terms, what had he gained from the *Hassler* trip was thousands of specimens, for sure—100,000 fish alone, by at least one estimate.[73] But even if we go by Agassiz's surprisingly conservative assessment, Steindachner's bounty was substantial. Agassiz

---

[70] Steindachner to Anna ("Netti") Steindachner, 23 January 1873, NHMW.
[71] Steindachner to Anna ("Netti") Steindachner, 24 June 1873, NHMW.
[72] Steindachner, *Reisebriefe* 77.
[73] See Riedl-Dorn, "Steindachner, Franz."

claimed that the *Hassler* had netted 30,000 specimens. Publicly Steindachner insisted that, per his original deal with Agassiz, he had only taken duplicates.[74] But only 7,000 specimens actually made it to Harvard—you do the math.[75] "Ich tue, was ich verantworten kann, für Wien." I will do whatever I can justify for Vienna, Steindachner said.[76]

***

When he revised the official visitor's guide to his museum, Steindachner included a lengthy section explicating the thirty-four statues and sixty-four busts mounted on the museum's roof and facades, a chronological gallery of men, beginning with Anaxagoras, all of whom had blazed a trail for the progress of science and expanded "the horizons of perception and insight." Agassiz's statue, sculpted by Gustav Deloge, was mounted (as it still is today) on the balustrade facing the Ringstrasse. Writing about his former employer in the guide, Steindachner praised his contributions to glaciology and paleontology but pointedly did not mention his achievements in the field of ichthyology. A few pages later, Steindachner pointed out the most recent acquisition in the museum's gallery, a bust of Charles Darwin, but here he no longer held back: "the most famous naturalist of modern times, whose teachings dominate all research that is currently being done in zoology, botany, and paleontology." Not coincidentally, Darwin was, Steindachner added, the only naturalist whose likeness had been added to the museum's hall of fame while still alive.[77] In 1909, Steindachner traveled to the other Cambridge for the centenary celebrations of Darwin's birthday to represent both the Imperial Austrian Academy of Sciences and his beloved Vienna museum.[78]

It is obvious where Steindachner's loyalties lay in the intense ideological battles that divided the nineteenth century—battles that are, at least in the United States, where more than one third of residents still do not accept the reality of evolution,[79] not over yet. For the problem was this:

---

74 See Winsor, *Reading the Shape* 76.

75 Irmscher, *Agassiz* 336.

76 Steindachner, *Reisebriefe* 79.

77 *Allgemeiner Führer durch das k.k. Naturhistorische Hofmuseum* 9, 13-14, 19.

78 See "The Darwin Centenary at Cambridge," *The London Times*, Tuesday, 22 June 1909, 9.

79 Quammen, *The Reluctant Mr. Darwin* 14-15.

during the more than three years he spent in the New World, Dr. Steindachner had discovered that Americans, rather than venturing out to see and genuinely appreciate the world in all its diversity, remained stuck in their own personal shells. Steindachner would spend hours immersing himself in his science, but he also loved showy, exotic flowers and, as Elizabeth Agassiz had noted with admiration, would not hesitate to enter the homes of Chileans and chat with them in bad Spanish. For Franz Steindachner, the next beautiful fish was waiting just around the corner or, rather, in the next, yet unexplored river. Interested in seeing confirmed what they already knew to be true, Americans were more than ready to settle for a monologizer and professional compartmentalizer such as Louis Agassiz. From that perspective, the glaring absence of liberalizing coffeehouses, those havens of rational debate,[80] which Steindachner had noted right after his arrival in Cambridge, was not a surprise at all.

WORKS CITED

Agassiz, Elizabeth Cary. The *Hassler* Letters (1871-72). Elizabeth Agassiz Papers. The Schlesinger Library, A-3/19. Harvard University.

Agassiz, Louis. Correspondence and Other Papers. Ms Am 1410. Houghton Library, Harvard University.

—. to Hon. Thomas Russell, 16 August 1871, Archives of the Ernst Mayr Library of the Museum of Comparative Zoology, Harvard University.

—. *Introduction to the Study of Natural History.* Edited and annotated by Christoph Irmscher. Basel: Springer, 2018.

Allgemeiner Führer durch das k.k. Naturhistorische Hofmuseum, unter Mitwirkung der Sammlungs-Vorstände verfasst von weil. Dr. Franz Ritter von Hauer, k.u.k. Hofrat und Intendanten. Dritte, neubearbeitete Auflage, herausgegeben von Dr. Franz Steindachner. Vienna: k. und k. Naturhistorisches Museum, 1914.

Böhme, Katrin. "Briefe Franz Steindachners von der Brasilien-Expedition 1903." *Annalen des Naturhistorischen Museums in Wien. Serie B für Botanik und Zoologie* 98 (1996): 545-68.

Darwin, Charles. *Voyage of the Beagle: Charles Darwin's* Journal of Researches. Ed. Janet Browne and Michael Neve. 1839; London: Penguin, 1989.

[80] A nod to Jürgen Habermas' *The Structural Transformation of the Public Sphere.*

"The Darwin Centenary at Cambridge." *The London Times*, Tuesday, 22 June 1909, 9.

Habermas, Jürgen. *The Structural Transformation of the Public Sphere: An Inquiry into a Category of Bourgeois Society*. Trans. Thomas Burger. Cambridge, Massachusetts: The MIT Press, 1989.

Irmscher, Christoph. *Louis Agassiz: Creator of American Science*. Boston: Houghton Mifflin Harcourt, 2013.

—. *The Poetics of Natural History*. 2nd ed. With a foreword and photographs by Rosamond Purcell. New Brunswick, NJ: Rutgers UP, 2019.

Kähsbauer, Paul. "Intendant Dr. Franz Steindachner, sein Leben und Werk." *Annalen des Naturhistorischen Museums Wien* 63 (1959): 3-30.

Pietschmann, Viktor. "Franz Steindachner." *Annalen des Naturhistorischen Museums in Wien* (1919): 47-8.

Quammen, David. *The Reluctant Mr. Darwin: An Intimate Portrait of Charles Darwin and the Making of His Theory of Evolution*. New York: Atlas, 2006.

Riedl-Dorn, Christa. "Steindachner, Franz." *Neue Deutsche Biographie* 25 (2013): 171-2; https://www.deutsche-biographie.de/pnd139157395.html#ndbcontent.

Stagl, Verena. "Steindachner, Franz." *Österreichisches Biographisches Lexikon 1815-1950*, vol. 13.60. Vienna: Austrian Academy of Sciences, 2008. 164.

Stagl, Verena, Helmut Sattmann, and Peter C. Dworschak. "The Material of the 'Pola' Red Sea Expeditions (1895-1898) in the Collections of the Natural History Museum in Vienna." *Deep-Sea and Extreme Shallow-Water Habitats: Affinities and Adaptations*. Ed. Franz Uiblein, Jörg Ott, and Michael Stachowitsch. Vienna: Austrian Academy of Sciences Press, 1996. 29-41.

Steindachner, Franz. Briefnachlass. Archive of the Natural History Museum, Vienna.

—. *Reisebriefe Franz Steindachners aus Amerika*. Ed. Hans Rebel. Vienna: privately printed, 1938.

—. *Die Schlangen und Eidechsen der Galapagos-Inseln. Mit 7 Tafeln*. Vienna: Zoologisch-Botanische Gesellschaft, 1876.

—. "Die Süsswasserfische des südöstlichen Brasilien, IV." *Sitzungsberichte der kaiserlichen Akademie der Wissenschaften, Mathematisch-naturwissenschaftliche Classe* 76.1 and 2 (June and July 1877): 217-30.

Winsor, Mary P. *Reading the Shape of Nature: Comparative Zoology at the Agassiz Museum*. Chicago: The U of Chicago P, 1991.

Winston, Judith E., Leandro M. Vieira, and Robert Woollacott. "Scientific Results of the Hassler Expedition. Bryozoa. No. 1. Barbados." *Bulletin of the Museum of Comparative Zoology* 159.5 (2009): 239-300.

—. "Scientific Results of the Hassler Expedition. Bryozoa. No. 2. Brazil." *Bulletin of the Museum of Comparative Zoology* 161.5 (1 Dec. 2014): 139-239.

PART II

Political Relations between the USA and Europe before and after World War II

TIBOR FRANK

The Blind Eyewitness: Joseph E. Davies, U.S. Ambassador to Moscow (1936–1938)

Even though the United States had not established diplomatic ties with the Soviet Union until 1933, it had been making efforts, since 1917, to be of service to the Union of Soviet Socialist Republics (USSR), for instance by adopting significant charity measures to alleviate the famine taking off in 1921. Herbert Hoover (1874–1964), who would be President, and who had distinguished himself during World War I by the aid missions he led, was authorized by Congress to provide medical supplies valued at USD 4 million, through the mediation of the Red Cross. Despite that the government's initiative seemed merely symbolic in comparison with the USD 80 million's worth of relief funneled into Russia from private funds. In 1922, Hoover, a former mining engineer, benefited from his extraordinary gifts as an organizer to deliver 900,000 tons of food, clothing, and medication to 10.5 million needy Russians at 18,000 points of distribution. The writer Maxim Gorky (1868–1936), then living in exile from Russia, expressed his heartfelt gratitude to Hoover in these words: "The generosity of the American people resuscitates the dream of fraternity among people at a time when humanity greatly needs charity and compassion." On his home turf, at an official banquet in Moscow, the President of the Council of People's Commissars thanked Hoover "in the name of the millions of people who have been saved."[1]

EARLY SOVIET-U.S. DIPLOMATIC RELATIONS

Throughout the 1920s, the two countries did not wish even to talk about assuming diplomatic relations, for two reasons. For its part, the Soviet Union refused to repay a state debt incurred by Tsarist Russia. In addition, the United States claimed that the Soviet Union had been pursuing a

[1] Daniel J. Boorstin, *The Americans: The Democratic Experience*, New York: Random House, 1974, 573.

Central American policy detrimental to American interests, for instance by supplying arms, via Mexico, to the revolutionaries in Nicaragua, spearheaded by Augusto César Sandino (1896–1934). Meanwhile, American business had set foot in the Soviet Union, with Armand Hammer developing assets in asbestos and graphite, General Electric building a power plant on the Dnieper River, and Henry Ford setting up a car manufacturing plant in Novgorod.[2]

It was not until sixteen years after the Bolshevik revolution that the United States recognized the Soviet Union. The decision to establish diplomatic ties was made, in November 1933, by the government of Franklin Delano Roosevelt (1882–1945). The move had been urged by prominent American businessmen, such as Henry Ford (1863–1947) and General Electric chairman Gerard Swope (1872–1957), on account of the enormous magnitude of the Soviet market, although the Soviet government also welcomed it enthusiastically in the hope of putting the reins on Japan's expansionist efforts. By then, the U.S. itself had been setting great store by an anti-Japanese stance to be adopted by the Soviet Union—an orientation fostered diligently by Stanley Kuhl Hornbeck (1883–1966), a Far East expert in the State Department,[3] who was to call for economic sanctions against Japan in 1938.[4] Yet it was not a career diplomat Roosevelt entrusted with the task of paving the way toward diplomatic relations, but William C. Bullitt (1891–1967), a close friend and confidant of his at the time. In October 1933, Bullitt offered Moscow the invitation of a senior negotiating partner for talks in Washington, D.C. Between 8 and 16 November 1933, People's Commissar of Foreign Affairs Maxim Litvinov (1876–1951) then conferred with Roosevelt, whose first request was for American nationals residing in the Soviet Union to be granted the freedom to exercise their religion. Beyond complying with this request, Litvinov also pledged that the Soviet Union would repay its wartime debt of USD 70 to 150 million. Although this diplomatic overture was a success in formal terms, it failed to deliver the expected and

---

[2] Cf. Tamás Magyarics, *Az Egyesült Államok külpolitikájának története. Mítosz és valóság: érdekek és értékek* 271.

[3] Robert D. Schulzinger, *U.S. Diplomacy Since 1900* 156.

[4] "Stanley K. Horbeck Urges Economic Sanctions Against Japan, 1938," *U.S. Department of State: Foreign Relations of the United States*, 1938. Washington, D.C., 1954, 572–73. Cited by Dennis Merrill and Thomas G. Patterson, eds. *Major Problems in American Foreign Relations*. Vol. II. *Since 1914*, 121–2.

promised results for the next five years. The Soviets did not grant freedom of religious pursuit to American citizens living on their territory and defaulted on their wartime debts. Conversely, American trade proved unable to make inroads into the Soviet economy, nor did the United States live up to Soviet hopes that it would help stifle Japan's imperialistic ambitions. By late 1934, relations between the two great powers were marked by mutual mistrust.[5]

The first U.S. ambassador to Moscow, William C. Bullitt, had an excellent staff of Soviet experts to rely on. After two years on the job, however, his initial enthusiasm for the Soviet system gave way to a fierce anti-Communism, and he was reassigned to Paris in 1936. The embassy staff he left behind—including Charles E. Bohlen (1904–1974) and Loy W. Henderson (1892–1986), and led by George F. Kennan (1904–2005), who would play a vital role at the onset of the Cold War—watched with mounting trepidation as Stalin's project of "cleansing," i.e. the elimination of the Bolshevik old guard, gathered speed. It was around this time that the State Department, then under Robert F. Kelley (1894–1976), the staunch anti-communist supervisor of the Eastern Europe division, launched a campaign with the aim of alerting the political elite to the perils of Communism.[6] In the 1930s, this circle of American diplomats and their experiences at the time were instrumental in fueling the profound anti-Soviet sentiments characterizing the Cold War at its inception.[7] American historians today hasten to point out that, as early as during the 1940s, Kennan described the Communist system in terms of gender, representing the Soviet people as a woman raped by its government, while casting himself as a genuine admirer of Russians.[8] All American diplomats in Moscow agreed that any cooperation with the Soviet Union was out of the question. Indeed, during the 1930s, there were not even signs of the possibility of marshaling Soviet help in the face of common enemies. In short, the show trials and purging operations staged by Stalin cemented the anti-Soviet stance of these diplomats for the length of their careers.

---

[5] Schulzinger, 157; Alan Brinkley, *The Unfinished Nation. A Concise History of the American People* 657–8; Magyarics 271–2.

[6] Schulzinger, *U.S. Diplomacy Since 1900* 157–8.

[7] Frank Costigliola, "George F. Kennan and the Gendering of Soviet Russia," Merrill and Patterson, 255.

[8] *Ibid.*

A LAWYER TURNED AMBASSADOR

In Moscow, Bullitt was succeeded as ambassador by Joseph Edward Davies (1876–1956), with a mandate from 16 November 1936 to 11 June 1938. Born in Watertown, Wisconsin, Davies studied law at the University of Wisconsin (1898, 1901), then obtained his doctorate from the Presbyterian College in South Carolina (1937). After taking jobs as a lawyer, he immersed himself in Democrat party politics. In 1912, having secured the support of states in the West, he became a major force in clenching victory at the presidential elections for Woodrow Wilson (1856–1924). Thus turned into a close ally of the new President, Davies was appointed Commissioner of Corporations in 1912, and first Chairman of the Federal Trade Commission (1915–16),[9] and even ran for Senator (1918) at the express behest of Wilson himself. However, he was beaten by his Republican opponent, causing the Democrats to lose their majority in the Senate, thereby ultimately contributing to the fall of President Wilson. Davies advised Wilson on issues of economic policy at the Paris Peace Conference (1919). After Paris, Davies withdrew to his own legal practice, serving as counsel in several matters involving foreign countries such as Mexico, Peru, The Netherlands, Greece, and the Dominican Republic. As a lawyer, he remains best known for defending Ford shareholders against the United States. He won the lawsuit, pocketing a record fee of 2 million dollars. In general, he preferred anti-trust assignments, representing large corporate clients such as Seagrams, National Dairy, Copley Publishing, Anglo-Swiss, Nestlé, and Fox Films.[10]

A recent millionaire, Davies spent generous sums from his private fortune on helping fund the presidential campaign of 1932 on behalf of Roosevelt, with whom he had been working closely since Wilson's term.[11] It was in recognition of his diverse legal and international experience, as well as his staunch support of the Democratic Party, that Roosevelt chose

[9] Elizabeth Kimball MacLean, "Joseph E. Davies: 'The Wisconsin Idea and the Origins of the Federal Trade Commission'," *Journal of the Gilded Age and Progressive Era* 6.3 (2007): 248–84.

[10] For this brief biography of Davies, I have drawn on *Who Was Who in America*, vol. 3, and the *Wikipedia* entry on Joseph Edward Davies: https://en.wikipedia.org/wiki/Joseph_E._Davies. Accessed 5 July 2016.

[11] MacLean, "Joseph E. Davies and Soviet-American Relations," 1941–43. *Diplomatic History* 4.1 (1980): 73.

him to lead the mission in Moscow. Afterwards, Davies represented the United States in Belgium and Luxembourg (1938–39), then became special advisor to Cordell Hull (1871–1955), the Secretary of State and later Nobel laureate, whom he advised on steering initial American foreign policy during World War II. In 1942, he was appointed Chairman of the War Relief Control Board, the agency overseeing aid, reparations, and reconstruction programs necessitated by the war. In 1945, again as ambassador, he served as special advisor to President Truman (1884–1972) and Foreign Secretary James F. Byrnes (1882–1972) in Potsdam.

By way of a detour into personal details, it is worth mentioning that Davies's second wife (from 1935 to 1955, i.e. in part during his tenure in Moscow) was Marjorie Merriweather Post (1887–1973), the wealthiest (and perhaps most attractive) heiress in all of the United States, proprietress of the Postum cereal firm and founder of General Foods, Inc. The couple spent some of their vacation time at Mar-a-Lago, Ms. Post's soon famous summer residence in Palm Beach, Florida. The mansion, then comprising no fewer than 126 rooms, was later acquired by a multi-billionaire named Donald Trump, in 1985. It still has 118 rooms.

Ill.1: Marjorie Merriweather Post

MISSION TO MOSCOW

As early as in 1941, Davies had published a book, a veritable international bestseller at the time, under the title of *Mission to Moscow*. It was printed in hundreds of thousands of copies, translated into several languages, and even turned into a script in Hollywood.[12] This book by an American diplomat proved extremely useful for Soviet propaganda during and after the war. In 1943, it was adapted for the screen, courtesy of director Michael Curtiz, with Walter Huston and Ann Harding cast in the leading roles as Davies and Post, respectively. The film marked the efforts of wartime Hollywood to show support for the Soviet Union as an ally of the U.S. Meanwhile, Davies maintained and actually exercised his full rights

[12] Joseph E. Davies, *Mission to Moscow*, https://archive.org/details/missiontomoscow035156mbp. Accessed 31 Aug. 2019.

over the script, managing to hammer through his false perceptions and judgments. “Davies had absolute control over the script and could veto any dialogue not to his liking.”[13] Like his book itself, the film ultimately painted a picture of the Soviet Union so unabashedly biased toward Stalin that even its producer Robert Buckner called it "an expedient lie for political purposes, glossily covering up important facts with full or partial knowledge of their false presentation.”[14] Indeed, the film presented the victims of the Moscow show trials as fifth columnists working for Nazi Germany.[15] Davies’s mission in Moscow is now subject to substantial scholarly inquiry, as a result of books (among others) by David H. Culbert (1980), Elizabeth Kimball MacLean (1993) and an article by Todd Bennett.[16]

Davies’s book[17] is a tapestry woven from the ambassador’s journal entries and official reports. As such, it makes a number of interesting observations about the Soviet Union in the period between 1936 and 1938, including politics, social affairs, the economy, public figures, daily life, the international situation, and foreign policy. It divulges a confidential report to Cordell Hull, dated 12 March 1937, in which the author recounts his tour of the Soviet Union, surveying key economic centers and visiting several factories and corporations. He was impressed by the Donets Basin, with “the largest steel plants, heavy-machine-building and electrical turbine plants, aluminum plant, tractor and chemical plants, agricultural machinery, and other large industrial operations”[18] and particularly by the fact that “these plants have been built, operative trained, and production secured, some employing as high as 38,000 men and women, all within the past six or seven years."[19]

On 26 February 1937, Davies got on the road. “Accompanied by my daughter, a secretary, and four journalists … we left for Kharkov on a six-

---

[13] https://en.wikipedia.org/wiki/Mission_to_Moscow. Accessed 31 Aug. 2019.

[14] *Ibid.*

[15] *Ibid.*

[16] David H. Culbert, *Mission to Moscow*, 16–17; Todd Bennett, *The Journal of American History* 88.2 (2001): 489–518.

[17] In what follows, all quotations are from the London edition of the book, https://archive.org/details/missiontomoscow035156mbp. Accessed 31 Aug. 2019.

[18] Davies 73.

[19] *Ibid.* 73.

day tour" in the Ukraine.[20] After visiting some of the largest industrial plants, they went to see

> the first Young Pioneer House, an establishment of 280 rooms, adapted to the development of school children (27,000), outside of regular school hours, in scientific, artistic, airplane, transportation, and other lines of manual training (320 teachers). These latter institutions are one of the most interesting developments in the Soviet Union and are being established in all the large centres, predicated upon the Stalin idea that the most precious capital of the state is the brains of the youth.[21]

On 28 July 1937, Davies prepared an in-depth report for Cordell Hull reflecting on the concerns and rumors about the state of Soviet industry. In this, he stated that

> it is the enormous wealth of the country which enables this communistic and socialistic experiment to project and sustain itself with the apparent success which it has.
>
> Not only can it withstand inefficiency and waste in industry, but it could afford to blot out the entire contribution of industry and scarcely feel the impact in the economic or financial administration of the state. With control of the army, it could afford even to disregard the social effects thereof.
>
> The conclusion seems to be established that the plight of the economic industrial organization of the Soviet Union was not as serious as is currently believed; and further it seems probable that even though the most dire predictions of complete industrial and economic disintegration were in fact justified, the complete disruption of industry would not have so serious an effect upon the whole Soviet organism as might be generally accepted, because of its relative insignificance in contrast to the enormous resources and strength which go to make up the life of the state.[22]

Then, on 10 June 1937, Davies expressed sheer admiration for the Soviet Union to Deputy Secretary of State Sumner Welles (1892–1961):

> The man power here is tremendous. The capacity for ideological concept and devotion to 'the cause' found in these people is extraordinary and commands admiration. Moreover, this country is tremendously rich and in spite of all the inefficiencies of bureaucracy and political control of industry, there must be and will be a residue of accomplishment which, because of the size of the country, will be very powerful. Moreover, they have done some extraordinarily good things over here and there is much I see to admire and respect.[23]

---

[20] *Ibid.* 74.
[21] *Ibid.* 74.
[22] *Ibid.* 128.
[23] *Ibid.* 119.

However, the ambassador also added: "But the price they pay is too high."[24]

Davies refers to his talks with Soviet President Mikhail Ivanovich Kalinin (1875–1946), who affirmed that "they had every confidence in their army and felt secure against attack, even though it were simultaneous on both sides."[25] In this respect at least, Davies proved to be an astute, even prophetic observer when he added that "At the same time, the ambassador clearly realized that 'Their industries have been so located in the country as to indicate that the industrial plan was organized and projected, in part, as a war measure.' … While not nearly so efficient as the industry of capitalist countries, it is quite probable that Soviet industry would give a very fair account of itself in case of emergency."[26]

The U.S. ambassador essentially followed the same argument on April 14, 1938, in his letter to Senator Millard Tydings (1890–1961), in which he forecast a surprisingly accurate vision of Soviet isolation within Europe. "As things are going in this cockeyed world," Davies wrote,

> I am not sure but what the democracies of the world might not be damn glad some day to have the friendship and the power and the devotion to peace which this government could supply in case of another world crisis. And believe me, if these Fascist dictators continue going haywire that crisis is bound to come, and in the opinion of many people whom I know life would not be worth living if it had to be on terms which they would dictate, and it is very close. There is too much wishful thinking – and a refusal to see the simple elemental factors in this Europe.[27]

STALIN

The U.S. ambassador wasted no time in observing and reporting on the cult surrounding Stalin. He provided the Foreign Secretary with a detailed account of the festivities celebrating the twentieth anniversary of the October Revolution, held on 6 to 8 November 1937. Struck by the enormous papier-mâché statues, the projected images, and the inevitable cheers from the masses every time Stalin's name was uttered, he observed that "there were many babies and small children carried on the shoulders

---

[24] *Ibid.*
[25] *Ibid.* 129.
[26] *Ibid.* 129.
[27] *Ibid.* 208.

of parents so that they might catch a glimpse of Stalin."[28] And yet, Ambassador Davies believed, in 1938, that "Stalin, historically, will be recognized probably as the great builder in Russia, following Peter the Great."[29] By way of an explanation he adds that "One hundred and fifty-seven schools are alleged to have been built in Moscow alone during the last year."[30] Indeed, Davies had himself almost venerated Stalin ever since he had been assigned to Moscow, and thus could not help but succumb to the cult surrounding the leader:

> Stalin is a simple man, everyone says, but a man of tremendous singleness of purpose and capacity for work. He holds the situation in his hand. He is decent and clean-living and is apparently devoted to the purpose of the projection of the socialist state and ultimate communism, with sufficient resiliency in his make-up to stamp him as a politician as well as a great leader.[31]

On 5 June 1938, just before his reassignment to Brussels, the ambassador paid a farewell visit to President Kalinin and Prime Minister Vyacheslav Mikhailovich Molotov in the Kremlin. On the occasion, as before, Kalinin expressed to him the recognition of the Soviet leadership

> for the serious manner in which the Ambassador had taken his work and particularly by his studious application to industrial and social conditions in the Soviet Union and the objectivity and honesty with which he had sought the facts, and that while he had always been very frank in his attitude, non-belief in their political idea, and had always asserted his fundamental confidence in his own country's political philosophy.[32]

Then Davies was escorted to Molotov's residence, where he had the opportunity to meet Stalin in person. To the utter surprise of Davies, he "was perfectly amazed and almost struck dumb with surprise to see the far-end door of the room open and Stalin come in alone."[33]

---

[28] *Ibid.* 159.
[29] *Ibid.* 197.
[30] *Ibid.* 197.
[31] *Ibid.* 54.
[32] *Ibid.* 229.
[33] *Ibid.* 230.

Ill.2: Ambassador Davies with Stalin and Molotov

The ambassador offered a detailed account of the meeting in a memorandum dated the same day, noting that the Soviet leader "was quite 'slight' in appearance. His demeanour is kindly, his manner almost deprecatingly simple, his personality and expression of reserve strength and poise very marked."[34] Davies in turn addressed the party chief with great reverence, attributing personally to him "these extraordinary achievements, which had been conceived and projected in the short period of ten years," which "had commanded my great admiration."[35] As he told Stalin himself, he "had heard it said that history would record Stalin as the man who was responsible for this achievement and that he would be recorded as a greater builder than Peter the Great or Catherine."[36] "I was honoured by meeting the man who had built for the practical benefit of common men," Davies added.[37] Stalin replied without delay "and stated that the credit was not his; that the plan had been conceived and projected by Lenin, who had projected the original Dnieperstroges Dam project; that the ten-year plan was not his work; that it was due to the three thousand

---

[34] *Ibid.* 222.
[35] *Ibid.*
[36] *Ibid.*
[37] *Ibid.*

able men who had planned this work and those others of his associates; and above all that it was the 'Russian people' who were responsible, and that he disclaimed any personal credit therefor."[38] Davies commented on Stalin's words with sincere conviction: "He gave me the impression of being sincerely modest."[39]

Stalin asked Davies to stay a little longer so he could ask a few questions. At this point it became clear why he attached such great importance to the conversation with the ambassador, for which he had apparently prepared thoroughly. He wanted to discuss two issues of vital interest, notably for the development of Russian military capabilities, which formed particularly neuralgic nodes in U.S.-Soviet relations. First, Stalin wanted to know the reason for the American delay in building a warship on the orders of Moscow, which would be used as a model for further replica vessels to be built on Soviet soil. Davies offered a competent reply: "there were also restrictions imposed by law that would prevent the giving of plans for battleships, or giving access to manufacturing plants which were building battleships to foreign countries, unless the army and navy would declare that this would not be prejudicial to the military or naval defence of the United States."[40] For his part, the ambassador wished to find out the identity of the American company the Soviets were negotiating with. Stalin identified the firm as Carp, co-owned by a Soviet-American multimillionaire named Sam Carp, who was Molotov's brother-in-law and had presumably been under Soviet influence.[41] By then, the case had been dragging on for a while owing to

[38] *Ibid.*
[39] *Ibid.*
[40] Davies 223.
[41] Ellen McClay, *In The Presence of Our Enemies* 67. Molotov's wife was known to the Communist movement as Polina Semyonovna Zhemchuzhina (1897–1970, born Perl Semyonovna Karpovskaya). According to an editorial published in the 1 December 1953 issue of the *Milwaukee Sentinel* (12), Carp had been visiting the Soviet Union annually until the late 1930s, regularly returning to the U.S. carrying wads of thousand dollar bills. The House Committee on Un-American Activities (HCUA) interrogated Carp on two occasions, but the businessman was unable to specify the exact amount in question or indeed say where the money had gone. The article claims that Carp wielded such powerful influence that he was in position to summon to his New York office the Soviet ambassador to Washington, and even Stalin in Moscow took his phone calls. David A. Rosoff, mentioned by Davies later in the book, had been working for

the strong resistance of senior officials of the Department of the Navy to the idea of war ships to be built for the Soviet Union on American soil. Given that the Navy had remained the number one client of the firms Carp contacted, they had good reason to fear for the loss of future orders if they contravened the warnings of the Navy.[42] Davies prudently suggested only that Roosevelt was probably not privy to these affairs, and that he wanted to make sure that "as a practical matter it would clarify the situation for the authorities of the United States to know clearly that the agency presenting this matter spoke authoritatively, and had both his confidence and that of the Soviet government."[43]

Stalin then came to the second question, concerning the settlement of state liabilities to the United States, known as the Kerensky debt.[44] During World War I, the government of Tsarist Russia had taken out a loan of some USD 86 million from the United States through the mediation of First National City Bank, and added war bonds valued at USD 11 million, which it proceeded to sell in American financial markets. Then, after recognizing the Kerensky government, the United States opened for the new Russian régime a line of credit initially of USD 100 million, later raising the ceiling to USD 325 million. Of this amount, the Russian government actually drew USD 187 million, encumbering the country with an enormous liability to the United States. This massive sum should be augmented by the value of American investments effected in Russia preceding the Revolution, estimated to total USD 60,594 million.[45]

Carp as chairman of Amtorg, the Soviet trade firm. Cf. https://news.google.com/newspapers?nid=1368&dat=19531130&id=A44xAAAAIBAJ&sjid=XRAEAAAAIBAJ&pg=4284,3925861&hl=en. Accessed 22 July 2016.

[42] Thomas R. Maddux, "Relations in the 1930s. The Soviet Union's Efforts to Purchase Naval Vessels," Donald J. Stoker Jr. and Jonathan A. Grant, eds. *Girding for Battle. The Arms Trade in a Global Perspective, 1815–1940*, 206.

[43] Davies 224.

[44] Alexander Fyodorovich Kerensky (1881–1970) was a Russian lawyer, member of the Duma, minister in 1917, and briefly Prime Minister. In 1918 he was forced into exile, and died on foreign soil.

[45] "The Roosevelt Administration and the Russian Problem," *Soviet-American Political and Trade Relations*. CQ Researcher, http://library.cqpress.com/cqresearcher/document.php?id=cqresrre193302240. Accessed 1 Sept. 2019. The data tally with P. V. Ohl's numbers in *Foreign Capital in Russia*, Petrograd, 1922.

Ambassador Davies outlined the chronology of former proposals to settle the debt, going back to 1933. The Soviet Union had been seeking, particularly since its recognition by the United States on 16 November 1933, to apply to the U.S. for further loans. However, in 1934, Congress passed the *Johnson Debt Default Act*, named after the sponsor of the bill, Senator Hiram Johnson (1866–1945), banning loans to states that had defaulted on previously incurred debts to the U.S. Remarkably, the Act was not motivated by some anti-Soviet stance so much as by the exigencies of the international financial crisis that accompanied the Great Depression.[46] Under the circumstances, the U.S. was unable to grant the new Soviet loan application. As the passing of Johnson's bill was only to be expected, already in this early phase of Soviet-U.S. negotiations, foreign affairs commissar Litvinov and the recently elected U.S. President worded their 1933 memorandum to say that the new loan would not be issued by the U.S. government but by private American individuals. Davies, who had instructions not to aggravate the conflict, felt reassured when Stalin pledged that "the Soviet government was seeking to find a way to settle at least a portion of this debt situation."[47] What this oracular proclamation actually meant was that the Soviet Union would not be able to repay all of its international debts (including to Britain and France) all at once, and therefore undertook only to settle Russian/Soviet debts owed to the U.S. government itself. Davies insisted that his questions targeted no more than the specifics of the Soviet proposal, since he was not authorized to make judgments on the merits of the case, nor aware of "what would or would not be acceptable to my government."[48]

Following his exchange with Stalin, Davies immediately set about studying the subject of Russian debts. A few days later, on 8 and 9 June, he visited Molotov, who presented him with a written proposal detailing plans to settle the debt.[49] Molotov expressed his willingness "to show its high regard for the good opinion of the President and the Secretary of State. Whether or not it failed, he said, it at least would be a manifestation

---

[46] http://en.citizendium.org/wiki/Johnson_Debt_Default_Act_of_1934. Accessed 16 June 2016. For background, see Katherine A. S. Siegel, *Loans and Legitimacy. The Evolution of Soviet-American Relations, 1919–1933*, 138 – by any reckoning, a superb book by a former student of mine in the United States.

[47] Davies 225.

[48] *Ibid.* 226.

[49] Davies talks about "Russia" and "the Russians," rather than "Soviets."

of their good will," Davies added in a note.[50] The press was never briefed about these talks.

On 17 January 1939, then in the capacity of ambassador to Brussels, Davies revisited the history of Molotov's proposal one last time. In his summary report to the Secretary of State, he recalls being empowered, in the summer of 1938, by the President and the Secretary, to propose to the Soviet government more favorable terms on settling the Kerensky debt. The plan was for the U.S. to offer compensation loans to the Soviet Union, on condition of receiving settlement only of the Kerensky debt, instead of the entire loan amount owed by Russia and the Soviet Union.

THE MOSCOW TRIALS

The longer one dwells on ambassador Davies's views on Soviet economy, society, and international role and on Stalin's significance, the more astonished one will be by the political myopia and deafness that characterizes his contemplation of the show trials in Moscow during his tenure. In many cases, not only did Davies have cognizance of these trials, but he often witnessed them directly in person as a diplomat invited to the hearings. The ambassador's political lack of insight invited criticism from many corners, including close associates such as George F. Kennan, who went so far as to recommend his recall from the job. Yet even Kennan proved unable to exert a meaningful influence on his boss.[51] Incidentally, some hints dropped by Davies make it clear that the trials were the subject of heated debate among diplomats assigned to Moscow. In his journal, Davies mentions a dinner hosted by the Ambassador of Afghanistan, then regarded as the doyen of the diplomatic corps in Moscow, where a dispute over a trial broke out. Followed keenly by Davies, the argument of his Afghan colleague proceeded as follows:

> In discussing the trial, the Ambassador remarked that—from our point of view—the criminal procedure in Russia based upon the Napoleonic Code did not provide those protections for the accused which the common-law system affords. He then went on to tell me how the provisions of the Mohammedan law in his country made provision for such protections. Nothing, said he, contributed so much to the dignity of the human

---

[50] Davies 228.

[51] Wilson D. Miscamble, "George Kennan. A Life in the Foreign Service." *Foreign Service Journal* 81.2 (2004): 23.

> mind and personality of man as the protections which the law provided for his freedom from persecution by those in power in any country. The extent of the advance of civilization, he thought, was the degree to which the individual was protected even against the state itself in charges of crime. He commented upon the right of the accused to refuse to testify against himself and the right of the accused to a presumption of innocence.[52]

Davies comments: "This wise and fine man impressed me with his sincerity and his philosophy."[53]

Yet this "impression" remains very hard to glean upon reading Davies's book, despite the fact that he paid extremely close attention to the proceedings. For instance, early on in his book, he quotes his own diary entry (dated just before he received his credentials) on the Radek trial,[54] which he claims was "particularly fascinating and interesting to me."[55] Yet Davies's ears also remained open to voices warning of the true nature of these trials. As he could clearly infer from the words of an unnamed ambassador on 30 January 1937, diplomatic circles in Moscow regarded the trial as "the sensation of the Diplomatic Corps this week, he thinks it is all a put-up job and an internal fight among the old Bolsheviks. He believes that the confessions were induced by all manner of threats and physical police methods."[56] In early February, Davies talked with the Ambassador of Lithuania, who "discussed at length the various theories as to why these defendants confessed. He didn't believe that direct physical cruelties (contradistinguished with nervous cruelties) were employed …. He thinks highly of this regime in many ways."[57]

At this point, it is worth recalling what the Hungarian author Ervin Sinkó said in his Moscow journal:

> Was there a single voice to be heard that would have attested to a modicum of moral courage on the part of the defendants or those who commented the trial in public? And

[52] Davies 56.

[53] *Ibid.* 56.

[54] Karl Bernhardovich Radek (1885–1939) was a Soviet politician who first followed Trotsky then repudiated him. In August 1936 he was arrested and he stood trial in January 1937 as one of The Seventeen, including Piatakov, Sokolnikov, and Serebriakov. He was sentenced to ten years in prison, then killed in the Gulag in 1939.

[55] Davies 26.

[56] *Ibid.* 44.

[57] *Ibid.* 55.

> did I have the slightest grounds … to deem my own conduct during the Radek-Pyatakov trial[58] in any way superior to that of any other person? Do I have the slightest reason to feel complacent, to regard myself as the exception immune to the ubiquitous, dehumanizing lack of morality to which everyone living in the Soviet Union succumbed in one way or another? … I did what everybody else did: I did nothing.[59]

During his visit to Washington in early April, Davies found Roosevelt deeply concerned about the Radek trial. During lunch in the White House, the ambassador briefed the President in general terms, but the latter zoomed in on the trial. "His interest was particularly directed to the charges of treasonable activities by the defendants with Germany and Japan. He wanted to know my impressions as to the judges, the prosecutors, and the criminal procedure."[60]

While the ambassador does keep track of the progress of Stalinist purging operations, he rarely voices doubts or even meaningful political commentary.[61] His gullibility comes into especially sharp focus in the summer of 1937, when a number of Red Army generals were executed. Davies devotes an entire chapter to the episode, with the title of "Why they shot Tukhatchevsky?"[62] As he writes, "I have been making an effort to probe those facts and procure the temperate judgments and opinions of people here, who are as well informed as any foreigners could be, in an effort to get a consensus as to what occurred; what is the present strength of the government and what its prospects are."[63] All the while, the author remains firm in his belief that the Soviet system had grown stronger than ever before as a result of the purges,[64] and he hastens to add that "It is generally accepted by members of the Diplomatic Corps that the accused must have been guilty of an offence which in the Soviet Union would merit the death penalty."[65] Moreover, Davies makes it clear that "Facts are not

---

[58] Georgy Leonidovich Pyatakov (1890–1937), a Ukrainian anarchist and terrorist turned Soviet politician, was one of the victims of the Stalinist trials.

[59] Ervin Sinkó, *Egy regény regénye. Moszkvai naplójegyzetek 1935–1937*, 537.

[60] Davies 99.

[61] *Ibid.* 130, 180, 184, 257-8.

[62] *Ibid.* 129-38. Mikhail Nikolayevich Tukhachevsky (1893–1937), marshal of the Soviet Union, deputy chairman of the Revolutionary Military Council and assistant in the People's Commissariat of Defence, also fell victim to Stalinist purges.

[63] Davies 131.

[64] *Ibid.* 131-2.

[65] *Ibid.* 137.

now available, and it is doubtful whether they will be for a long time to come, which would justify a statement as to exactly what happened and just what constituted the 'offence' of these officers of the Red Army. Opinion must be based largely on deductions from known facts and they are few."[66] Yet, by way of reassuring the Secretary of State, the recipient of his lengthy report, Davies explains in a footnote that "The Bukharin trial six months later developed evidence which, if true, more than justified this action. Undoubtedly those facts were all fully known to the military court at this time."[67] Under the circumstances, it is astonishing, particularly at this junction of history, that Davies should praise, even eulogize, Stalin, whom he regards as commanding

> a great deal of respect, outside of these terrible happenings. He is generally considered to be a clean-living, modest, retiring, single-purposed man, with a one-track mind, devoted to communism and the elevation of the proletariat. The responsibility is generally attributed to the 'action of the party' through its party leaders. Of course, in that connection, it is generally considered that Stalin is by far the strongest character, and he is what we might term the type of 'easy boss,' who permits it to appear that his associates make their own decisions.[68]

The most shocking chapter—the fifth—in the ambassador's book concerns the Bukharin trial. Apart from reports to the Secretary of State, it contains various fragments from journals and correspondence, as well as, most interestingly, a section discussing notes by the ambassador from the summer of 1941 "inserted here because this seems the logical place to illustrate how the treason trials destroyed Hitler's Fifth Column in Russia."[69] Davies, who from 4 to 12 March was present at the Bukharin trial,[70] himself admits that on 8 March 1938 he heard the testimony of Dr. Levin against "Yagoda, chief of secret police," who, Davies adds, compelled Levin and associates "to 'cure to death' Maxim Gorky and his son and others, as a part of the plot to discredit the Kremlin. It was a gruesome and bizarre tale."[71] What ostensibly happened was "that

---

[66] *Ibid.* 136.
[67] *Ibid.* 137.
[68] *Ibid.* 131. Davies's views of Stalin can be readily compared with reality on the basis of on the enormous corpus of literature on Stalin.
[69] Davies 179.
[70] *Ibid.* 177-8.
[71] *Ibid.* 176.

Yagoda, one of the defendants, was infatuated with young Gorky's beautiful wife and that Gorky Senior had aroused Yagoda's enmity because of his interposition in that triangle. Yagoda, it was said, feared the elder Gorky because of his great popularity with the Russian people."[72]

It was not just to his superiors that Davies displayed signs of a naiveté that is rather uncommon among men of law. In his letter of 8 March 1938, to his daughter Emlen Grosjean, who was familiar with the scene in Moscow, the ambassador plainly states his belief that

> the extraordinary testimony of Krestinsky, Bukharin, and the rest would appear to indicate that the Kremlin's fears were well justified. For it now seems that a plot existed in the beginning of November 1936, to project a *coup d'état*, with Tukhatchevsky at its head, for May of the following year. Apparently it was touch and go at that time whether it actually would be staged.
>
> But the government acted with great vigour and speed. The Red Army generals were shot and the whole party organization was purged and thoroughly cleansed. Then it came out that quite a few of those at the top were seriously infected with the virus of the conspiracy to overthrow the government, and were actually working with the Secret Service organizations of Germany and Japan.[73]

In his diary, Davies makes quite a surprising connection between these impressions of the "great trial" and the issue of the Russian/Soviet state debt.

> The 'last words' of Pletnov, Rosengoltz, and other defendants were harrowing in their interest and tragedy. Rosengoltz particularly so. It was only a year ago that we were at his country home for the day with Grinko, Krestinsky, the prosecutor Vyshinsky, Judge Ulrich, Mikoyan, Rosoff, and Voroshilov at dinner. I then made no impression upon some of them in stressing the dangers of foreign war as an inducement for them to pay their debt to us. The defendants in this trial, including some of these men, according to their statements wanted war! Not so Voroshilov and some of the others. He was then, a year ago, strong for the debt payment to the U.S.[74]

---

[72] *Ibid.* 176.

[73] *Ibid.* 177.

[74] *Ibid.* 178. References are made to Dmitry Pletniev (1872–1953), Arkady Pavlovich Rosengoltz (1889–1938), Grigory Fedorovich Grinko (1890–1938), Nikolai Ivanovich Krestinsky (1883–1938), Andrey Yanuaryevich Vyshinsky (1883–1954), Vasiliy Vasilievich Ulrikh, Anastas Ivanovich Mikoyan (1895–1978), Kliment Yefremovich Voroshilov (1881–1969). Data for David A. Rosoff are still unavailable.

A few days after the verdict was read at dawn on 13 March, Davies reported to Secretary Cordell Hull that

> … it is my opinion so far as the political defendants are concerned sufficient crimes under Soviet law, among those charged in the indictment, were established by the proof and beyond a reasonable doubt to justify the verdict of guilty of treason and the adjudication of the punishment provided by Soviet criminal statutes. The opinion of those diplomats who attended the trial most regularly was general that the case had established the fact that there was a formidable political opposition and an exceedingly serious plot, which explained to the diplomats many of the hitherto unexplained developments of the last six months in the Soviet Union. The only difference of opinion that seemed to exist was the degree to which the plot had been implemented by different defendants and the degree to which the conspiracy had become centralized.[75]

A few days after National Socialist Germany attacked the Soviet Union in 1941, Davies gave a talk at the club of the University of Chicago, his alma mater. When it came to taking questions, someone in the audience wanted to know "What about Fifth Columnists in Russia?"[76] Davies answered, "There aren't any – they shot them."[77]

Mentally revisiting the scene and period of his mission to Moscow, Davies wrote in 1941:

> As I ruminated over this situation, I suddenly saw the picture as I should have seen it at the time. The story had been told in the so-called treason or purge trials of 1937 and 1938 which I had attended and listened to. In re-examining the record of these cases and also what I had written at the time from this new angle, I found that practically

[75] Davies 178-9. The literature of the Moscow show trials is extensive and rife with controversy. The following works stand out: Robert Conquest: *The Great Terror. A Reassessment*; Robert Tucker: *Stalin in Power. The Revolution from Above, 1928–1941*; Vadim Z. Rogovin, *1937. Stalin's Year of Terror*; Jörg Baberowski, *Der rote Terror. Die Geschichte des Stalinismus*; Karl Schlögel, *Terror und Traum. Moskau 1937*; Vadim Z. Rogovin, *Stalin's Terror of 1937–38. Political Genocide in the USSR*; Jörg Baberowski, *Verbrannte Erde. Stalins Herrschaft der Gewalt*; Stephen Kotkin, *Stalin. Volume I: Paradoxes of Power, 1878–1928*; Douglas O. Linder, *The Moscow Purge Trials (1936–38).* Selected Links & Bibliography:
http://law2.umkc.edu/faculty/projects/ftrials/moscowpurge/moscowlinks.html. Accessed 1 Sept. 2019.

[76] Davies 179.

[77] *Ibid.* 179.

> every device of German Fifth Columnist activity, as we now know it, was disclosed and laid bare by the confessions and testimony elicited at these trials of self-confessed 'Quislings' in Russia.[78]

The German attack forced Davies to rethink the Moscow purge trials. In a note penned in 1941, he admits that, during the trials, neither he nor the American journalists in Moscow cared about the potential German and Japanese implications of the proceedings. They devoted all their attention to the "dramatic struggle for power between the 'ins' and 'outs'—between Stalin and Trotsky—and the clash of personalities and policies within the Soviet government, rather than upon any possible German Fifth Column activities, which we were all disposed to discount at the time."[79]

Later, however, the German offensive made it clear to him, so to speak, that "The story which was unfolded in these trials disclosed a record of Fifth Columnist and subversive activities in Russia under a conspiracy agreement with the German and Japanese governments that were amazing."[80] At this point, Davies reiterates the well-known accusations of the show trials and, in an attempt to justify his own "realization," quotes from the defendants' testimony based on the courtroom minutes.

> All of these trials, purges, and liquidations, which seemed so violent at the time and shocked the world, are now quite clearly a part of a vigorous and determined effort of the Stalin government to protect itself from not only revolution from within but from attack from without. They went to work thoroughly to clean up and clean out all treasonable elements within the country. All doubts were resolved in favour of the government.[81]

These claims attest to the fact that, rather than simply misjudging the show trials and Stalin's purges in general, Davies sought to interpret and explain them with a strong bias as dictated by the daily needs of the Soviet Union. Davies's endeavors benefitted the policies favored by Roosevelt and the Democrats, particularly in terms of improving Soviet-American relations during World War II, ultimately serving the cause of the emerging anti-Hitler coalition. In these efforts, he tried to find rational

---

[78] *Ibid.* 180.
[79] *Ibid.* 181.
[80] *Ibid.* 181.
[81] *Ibid.* 184.

explanations for the unintelligible and unreasonable reality that was Stalin's paranoia.[82]

Ill.3: Joseph E. Davies

RETURN TO MOSCOW

During and after World War II, Davies continued to enjoy the trust of Roosevelt and Truman, and performed high-priority assignments involving the Soviet Union. In May 1943, he was sent on another mission to Moscow, this time carrying a top secret letter from Roosevelt to Stalin. Since the war raging on the Continent made it seem unwise for him to

[82] Cf. Robert Dallek, *Franklin D. Roosevelt and American Foreign Policy, 1932-1945: With a New Afterword. 1979;* Justus D. Doenecke, Mark *A.* Stoler, *Debating Franklin D. Roosevelt's Foreign Policies, 1933-1945.*

travel across Europe, he chose a detour of nearly 26,000 miles, reaching Moscow from New York via Brazil, Senegal, Egypt, Iraq, Iran, Kuybishev, and Stalingrad. On the way back, he entered the United States via Novosibirsk and Alaska—completing a journey totaling 41,246 kilometers.[83] In the letter, Roosevelt proposed a one-to-one meeting with Stalin, with no one else present other than an interpreter and a stenographer. Stalin recommended Fairbanks, Alaska, as the venue, and named several dates between 15 June and 15 August. He asked Davies to convey to Roosevelt the emphatic message that, owing to Hitler's massive advances, the Soviet Union would be needing more of everything under Lend-Lease.[84] Davies was surprised to find at the U.S. Embassy in Moscow the same hostile and prejudiced climate that he had experienced as ambassador in his day. On the evidence of his own notes, Davies (now Roosevelt's special envoy) did his best to explain to embassy staff that any public criticism of the Soviet Union on the part of the United States could be extremely damaging to the war-time alliance.[85]

Following the war, Davies resumed his diplomatic service, finding himself in the epicenter of world politics over and over again. In May 1945, Truman dispatched him to Potsdam to organize talks with British Prime Minister Winston Churchill. In a diary entry, Davies claims to have been told by Truman about his plans to postpone the talks with Stalin and Churchill to July, when the atomic bomb had already been tested.[86] At the Potsdam Conference, Davies served as advisor to Truman, with the rank of ambassador.

---

[83] *Life* magazine, 4 October 1943.

[84] Passed on 11 March 1941, the Lend-Lease Act permitted American shipments of weapons and military supplies to the Soviet Union and Great Britain.

[85] Joseph E. Davies, *Missions for Peace – 1940–1950*; unpublished manuscript held by the Library of Congress. https://en.wikipedia.org/wiki/Joseph_E._Davies. Accessed 5 June 2016. Cf. also Elizabeth Kimball Maclean, "Joseph E. Davies and Soviet-American Relations, 1941–43," 73–94.

[86] Diary entry by Davies, 21 May 1945. Joseph E. Davies Papers, Library of Congress, Box 17. Published in: William Burr, ed., *National Security Archive Electronic Briefing Book,* No. 162. http://nsarchive.gwu.edu/NSAEBB/NSAEBB162/. Accessed 26 July 2016. Robert D. Schulzinger, ed., *A Companion to American Foreign Relations,* http://onlinelibrary.wiley.com/doi/10.1002/9780470999042.biblio/pdf. Accessed 28 July 2016.

HUNGARIAN TIES

Joseph E. Davies visited Hungary as well.

During his trip to Europe, in 1937, he had personally talked with Czechoslovak President Edvard Beneš (1884–1948), who addressed issues concerned with the Little Entente and Hungary. At the meeting, Beneš identified Hungary partly as a "totalitarian-autocratic" state, while conceding certain improvements in Czechoslovak-Hungarian relations. Davies was deeply impressed by Beneš, whom he described as one of the most capable and brilliant statesmen in Europe.[87]

In late September Davies arrived in Budapest (he had been to the city before). Although Minister Montgomery did not happen to be in to greet him, Davies had a great time. He enjoyed the Hungarian capital and was fond of Hungarians in general.[88] On the occasion, he had a lengthy conference with Regent Miklós Horthy (1868–1957), whom he described as strong, with temperament and balance.[89]

Davies nurtured intimate relations with and cultivated the friendship of John F. Montgomery (1878–1954), U.S. Minister to Budapest.[90] In June 1938, the two crossed the Atlantic from Southampton to New York together on board SS *Washington.*[91]

---

[87] Joseph E. Davies to Secretary of State Cordell, Villefranche, 13 September 1937. In: *Foreign Relations of the United States. Diplomatic Papers 1937,* Vol. 1: *General*, 124–7.

[88] Joseph E. Davies – John F. Montgomery, Budapest, 27 September 1937; John F. Montgomery – Joseph E. Davies, 26 October 1937; Joseph E. Davies – John F. Montgomery, Moscow, 3 November 1937. John F. Montgomery Papers, Sterling Memorial Library, Yale University, MS Group #353, Vol. IV.

[89] Zsuzsa L. Nagy, "Amerikai diplomaták jelentései Horthy Miklósról," *História* 5–6 (1990): 20.

[90] Tibor Frank, ed., *Discussing Hitler. Advisers of U.S. Diplomacy in Central Europe 1934-1941*, 13–4.

[91] Diary entry by Davies on 17 June 1938. In Davies 239.

Ill. 4: *John F. Montgomery and Joseph E. Davies*

The correspondence between the two friends between 1937 and 1939, devoted mainly to personal issues important for Montgomery, contains little worthy of mention in terms of politics, even though it clearly manifests Davies's ill-advised political views and wide-of-the mark predictions. On 13 February 1939, in a letter to Montgomery from Brussels to Budapest, Davies, for example, wrote that the year would not bring about the outbreak of actual hostilities.[92]

Davies's book was published in Hungarian, and in two editions at that, directly after World War II [*Moszkvai jelentés*, translated by Vilmos Juhász, nearly 500 pages in length (Budapest: Anonymus, 1945).] In 1984, Oxford Engineering Professor László Solymár, member of the Royal Society, briefly compared the English text with the Hungarian version, and came to the conclusion that the numerous deviations and omissions from

[92] Joseph E. Davies – John F. Montgomery, Brussels, 13 February 1939. John F. Montgomery Papers, Sterling Memorial Library, Yale University, MS Group #353, Vol. V.

the original had invariably been occasioned by the resolve to toe the line of Stalinist Soviet policy.[93] The bottom line is that the Hungarian text must have been revised by censors thoroughly in 1945, in an attempt to achieve a better fit with Soviet interests in Hungary.

TRACING A MYSTERY

Davies was, of course, completely wrong, and not for the first time. It is extraordinary that a successful, professionally experienced American lawyer and legal counsel failed to discern the true nature of the Moscow show trials. How can we comprehend the fact that Davies, sitting in the first row of the court room, was not astonished by the terribly stolid faces, broken figures, and blatantly fabricated testimonies of senior government officials and politicians, all of them good acquaintances of his, turned into abject, tortured defendants in the blink of an eye? Is it possible that this prominent bureaucrat, despite the confidence of his superiors, was ultimately lost in the maze of world politics, led astray simply by poor judgment of character, mistaken thinking, and a quintessentially American naiveté? The Order of Lenin[94] awarded to him in 1945 does not provide evidence that he may have made a secret pact with the Soviets. Was he perhaps vulnerable to blackmail? Not that unlikely. Was he afraid himself? Of what or of whom, and why? Why did he not believe his astute peers and embassy staff, who gauged the situation accurately, seeing it for what it was?

The answer probably lies in the biographical writings of Davies's wife published to date. Davies and Ms. Post regularly received invaluable art

[93] Mr. László Solymár of Oxford called my attention to the blatantly intentional distortions in the Hungarian translation of Davies's book, and to a brief article he had published on the subject: cf. L. R. Somlay (=László Solymár), "Submission to Moscow" (in Hungarian). *Survey* 28.4 (1984): 188–92. Davies and his incomprehensible approval of Stalin had for a long time been criticized in the harshest terms by international experts, such as Charles E. Bohlen (1904-1974), who was to become Ambassador to Moscow (1953-1957). See also David Mayers, *George Kennan and the Dilemmas of US Foreign Policy*, 43-44, 91, quoting Charles E. Bohlen, *Witness to History, 1929–1969*, 44, 56.

[94] https://en.wikipedia.org/wiki/Order_of_Lenin. Accessed 5 Sept. 2019.

objects from the Soviet authorities to enrich their own collection,[95] either as a gift or for a ridiculously low price, originally confiscated from the Tsar's family estate or the Russian aristocracy, or spirited away from the State Tretyakov Gallery in Moscow—even sometimes from the victims of Stalinist terror.[96] It is quite probable that these gifts swayed Davies in favor of Stalin's régime, although his precise motives remain to be investigated by further research, notably in the archives in Moscow.

Additionally, as previously mentioned, Davies adamantly served the policies of Roosevelt and the Democratic Party, including the cause of thawed Soviet-American relations and of the nascent coalition against Hitler. In these efforts, he tried to find rational explanations for the unintelligible and unreasonable reality that was Stalin's paranoia.[97]

One thing is certain: Davies's written and oral reports steered President Roosevelt and Secretary of State Hull in a Soviet-friendly direction, including their acceptance of Stalin, thereby helping to build and maintain the Soviet-American coalition against Hitler. The heavily censored and revised Hungarian translation of his book merely amplifies his pro-Soviet and pro-Stalin voice. For all of his egregious errors of judgment, it remains an indisputable fact that, in his own way, Davies made a meaningful contribution to the ultimate triumph of the Allies in World War II.

An earlier version of this article, mainly on the Hungarian translation of *Mission to Moscow (1945)*, was published in Hungarian by Tibor Frank, ed., *Az orosz birodalom születései. Magyar kutatók tanulmányai az orosz történelemről*, Budapest: Gondolat, 2016, 255–78;

---

[95] For Post's Russian art collection see the catalogue of the Hillwood Estate, Museum & Gardens, https://www.hillwoodmuseum.org/. Accessed 10 Sept. 2019.

[96] https://en.wikipedia.org/wiki/Marjorie_Merriweather_Post (accessed 28 April 2018) identifies the source of these claims as William Wright, *Heiress: The Rich Life of Marjorie Merriweather Post*, Nancy Rubin Stuart, *American Empress: The Life and Times of Marjorie Merriweather Post*; Estella M. Chung, *Living Artfully: At Home with Marjorie Merriweather Post*; Liana Paredes, *Spectacular: Gems and Jewelry from the Merriweather Post Collection*; Howard Vincent Kurtz, *Ingenue to Icon: 70 Years of Fashion from the Collection of Marjorie Merriweather Post.*

[97] *Life* magazine, 4 October 1943.

a different version in Russian: Тибор Франк, Слепой свидетель. Американский посол Джозеф Э. Дэвис в Москве, 1936–1938. *RussianStudiesHu*, DOI: 10.38210/RUSTUDH.2020.2.4, 1-30.

WORKS CITED

Baberowski, Jörg. *Der rote Terror. Die Geschichte des Stalinismus.* Munich: DVA, 2003.

—. *Verbrannte Erde. Stalins Herrschaft der Gewalt.* Munich: C. H. Beck, 2012.

Bohlen, Charles E. *Witness to History, 1929–1969*. New York: Norton, 1973.

Brinkley, Alan. *The Unfinished Nation. A Concise History of the American People*. New York: McGraw Hill, 2010.

Conquest, Robert. *The Great Terror. A Reassessment.* Oxford – New York: Oxford UP, 1968, 40th anniversary ed. 2008.

Chung, Estella M. *Living Artfully: At Home with Marjorie Merriweather Post*. London: Giles, 2013.

Culbert, David H. *Mission to Moscow.* Madison, WI: U of Wisconsin P, 1980.

Dallek, Robert. *Franklin D. Roosevelt and American Foreign Policy, 1932-1945*. With a New Afterword. New York: Oxford UP, 1979.

Davies, Joseph E. *Mission to Moscow*. New York: Simon and Schuster, 1941; London: Victor Gollancz, 1942, 10th impr. 1945.

—. *Missions for Peace – 1940–1950*; unpublished manuscript held by the Library of Congress. https://en.wikipedia.org/wiki/Joseph_E._Davies. Accessed 5 June 2016.

—. Papers, Library of Congress. Published in: William Burr, ed., National Security Archive Electronic Briefing Book, No. 162. http://nsarchive.gwu.edu/NSAEBB/NSAEBB162/. Accessed 26 July 2016.

Doenecke, Justus D., and Mark A. Stoler. *Debating Franklin D. Roosevelt's Foreign Policies, 1933-1945*. Lanham: Rowman & Littlefield, 2005.

Foreign Relations of the United States. Diplomatic Papers 1937, Vol. 1: General. Washington: United States Government Printing Office, 1954.

Frank, Tibor, ed. *Discussing Hitler. Advisers of U.S. Diplomacy in Central Europe 1934-1941*. Budapest—New York: CEU Press, 2003.

Kotkin, Stephen. *Stalin*. Volume I: Paradoxes of Power, 1878–1928. London: Penguin Press, 2014.

Kurtz, Howard Vincent. *Ingenue to Icon: 70 Years of Fashion from the Collection of Marjorie Merriweather Post*. Washington, D.C.: Hillwood Estate, Museum & Gardens, 2015.

Linder, Douglas O. *The Moscow Purge Trials* (1936–38). Bibliography and Selected Links.https://www.google.com/search?client=firefox-b-d&q=Linder%2C+Douglas+O.%2C+The+Moscow+Purge+Trials+%281936%E2%80%9238%29.+Bibliography+and+Selected+Links. Accessed 17 December 2019.

L. Nagy, Zsuzsa. “Amerikai diplomaták jelentései Horthy Miklósról.” *História* (1990): 5-6.

MacLean, Elizabeth Kimball. “Joseph E. Davies and Soviet-American Relations, 1941–43.” Diplomatic History 4.1 (1980): 73-93.

—. “Joseph E. Davies: ‘The Wisconsin Idea and the Origins of the Federal Trade Commission.’” *Journal of the Gilded Age and Progressive Era* 6.3 (2007): 248–84.

—. *Joseph E. Davies: Envoy to the Soviets*. Westport, CT: Praeger, 1992.

Mayers, David. *George Kennan and the Dilemmas of US Foreign Policy*. New York—Oxford: Oxford UP, 1988.

McClay, Ellen. *In The Presence of Our Enemies*. Bloomington, IN: AuthorHouse, 2006. Accessed 22 July 2016.

Merrill, Dennis, and Thomas G. Patterson, eds. *Major Problems in American Foreign Relations*. Vol. II. Since 1914. Boston – New York: Houghton Mifflin, 2000.

Miscamble, Wilson D. “George Kennan. A Life in the Foreign Service.” *Foreign Service Journal* 81.2 (2004): 22-34.

Montgomery, John F. Papers, Sterling Memorial Library, Yale University.

Ohl, P. V., *Foreign Capital in Russia*. Petrograd: Institute of Economic Research, 1922.

Paredes, Liana. *Spectacular: Gems and Jewelry from the Merriweather Post Collection*. London: Giles, 2017.

Rogovin, Vadim Z. *Stalin’s Terror of 1937–38. Political Genocide in the USSR*. Oak Park, MI: Mehring Books, 2009.

Schlögel, Karl. *Terror und Traum, Moskau 1937*. Munich: Hanser, 2008.

Schulzinger, Robert D., ed. *A Companion to American Foreign Relations*. Oxford: Blackwell Publishing Ltd., 2003.

Schulzinger, Robert D. *U.S. Diplomacy Since 1900*. 6th ed., New York – Oxford: Oxford UP, 2008.

Siegel, Katherine A. S. *Loans and Legitimacy. The Evolution of Soviet-American Relations, 1919–1933*. Lexington, KY: The UP of Kentucky, 1996.

Sinkó, Ervin. *Egy regény regénye. Moszkvai naplójegyzetek 1935–1937.* Budapest-Újvidék: Magvető–Forum, 1988.

Soviet-American Political and Trade Relations. CQ Researcher. http://library.cqpress.com/cqresearcher/document.php?id=cqresrre1933022400.

Stoker, Donald J. Jr., and Jonathan A. Grant, eds. *Girding for Battle. The Arms Trade in a Global Perspective, 1815–1940*. Westport, CT – London: Praeger, 2003.

Stuart, Nancy Rubin. *American Empress: The Life and Times of Marjorie Merriweather Post*. Lincoln, NE: iUniverse, 2004.

Tucker Robert. *Stalin in Power. The Revolution from Above, 1928–1941*. New York: Norton, 1992.

U.S. Department of State: Foreign Relations of the United States, 1938. Washington, D.C., 1954, Government Printing Office.

Wright, William. *Heiress: The Rich Life of Marjorie Merriweather Post*. Washington, D.C.: New Republic Books, 1978.

PHILIPP GASSERT

One World, Or War? Politics, Science, and Popular Culture in the Transatlantic Resistance to the Cold War

From today's vantage point of the recent turmoil in transatlantic relations the Cold War presents itself as an era of remarkable stability. After the post-World War II civil wars had ended in the Balkans, Europe did not see a major military conflagration for more than forty years. When tensions were on the rise, such as during the 1962 Cuban Missile Crisis or the 1953, 1956, and 1968 Soviet crackdowns on Eastern European uprisings, common sense always prevailed. Hence, the "nuclear stalemate" led to the most prolonged period of peaceful coexistence in modern European history. While decolonization and U.S.-Soviet rivalry produced violent confrontations in the so-called "Third World," some smoldering for decades, the Cold War in Europe was notable for the absence of large-scale hot wars. Even the Arab-Israeli conflict was largely contained. Compared to what came later in places like the former Yugoslavia, Rwanda, Afghanistan, Iraq, and most recently Syria, the postwar decades have attained the nostalgic tinge of a "long peace."[1]

Of course, this was not the prevailing sentiment at the time. The post-1945 "Cold War order" was always contested, especially in divided Europe, but also in the United States.[2] In Europe, as well as in similarly divided East Asia, the consolidation of the two superpower empires meant that centuries-old lines of communication were cut, families torn apart, and people prevented from going about their businesses across newly erected borders. That was most visible in places like Berlin or the Korean Demilitarized Zone (DMZ), situated a few miles from Korea's historical capital. Vienna, too, moved from the center of Europe to the margins. As the Czech writer Milan Kundera lamented in his famous essay *Un occident kidnappé*, the "golden city" of Prague had once been a proud cultural,

---

[1] This being the title of Cold War historian John Lewis Gaddis's iconic essay, which had been published even before the Berlin Wall came down; see Gaddis, "The Long Peace."

[2] Gassert, "Internal Challenges."

economic, and political crossroads of Europe. It was now relegated to the place of a provincial capital in an isolated Russian-dominated East, of which it never had felt to be part.[3]

Europeans, East Asians, and even Americans and Russians frequently detested and sometimes challenged this "unnatural" situation at ancient centers of European and Asian civilizations. While West Europeans and the people of Japan (as well as later the South Koreans, Taiwanese, Hong Kong Chinese, Greeks, Portuguese, and the Spanish) were living in relative prosperity, those living to the north and east of those borders were punished for Cold War stability, as were those living in the so-called "Third World" countries, where the superpowers were fighting "proxy wars." Moreover, while many were going about their daily business, forgetting about the nuclear threat and the "division of the world," others perceived the situation along the geopolitical fault lines as a dangerous powder keg that could detonate at any moment. Popular culture was rife with imaginations of accidental or not so accidental Armageddons.[4] Millions took to the streets during the 1950s and 1980s to prevent impending nuclear doom. The "struggle against the bomb" became one of the most prolonged transnational social movements in history, finding supporters across the globe.[5]

This contribution looks at those American, transatlantic and European voices who opposed the status quo of the Cold War, which included political parties, social movements, artists, filmmakers, intellectuals, scientists, and politicians. While that opposition took up a range of issues, including a general critique of the militarization of societies, my focus is on the debate on "nuclear death." The vision of total nuclear annihilation became the most powerful symbol of those critical of an international order that seemed to have become utterly unpredictable, dangerous, and inhumane. This debate played itself out in an interactive transatlantic and to some extent global framework. While opponents to governmental Cold War politics were often labelled "anti-Western" or "anti-American," many were in fact deeply influenced by Henry David Thoreau, Martin Luther King, Jr., Mahatma Gandhi, and other protagonists of the nonviolent resistance tradition equally revered by the U.S. peace movement.[6]

---

[3] Kundera, "Die Weltliteratur."

[4] Shapiro, *Atomic Bomb Cinema*; DeGroot, *The Bomb*.

[5] Wittner, *Struggle Against the Bomb*.

[6] Gassert, "Conflict."

My general argument is that the Cold War should be conceived as much as the history of a transatlantic conversation among those opposed to the nuclear stalemate as it has been conceived as the history of the interaction of those who accepted the Cold War division of the world as the inevitable outcome of a power struggle between two military and ideological blocs. Therefore on many occasions a critique of the Cold War order included a critique of the domestic status quo in Western societies. During its first two decades (1940s and 1950s) as well as during the last decade (the 1980s) the main bearers of anti-nuclearism were political parties, activist political networks (including social movements) as well as popular culture, with the last playing a much more prominent role in "bringing the war home" during the 1980s than during previous decades. During the middle decades (1960s and 1970s) the main opposition came from academic peace research. In this context, intellectual networks played a most significant role. While neither social movements nor producers of nuclear catastrophes in popular culture were in a position to bring the Cold War to an end, they were part and parcel of "making sense" of what they perceived as a senseless and dangerous order.

FOR THE UNITY OF MANKIND: EARLY CHALLENGES TO THE COLD WAR ORDER

On both sides of the Atlantic, the early resistance to the Cold War and a looming arms race was mostly taken up by established political figures. They tended to cling to those visions of "one world," with which World War II had been fought and to some extent been won. Yet, given the difficulties of peacemaking in Yalta and Potsdam, they could not be sustained long beyond the cessation of hostilities.[7] The idea that in "Yalta" the potential for a "better world" had been in the balance, would fire up those who during the Cold War period were convinced that the West had betrayed the Eastern Europeans in Yalta.[8] And whereas international relations "realist" thinkers conceived the Soviet-American rivalry as a natural outcome of the power vacuum that had opened up in Central

[7] Numerous publications include Miscamble, *From Roosevelt to Truman*; Neiberg, *Potsdam*.

[8] Roberts, "Antipodes or Twins."

Europe after the fall of Hitler's Germany, others resisted the idea that a new conflict was a historical given.[9]

One prominent American example is that of Henry A. Wallace, a staunch New Dealer, former Secretary of Agriculture and Vice President during Roosevelt's third term as President. After briefly serving as Secretary of Commerce in the first Truman administration, Wallace became notable for his unwillingness to accept force and heightened conflict as the way things were going in Soviet-American relations. Even though his 1948 third-party presidential bid would be unsuccessful, he served as a figurehead for those questioning the Cold War paradigm, that by the late 1940s had become so firmly entrenched among the members of the administration. In particular, Wallace opposed Winston Churchill on the premises of the latter's 1946 "Fulton Speech," in which the former British Prime Minister had warned of aggressive Soviet tendencies. Churchill, who had spoken at the invitation of Truman, also popularized the term "iron curtain," referring to the barrier which had supposedly "descended across the continent."[10] Wallace went against this reasoning in full force, and soon found many detractors and enemies in the U.S. as well as in Europe.

Although Wallace was a very peculiar American mixture of mid-Western Presbyterianism and progressivism, globalist idealism, and naivety toward Joseph Stalin, he developed his critique of the Truman administration's growing hostility toward the Soviet Union to some extent in a dialogue with Europeans who were opposed to the Cold War as well. Among them he found more sympathetic and enthusiastic audiences than back home. After having been ousted by Truman, Wallace accepted the position of editor of the progressive-leaning magazine *New Republic*. In this capacity he traveled to Europe, speaking in England, Norway, Sweden, Denmark, and France. There, he advertised his vision of a united postwar world, which would share the secrets of atomic energy and the bomb.[11] As he said to a cheering crowd in London: "The world is devastated and hungry; the world is crying out, not for American guns and tanks to spread more hunger, but for American plows and machines to

[9] Cortright, *Peace* 109-10.
[10] Churchill, "The Sinews of Peace."
[11] Shimamoto, *Wallace* 158-9; Walker, *Wallace* 170-2.

fulfill the promise of peace."[12] While aiming at the American presidency, Wallace felt that he had to interact with those Europeans who supported him in his conviction that the world could not be saved if Europeans and Americans did not show "belief in the unity of all mankind."[13]

A second increasingly harsh critic of Churchill's and Truman's fixed belief in an "iron curtain descending across Europe," and their exhortations that the Soviet Union must be confronted, was the journalist and writer Walter Lippmann. Truly a transatlantic intellectual, he had been a member of the 1918-19 U.S. Armistice Commission, traveling frequently to Europe during the interwar years. In 1938, with the threat of Fascism looming large over Europe, he co-sponsored the famous Paris Colloquium that came up with the term "neo-liberalism."[14] Shortly after Churchill's 1946 Fulton speech, Lippmann went on a five-week trip to Europe, stopping in Paris, Berlin, Munich, Vienna, Prague, Rome, and Florence. While Lippmann did not harbor any illusions about Soviet intentions, he urged his compatriots to resist the temptation of "talking tough" to the Russians. Like Wallace, he contradicted Truman's and Foreign Secretary George C. Marshall's idea that Soviet intentions were aggressive and that the American people must prepare for the consequences.[15]

After visiting Europe for a second time in 1947, Lippman summarized his findings in a series of articles, which were published in a small booklet bearing the eponymous title *The Cold War.*[16] He did so, however, from a critical, "one world" perspective. Lippmann argued that the Russians had already lost the "Cold War."[17] The West should back down, remain confident, and relax tensions. Cooperation with the Soviets would be entirely in the interest of the United States. Reacting to former U.S. deputy chief of mission in Moscow and then State Department Policy Director

---

[12] Quoted in Walton, *Wallace* 153; on the trip to Europe see Walker, *Wallace* 149-65.

[13] Wallace, *Toward World Peace* 117-18.

[14] Although, in 1938 the term "neo-liberal" had a very different meaning from today: then it referred to a new thinking with regard to the failures of liberals to oppose Fascism, Communism, and totalitarianism effectively; see *Walter Lippmann Colloquium.*

[15] Steel, *Lippmann* 430-1.

[16] Lippmann, *Cold War* 42-5; while he did not invent the term "Cold War," he certainly popularized it.

[17] Steel, *Lippmann* 447.

George F. Kennan's famous "Mr. X" article, which provided the intellectual underpinnings of the policies of containment,[18] Lippmann did not think that the conflict with the Soviet Union was imaginary. Having traveled to Europe, however, he was convinced that "the strength of the western world is great." The Red Army was in no way in a position to occupy Western Europe: "Though impoverished and weakened, the nations of the Atlantic community are incomparably stronger, richer, more united, and politically more democratic and mature than any of the nations of the Russian perimeter." The Soviets could keep their grip on Eastern Europe with military might only. Therefore, it made no sense to aim "to make Jeffersonian democrats out of the peasants of eastern Europe […], but to settle the war and to restore the independence of the nations of Europe by removing the alien armies – all of them, our own included."[19]

Similarly, in Europe much of the early opposition to the Cold War was to be found less within civil society, than within established Social Democratic Parties and Labor Unions. West German unions in particular, even though they were critical of the Stalinization of East Germany, were strongly opposed to the rearmament of the country and sought allies within the American political establishment.[20] Yet, neither in the U.S. nor in Western Europe could Social Democratic and Communist parties win majorities with campaigns against nuclear armament. Conservative leaders such as Konrad Adenauer in Germany, Alcide de Gasperi in Italy, and Winston Churchill in England combined the promise of stability, security and prosperity in a nascent consumer society with a firm commitment to prioritize Western integration as well as anti-Communism over "one world" and the overcoming of the division of Europe. In most of Western-leaning, liberal Europe, with the exception of maybe Austria, the "peace party" remained in a minority position. Nudged on by U.S. labor unions and anti-Communist "Cold War liberals," West European labor unions as well as Social Democrats moved toward the center during the second half of the 1950s, basically accepting the premises of the Cold War.[21]

---

[18] X, "Sources of Soviet Conduct"; for Kennan's original Moscow Embassy "Long Telegram" see Etzold 50-63.

[19] Lippmann, *Cold War* 15, 26, 44-5.

[20] Fichter, "Support and Dissent" 572.

[21] Angster, "Finest Labor Network" 110-11.

Thus, during the 1950s, "prosperity," "freedom," "anti-Communism" and "Cold War" came to trump "peace" and "one world," or, to be more precise: Fears of a new, possibly catastrophic nuclear war never were strong enough to overcome skepticism toward those parties who were arguing in favor of an East-Western rapprochement and decisive moves toward détente. The political reactions to the testing of a hydrogen bomb at the Bikini Atoll in the South Pacific by the U.S. in 1954 is a good example: it certainly led to rising public concerns over the long-term health effects of nuclear radiation, when 28 Americans, 239 Marshall Islanders, and 23 crew members of a Japanese fishing boat, the *Lucky Dragon*, were contaminated by nuclear fallout. Soon, nuclear fiction was on the rise in both the U.S. and Europe. Japanese as well as American movie production companies reacted with a spectacular series of movies. That same year, the first *Godzilla* movie came out in Japan. Shortly thereafter, against the backdrop of the debates about nuclear fallout and its effect on human genetic material, mutants became endemic in Hollywood.[22]

Yet trashy movies like *Them!* (1954), *The Monster that Challenged the World* (1957) or even the more upscale, Kafkaesque story in the *The Incredible Shrinking Man* (1957) did not lead to any prolonged resistance to "nuclearism" and the Cold War. In her famous essay, "The Imagination of Disaster," the journalist and philosopher Susan Sontag has argued that popular science-fiction scenarios have the potential to normalize and trivialize real dangers.[23] And even though she was roundly criticized for her argument, there may be some truth in it, when we look at the paradoxical situation in the late 1950s: Popular culture was rife with scenarios of nuclear apocalypse. Moreover, Europe saw the rise of serious postapocalyptic "atomic literature" as well as the "physicist dramas," in which concerned and torn scientists like J. Robert Oppenheimer figured prominently.[24] Even though the ethics of atomic science was hotly debated, political resistance to the Cold War and the armaments race died down. While many, in theory, supported a test ban treaty as well as the prohibition of nuclear arms, the struggle for peace became the project of specialized organizations and social movements as well as the province of scientists.

---

[22] Weart, *Nuclear Fear*.

[23] Sontag, "Imagination of Disaster"; Broderick, "Surviving Armageddon."

[24] Stölken-Fitschen, *Atombombe*; Krah, *Weltuntergangsszenarien*.

Despite the sensational reports on nuclear testing, the transatlantic peace movements reached their low point during the mid-1950s. Later in the decade, a new type of peace organizations, which we today would call "social movements," such as the National Committee for a Sane Nuclear Policy (SANE) in the United States and the Campaign for Nuclear Disarmament (CND) in Britain renewed the "resistance to the bomb." British activists, who had been involved with American peace networks before, as well as the traditional Labour politics, took the lead with the first march from London to Aldermaston at Easter 1958. It adopted the symbol that has become the emblem of peace movements on both sides of the Atlantic: a circle encompassing a broken cross. The West German Easter March Movement, which originally grew out of the Social Democratic opposition to NATO's decision to arm West German forces with U.S. nuclear weapons, copied the CND.[25] But the very fact that they had sprung up outside the realm of established parties, was very telling with regard to the political salience of "peace" during the 1950s and early 1960s.

During the 1950s, in the U.S. domestic and international peace organizations, such as War Resisters' International (WRI), the International Fellowship of Reconciliation (IFR), and the Women's International League for Peace and Freedom (WILPF) renewed demands for nuclear disarmament. They clearly questioned the underlying paradigm of an arms race borne out of superpower rivalry.[26] And even though the 1963 Test Ban Treaty fell short of the expectations of peace activists, protesters could claim that they had contributed to a growing pressure forcing U.S. and Soviet governments to achieve a breakthrough at the negotiating table.[27] By politicizing a generation of young people and developing new forms of political action, the anti-nuclear campaign set the stage for the protests against the Vietnam War. The British CND as well as the German *Ostermarsch* movement, both were incubators of the movements of "1968." While the new protest movements of the late 1960s continued to challenge the Cold War status quo, they moved away from "peace" between "East" and "West," and tended to focus on decolonization and the "North-South" questions instead.[28]

---

[25] Nehring, "Searching for Security."
[26] Wittner, *Resisting the Bomb* 10-14.
[27] Rubinson, "Crucified on a Cross of Atoms."
[28] Klimke, *Other Alliance* 236-41.

In the mid to late 1960s transatlantic social movement activists began to prioritize "Third World" questions at the expense of campaigns "against the bomb." During the late 1960s, they mostly demonstrated against U.S. imperialism and the American War effort in Vietnam, and they sympathized with the efforts of Eastern Europeans to give Socialism a "human face" as happened during the Prague Spring in 1968. Therefore, during the 1960s, the social sciences emerged as the main agent of the opposition to the Cold War and the logic of mutually-assured destruction. In contrast, the "1968" student movements largely ignored nuclear death and sometimes acted as if the East-West conflict was already history. During the late 1960s, the North-South question took precedence, with student rebels mostly bored by the debates of the 1950s. On both sides of the Atlantic, the movements of 1968 focused on personal liberation, civil rights, and a Marxist critique of society, letting the East-West conflict fall by the wayside.[29]

AGAINST THE BOMB: THE RISE OF PEACE RESEARCH IN THE SHADOW OF DÉTENTE

Early on transatlantic scientific networks had been prominent in the struggles "against the bomb" and "for peace." Britain's anti-nuclear activists urged their government not to develop the hydrogen bomb as early as 1950. A key figure was the British mathematician and philosopher Bertrand Russell, whose BBC radio address on 23 December 1953 attracted international attention. It led to the creation of the Pugwash Movement, which was supported by a number of leading physicists, including several Nobel laureates on both sides of the Cold War barrier. Influenced by Western colleagues, Soviet physicists such as Andrei Sakharov apparently warned their government of the dangers of nuclear testing.[30] Across the Western world scientists made themselves heard with the Russell Einstein Manifesto, signed by many leading nuclear scientists on both sides of the Atlantic. Speaking as "members of the species Man, whose continued existence is in doubt," the signers urged people to set aside the strong political feelings, which the "titanic struggle between Communism and anti-Communism" engendered. Instead, they should

[29] Wittner, "Nuclear Threat Ignored."
[30] Rotblat, *Scientists*.

consider themselves "only as members of a biological species which has had a remarkable history, and whose disappearance none of us can desire."[31]

As social movement activism of the 1960s moved away from issues related to the Cold War and nuclear death, Peace and Conflict Studies (*Friedens- und Konfliktforschung*) became the main agent of the "resistance to the bomb." This scholarly field had originally emerged within both international relations theory and empirical social sciences. When it comes to the transatlantic circulation of ideas, Theodore Lentz's book *Towards a Science of Peace* (1955) was of particular importance. It earned him the title of "father of peace research." Lentz, a professor of Education at Washington University in St. Louis, had been born in Missouri, served in the U.S. military during World War I, and received his Ph.D. from Columbia University in 1925. First, he worked in "character studies," but by the mid-1930s he began circulating questionnaires to measure conservative-to-radical political opinions.[32] In the wake of the tumultuous end of World War II, he had established the Peace Research Laboratory. As a result during the final years of his tenure Lentz devoted most of his time to promoting peace research as a scientific discipline.[33]

In *Towards a Science of Peace* Lentz took what he called a "global perspective" (ix). His stark apocalyptic predictions had a normative basis in Wilsonian, or in that case rather "Rooseveltian" ideas of "one world," which had been the bedrock of Henry Wallace's critique of Truman's confrontational stance toward the Russians. Lentz suggested that while humanity had the scientific knowledge to move "toward a new worldwide golden age," this was not what was actually happening: "There is an extreme danger that the road we now travel will suddenly carry us over the cliff and into an abyss from which it would require centuries to recover, if ever. Amidst the dreams and hopes and promises of one world, we face the possibility of no world at all. The creative genius of man has fostered a towering structure of technology now threatened with cataclysmic

---

[31] "Russell Einstein Manifesto."

[32] Biographical information on the website of the State Historical Society of Missouri, Theodore Lentz Papers, https://collections.shsmo.org/manuscripts/stlouis/s0435.pdf (18 November 2019).

[33] Gleditsch, Nordkvelle, Strand, "Peace Research" 147.

collapse. Civilization seems to hang in the balance, sick and ill-suited to choose between sanity and suicide."[34]

Lentz's urgent call for action came at about the same time as the publication of the Russell Einstein Manifesto, taking a similar line. Both had a decisive impact in Europe. As David J. Dunn reports in *The First Fifty Years of Peace Research*, Lentz's book was read by a Lancaster physiotherapist, Patrick Deighan, who would soon become the founder of the Peace Research Center at Lancaster University. The Lancaster project, in turn, "was a seminal moment in the development of peace research in Britain."[35] At the same time, the Center for the Advanced Study of the Behavioral Sciences was started at Stanford, where, among others, the Austrian émigré Paul Lazarsfeld played a leading role. Among the first visiting scholars was the British political scientist Harold Lasswell, who took an interest in peace research there. These activities coalesced around the founding of the *Journal of Conflict Resolution*. In 1957, it began to appear under the auspices of the University of Michigan. Peace and Conflict Studies now had a highly visible platform for international scholarly exchange.[36]

During the second half of the 1950s and during the 1960s, Peace and Conflict Studies were able to gain a precarious foothold in American and European universities. The activities of concerned nuclear scientists, which peaked around the Einstein Russell Manifesto in Britain and the U.S. as well as the *Göttinger Appell* in West Germany, were coming together with the ambitious plans of social science entrepreneurs such as Theodore Lentz to make the new field of scholarly investigation permanent. However, one should not underestimate the difficulties. The beginnings of the "science of peace" had been so precarious, because "social science" itself was a problematic term during the late 1950s, often having to fend off the assumption that "social science" equaled "socialist science." It was with the Norwegian social scientist Johan Galtung that peace researchers were by and large able to shed the image of being "fellow travelers."

In 1960, Galtung, who had taught at Columbia University during the second half of the 1950s, returned to Norway to establish the International

---

[34] Lentz, *Towards a Science of Peace* 1; tellingly, the book was first published in Britain.

[35] Dunn, *First Fifty Years* 47.

[36] *Ibid.* 48.

Peace Research Institute in Oslo (PRIO). The timing was auspicious. The second Berlin crisis (1958-1962) and the Cuban Missile Crisis (1962) kept people on their toes. Political efforts were gaining speed in Western Europe, the United States as well as the Soviet Union, to slow the arms race and to establish procedures in order to prevent potentially catastrophic developments. The ensuing politics of détente, which became such a prominent feature during the Kennedy and Johnson administrations, opened up the space for a major social science research effort to help overcome the East-West conflict in the name of peace.[37] While the Nuclear Test Ban Treaty of 1963 did not satisfy most peace activists, it was an important first step toward détente. While it could not stop the build-up of nuclear arsenals, the end of testing in the atmosphere reduced a serious health hazard that for some time had been a concern to scientists and Western public opinion. Moreover, it was an important first step toward slowing nuclear proliferation.[38]

The transatlantic field of Peace Research soon went much further. During the 1960s, many of its practitioners took not only a decisive turn against the confrontation between the blocs and the atomic arms race. On both sides of the Atlantic, the "armaments race" was increasingly seen not as the result of the rivalry of great powers (as the "realist school" of international relations would have explained it), but related to the inner-societal causes of the Cold War. In 1969, in a seminal essay, Galtung popularized the idea of "structural violence" that was at the core of modern societies.[39] The German political scientist, Dieter Senghaas, spoke of an "organized lack of peace" (*organisierte Friedlosigkeit*).[40] Later, during the second "nuclear scare" of the 1980s, the psychologist Robert Jay Lifton and the political scientist Richard Falk compared "nuclearism" to a psychological dysfunction in Western societies (basically to madness) and made a strong connection between the arms race and the persecution of European Jews during the Holocaust.[41]

---

[37] Galtung, Fischer, *Johan Galtung* 6-9.

[38] Schrafstetter, Twigge, *Avoiding Armageddon* 120-1.

[39] Galtung, "Violence, Peace, and Peace Research."

[40] Senghaas, *Abschreckung und Frieden.*; on early German Peace Research see Weller, Böschen, "Friedensforschung und Gewalt"; Wasmuht, *Geschichte*; Hauswedell, *Friedenswissenschaften.*

[41] Lifton, Falk, *Indefensible Weapons*.

As the political scientist, peace studies pioneer, and founder of the "Correlates of War" project at the University of Michigan, J. David Singer, observed in 1963, U.S. intellectuals had finally adopted the notion "that we are drifting toward nuclear cataclysm and that the intellectual should – and perhaps can – do something about it."[42] Yet, during the 1960s, anti-nuclear activism was mostly limited to social scientific networks of inquiry. While social movements focused on American civil rights, the Vietnam War, and "Third World" liberation, the fight against the arms race continued in academic circles on both sides of the Atlantic, yet gained little traction in the wider public. Thus, the counter-hegemonial ideas of the peace movement of the 1950s, after having lost track in the political realm, became re-incarnated in the peace research of the 1960s. Peace research, however, acquired a leftist bent, which it had not yet had when Lentz came out with his manifesto in 1955: What became dominant during the 1970s and 1980s was the social-critical approach, that was represented by Galtung in Norway, Senghaas in Germany, and Falk in the U.S.[43]

Thus, by the 1980s, the now institutionalized Peace and Conflict Studies had become a highly politicized scholarly field. When the debate over nuclear weapons reached a new urgency during the "rearmament debate" of the 1980s and Ronald Reagan's "Star Wars" program, concerned scientists were ready to weigh in. Again, physicists played an important role. In 1983, for example, a meeting of natural scientists, organized by the German physicist Hans-Peter Dürr, released a joint declaration, the Mainz Appeal, which called for a European peace order. It was supported by American scientific royalty such as the Nobel Laureate Linus Pauling and the Austrian-born émigré Victor F. Weisskopf, who had been involved in the Manhattan Project and became a founding member of the Union of Concerned Scientists in 1969.[44] But whereas during the 1950s physicists had been the main bearers of a critical stance toward nuclear arms, the 1980s saw political scientists, social psychologists, and medical doctors in a much more prominent role. More than ever, knowledge was something the peace movement marshalled as a means to make its critical positions heard.[45]

---

[42] Singer "Peace Research."

[43] Dunn, *First Fifty Years* 94-6; Weller/Böschen.

[44] Dürr, *Verantwortung*; Moore, *Disrupting Science.*

[45] Zepp, "Rationality of Fear"; on doctors and psychologists: Kemper, "Nuclear Arms Race."

THE RETURN OF APOCALYPSE: THE 1980S AND THE REDUCTION OF THE SUPERPOWERS

When the thaw in superpower relations was giving way to new tensions during the late 1970s and early 1980s, many West Europeans and North Americans were not prepared to accept silently that a new cycle of a heightened Cold War confrontation was inevitable. During the late 1960s, while détente had been high on the minds of Western and Eastern politicians, first NATO and later the Soviet Union had begun to modernize their nuclear arsenals. This so-called "revolution in military affairs" forced military planners to come up with new ideas and weapons to keep the system of deterrence going. During the late 1970s, NATO members were increasingly at odds over strategy. These internal disagreements led to the so-called "NATO Dual Track Decision," which threatened the Soviets with the deployment of new medium-range nuclear missiles, if the U.S.S.R did not stop its nuclear build-up.[46] Then, the Soviet invasion in Afghanistan in December 1979 and, most importantly, Ronald Reagan's election to the American presidency in November 1980, once again provoked mounting fears of nuclear Armageddon in East and West.[47]

The 1980s peace movement was not an exact rerun of the peace movement of the 1950s. Most importantly, the context had changed. The superpowers had lost their dominance. During the 1960s and 1970s, allies of both the U.S. and to a more limited extent of the U.S.S.R. had made headway vis-à-vis the two hegemonic powers. The Soviet relationship with Poland was in a precarious state. As early as the late 1950s, the Sino-Soviet rift had severely limited Moscow's future capabilities in East Asia. China was becoming a full-blown nuclear power and was seeking a rapprochement with America. Western Europe, too, was much less dependent on America. Gaullist France went its own way. West Germany, Japan, but also smaller allies like the Netherlands and South Korea were flexing their economic muscles, while the U.S. seemed to be in economic decline.[48] The Federal Republic of Germany now made a huge military,

---

[46] Spohr "Conflict and Cooperation"; *Euromissile Crisis*; Geiger, "NATO Double Track Decision."

[47] Becker-Schaum, "Introduction."

[48] Kennedy, *Rise and Fall*; for the 1980s debate on "American decline" Gassert, "Erzählungen vom Ende."

economic, and increasingly political contribution to the Western alliance. With regard to the NATO Dual Track Decision, West European leaders like Prime Minister Callaghan of Britain, Chancellor Schmidt of West Germany, and President Giscard d'Estaing of France exercised leadership, while U.S. President Carter seemed to lack the resolve to lead the West.[49]

Moreover, the nature of anti-nuclear protest movements had changed. The European peace movements of the 1950s by and large had been nurtured by traditional parties and organizations of the "Old Left," including unions, the Labour Party in Britain, Social Democrats in continental Europe, and dissidents within the Democratic Party such as Henry A. Wallace, who wanted to stay true to Roosevelt's promises of "one world." The 1980s peace movements were connected to these older campaigns for peace, but their make-up resembled those of the new social movements that had come up during the late 1960s. While social movements have a long and rich history going back to the nineteenth century, Western societies had changed to an extent that the "new social movements" that had sprung up in the wake of the late 1960s protests were more global and more "single-issue"-minded than their predecessors in the "Old Left." To some extent, "protest" became "project driven," with the dynamic and fluent protest networks and social movements working along a shorter time scale.[50]

Protests against "nuclearism" and the Cold War "belligerence" exploded about two years after NATO's decision in 1979 to introduce a new generation of intermediate-range ballistic missiles in Europe if the Soviet Union did not remove its own nuclear armed SS-20 medium-range missiles. This second great anti-nuclear campaign in postwar history received most domestic support in Belgium and the Netherlands, where governments agreed to delay the NATO deployment schedule. In Britain CND was rejuvenated. The high point occurred in the fall of 1983, in the months and weeks before the deployment of NATO's new missiles was scheduled to begin if the disarmament talks between the U.S. and the

---

[49] Scholtyseck, "United States."

[50] To differentiate between an "Old Left" and a "New Left" is highly contentious. It has been argued that it mirrors the normative positions of the first generation of social movements scholars of the 1970s and 1980s, who followed modernization-theory approaches and were stressing the "newness" of their object, out of sympathy with the New Left; on the debate and the potential of social movement history for global history see Berger, Nehring, "Introduction."

Soviet Union did not yield any meaningful results. Millions demonstrated on both sides of the Atlantic. During the "hot autumn," as it was called in West Germany, the media overflowed with photos of human chains, sit-in blockades in front of military installations, and enormous rallies, which filled the *Hofgarten* in Bonn, the established space for large-scale demonstrations at the seat of the West German government, to capacity.[51]

Like the first anti-nuclear campaigns of the 1950s and the protests against the Vietnam War, the 1980s European peace movements did not originate in the United States. Yet, European protagonists more overtly stressed the fact that they were demonstrating in unison with their American peers as well as their peers in Eastern Europe. West European peace activists highlighted "transatlantic anti-nuclear unity" in order to combat the ubiquitous criticism of conservatives that they were visceral anti-Americans and Communist "fellow travelers." As the German-American peace activist, founding member of the German Green Party, and *Bundestag* Deputy Petra Kelly put it in a speech to parliament: "We are not standing alone, but together with the Freeze Movement in the U.S.A., with many Congress members and Senators, with our friends in [the Polish labor movement] Solidarność, the [Czechoslovak dissident group] Charta 77 as well as the Swords-To-Ploughshares Movement in the GDR, and activist networks all over the world. We also will do our duty to show civil disobedience."[52]

Thus European protesters saw themselves allied with American peace groups such as the National Freeze Campaign. But they also took a more pan-European approach to peace that transcended the East-West divide. In the 1980s, an originally British intellectual network, founded by the historian Edward P. Thompson, his wife Dorothy Thompson, and the social scientist Mary Kaldor, even succeeded in creating a transnational European protest movement, the European Nuclear Disarmament (END). The END founding pamphlet *Protest and Survive* was immediately reprinted in the U.S., with a foreword by the prominent military analyst and peace activist David Ellsberg (of *Pentagon Papers* fame).[53] END aimed at bringing Cold War dissidents on both sides of the "Iron Curtain" together. While END remained small and was criticized by Eastern European dissidents for being blind with regard to the repressiveness of

[51] Fahlenbrach, Stapane, "Visual and Media Strategies."
[52] Kelly, Speech in the Federal Parliament, 4 May 1983.
[53] *Protest and Survive.*

Communist regimes, it created a unique transatlantic and trans-European intellectual network for peace that allowed pacifist and anti-hegemonial ideas to transcend national borders.[54]

Popular culture too, took on a much larger role in the debates over nuclear weapons than had been the case during the 1950s. It took a turn toward representing nuclear death in stark "realistic" ways. During the 1960s, many European and American intellectuals had been skeptical with regard to the role of popular culture in communicating political dissent and making people aware of social and political dangers of nuclear weapons. Many followed Susan Sontag's line quoted above that imaginations of disaster were distracting from the real issues and helping to normalize threats. As the historian Philipp Baur has argued, 1980s producers of popular culture were quite aware of this early criticism: "A vast majority of nuclear disaster films of this period do not portray the survival of humankind."[55] In this respect the 1983 James Bond movie *Octopussy* was unusual, because the world is spared a nuclear war thanks to the skills of the famous British agent. In another 1983 movie, *War Games*, computerized nuclear warfare is stopped at the last second. But that was not how nuclear war was typically portrayed during the 1980s. Most movies were much less metaphorical and fantastical than the 1950s monster movies, and talked about nuclear death in much more direct ways.

The most prominent example of the realist apocalyptic nuclear disaster movie scenario was put forward by *The Day After* (1983). It played in American and European prime-time television and made a splash in various European countries as well as in North America. It reconstructs a nuclear exchange between the Soviets and the Americans in graphic detail. When it shows bomber pilots taking to the skies and getting ready to drop their nuclear payload, it is totally free of the kind of irony that made *Dr. Strangelove* such a huge artistic success. We see soldiers doing their duty, even though they have doubts. We also see how "middle America," the town of Lawrence, Kansas, is struck by nuclear weapons. We experience how people perish in this inferno, while others die a slow and painful death after they have been exposed to radiation.

The *Day After* also demonstrates that 1980s "peace" and "anti-nuclear" activism had a different relationship to emotions than previous

[54] Burke, "European Nuclear Disarmament."
[55] Baur, "Nuclear Doomsday Scenarios" 324.

movements. During the 1950s, activists had often resisted notions that they were effeminate and emotional. They had relied on the scientific basis of their resistance against the bomb. The anti-nuclearism of the 1980s often stressed the emotional qualities as well as the "rationality" of emotions in combatting the nuclear armament race. Left-liberal German journalists such as Ulrich Greiner, writing in the Hamburg weekly *Die Zeit*, were critical of the general thrust of the *Day After* and other apocalyptic nuclear fiction because they thought that "fear" prevented people from working toward the abolishment of nuclear weapons. Yet, even Greiner accepted that the movies as well as the proliferating apocalyptic literature of the 1980s had "broken a taboo" by showing the unimaginable and thus bringing the effects of nuclear war closer to home.[56] This new realism was further accentuated by using documentary material, when showing the launches of nuclear missiles.[57]

The shifting transatlantic balance of power within the narrative and discursive realm shows itself in the growing importance of European popular music and cinema as part of an emerging transatlantic nuclear culture. During the 1950s, with the exception of the Japanese *Godzilla* movies, popular nuclear fiction had been largely American in origin. In the 1950s the Europeans tended to specialize in high-end nuclear culture such as Friedrich Dürrenmatt's play *Die Physiker*. That changed during the 1980s, when Americans had already become used to mostly British, but also other European rock bands. The British animated movie *When the Wind Blows* (1986) became a classic of transatlantic atomic culture, also because of its harrowing soundtrack, which had been contributed by David Bowie and Roger Waters. The German singer Nena's hit *99 Luftballons* may be the most well-known anti-nuclear song of the 1980s and has been a rare German exception insofar as it reached number two on the American Billboard charts.[58] That nuclear death sold well is shown by the unlikely success of the German disco formation, Boney M., with *We Kill the World*. Even Europe's greatest summer hit of the early 1980s, *Vamos a la playa*, which was probably hummed by many beach-going Americans as well, talks not about the pleasures of vacationing by the sea, but about the

---

[56] Greiner, "Apocalypse Now."
[57] Shapiro, *Atomic Bomb Cinema* 186; Baur, "Nuclear Doomsday Scenarios" 324.
[58] Baur, "Nuclear Doomsday Scenarios" 332.

nuclear contamination of the oceans. Because it was sung in Spanish, not many caught the true meaning of the lyrics.[59]

How the critique of nuclearism had become more broadly imbedded in popular culture during the 1980s, is also obvious how Ronald Reagan's "Strategic Defense Initiative" (SDI) was perceived in the eyes of the public and how it was framed by its critics. Dubbed "Star Wars," it acquired the name of the George Lucas movie series to show that it was either out of reach of reality or part of a sinister plot to destroy the earth.[60] Even though the SDI was never realized, it received an extraordinary amount of public attention in both Europe and the United States. It served as a rallying cry for critical scientists and peace researchers. The astronomer Carl Sagan, who had originally worked for NASA, but had become the popular host of the PBS television show *Cosmos*, used his star power and membership of the Union of Concerned Scientist (UCS) to coordinate a campaign against "Star Wars." He was frequently quoted by German activists. In German-speaking countries he became well-known for popularizing the term "nuclear winter."[61] As the historian William Knoblauch has shown, the UCS went to great lengths popularizing its stance against Stars War, by enlisting James Earl Jones, the voice of Darth Vader in the original *Star Wars* trilogy, which was easily recognizable to American but also to European audiences.[62]

CONCLUSION

By the 1980s, transatlantic responses and resistance to the "Cold War order" and opposition to ideas of "Mutually Assured Destruction" as well as the "armaments race," had come to rest on a much broader base than during the 1950s. This can be demonstrated by the growing mass appeal of nuclear popular culture. The 1950s had been the decade of a "peace opposition" to the Cold War that recruited itself mostly from "established" political parties, labor unions, and networks of scientists, most of them nuclear physicists, who did not oppose nuclear energy in principle, but its weaponization. The 1960s saw the rise of a social science critique of the Cold War order in the form of the emerging transatlantic field of Peace

[59] Gassert, "Popularität der Apokalypse."
[60] Kalic, "Reagan's SDI Announcement."
[61] Sagan, *Atomkrieg und Klimakatastrophe*; Ehrlich, Sagan, *Die nukleare Nacht.*
[62] Knoblauch, "Selling Star Wars."

and Conflict Studies. While the latter was grounded in the disciplines of International Relations, Political Science, and Political Psychology, it was unique in how it connected the social sciences as well as the natural sciences, but also how it came into existence thanks to an intensive transatlantic dialogue. Many protagonists in the field, such as Johan Galtung in Norway and Dieter Senghaas in Germany, had built academic careers on both sides of the Atlantic. Important publications such as Theodore Lentz's book *Towards a Science of Peace* fell on fertile ground abroad.

These various strands of transatlantic conversations and exchanges of ideas coalesced into one big anti-nuclear field during the 1980s. While it would be misleading to speak of "one movement," there was a lot of cross-pollination between various actors. First, there were peace activists, who took to the streets in protest against NATO's Double Track Decision, Reagan's SDI, or in the case of the National Freeze Campaign against the Reagan build-up of intercontinental arsenals by the U.S. While specific grievances were not identical in Europe and the U.S., activists were in close interaction across national borders. Secondly, by the 1980s, peace and conflict studies had matured and to some extent become institutionalized. They also contributed to many theoretical and practical exchanges across the ocean. And finally, the media as well as popular culture had become much more international with regard to who would read, watch, and listen to "imaginations of disaster." Again, there were many national peculiarities in how the issue of "nuclear death" was framed by producers of popular culture. *When the Wind Blows* was very British in how it related a coming nuclear war to experiences during World War II, especially the Blitz. *The Day After* was very American, too, by taking nuclear war to Kansas. Yet, these movies were understood and consumed by Western European audiences as were the books by authors like Carl Sagan or Richard Falk.

People, social movements, and experts often make sense of their own situation by referring to ideas and visions that had first been expressed in a different national context. When ideas cross national borders, they often gain in legitimacy. During the Cold War, which heightened domestic as well as international conflicts over "freedom" and "peace," it was of particular importance for activists to show that they were in line with critics of governmental politics in other countries. The Cold War and most particular the fear of nuclear war provided a common framework and threat-perception for people in the U.S. as well as in Europe. The perceived discursive and political necessity to refer to outsiders often helped to speed the exchange of ideas, texts, images, sounds across the Atlantic Ocean. While in the end the critics did not really carry the day and could not prevent the nuclear arms race, they still made a contribution to the spreading of ideas of "one world" and of a transnational, "global" future into the post-Cold War period, whether they were politicians, movement activists, academics, authors or artists.

WORKS CITED

Angster, Julia. "'The Finest Labor Network in Europe': American Labour and the Cold War." *The US Government, Citizen Groups, and the Cold War: The State-Private Network*. Ed. Helen Laville and Hugh Wilford. London: Routledge, 2006. 100-15.

Baur, Philipp. "Nuclear Doomsday Scenarios in Film, Literature, and Music." *The Nuclear Crisis*, 322-37.

Becker-Schaum Christoph, and Philipp Gassert et al. "Introduction: The Nuclear Crisis, NATO's Double-Track Decision, and the Peace Movement of the 1980s." *The Nuclear Crisis*, 1-36.

Berger, Stefan, and Holger Nehring. "Introduction: Towards a Global History of Social Movements." *The History of Social Movements in Global Perspective: A Survey*. Ed. Stefan Berger and Holger Nehring. London: Palgrave Macmillan, 2017. 1-35.

Broderick, Mick. "Surviving Armageddon: Beyond the Imagination of Disaster." *Science Fiction Studies* 20 (1993): 362-82.

Burke, Patrick M. "European Nuclear Disarmament: Transnational Peace Campaigning in the 1980s." *Nuclear Threats, Nuclear Fears and the Cold War of the 1980s*. Ed. Eckart Conze, Martin Klimke, and Jeremy Varon. New York: Cambridge UP, 2006. 227-50.

Churchill, Winston. "The Sinews of Peace ('Iron Curtain Speech')." 5 March 1946, *The International Churchill Society*, https://winstonchurchill.org/resources/speeches/1946-1963-elder-statesman/the-sinews-of-peace/.

Cortright, David. *Peace: A History of Movements and Ideas*. New York: Cambridge UP, 2008.

DeGroot, Gerard J. *The Bomb: A Life*. Cambridge, MA: Harvard UP, 2005.

Dunn, David J. *The First Fifty Years of Peace Research. A Survey and Interpretation.* Aldershot: Ashgate, 2005.

Dürr, Hans-Peter. *Verantwortung für den Frieden: Naturwissenschaftler warnen vor neuer Atomrüstung.* Reinbek bei Hamburg: Rowohlt, 1983.

Ehrlich, Paul R., and Carl Sagan. *Die nukleare Nacht. Die langfristigen klimatischen und biologischen Auswirkungen von Atomkriegen.* Cologne: Kiepenheuer und Witsch, 1985.

Etzold, Thomas H. and John Lewis Gaddis. *Containment: Documents on American Policy and Strategy 1945-1950.* New York, 1978.

Fahlenbrach Kathrin, and Laura Stapane. "Visual and Media Strategies of the Peace Movement," *The Nuclear Crisis* 222-41.

Fichter, Michael. "Support and Dissent: German and American Labor's Transnational Ties." *Germany and the United States in the Era of the Cold War. A Handbook.* Ed. Detlef Junker, vol. 1: 1945-1968. New York: Cambridge UP, 2004. 566-72.

Gaddis, John Lewis. "The Long Peace: Elements of Stability in the Postwar International System." *The Long Peace: Inquiries into the History of the Cold War.* Oxford: Oxford UP, 1987. 215-45.

Galtung Johan, and Dieter Fischer. *Johan Galtung: Pioneer of Peace Research.* Heidelberg: Springer, 2013.

Galtung, Johan. "Violence, Peace, and Peace Research." *Journal of Peace Research* 6.3 (1969): 167-91.

Gassert, Philipp. "Conflict as a Moment of Integration: The Role of Transatlantic Protest Movements since the 1960s." *Transatlantic Democracy in the 20th Century: Transfer and Transformation.* Ed. Paul Nolte. Munich: Oldenbourg, 2016. 139-52.

—. "Erzählungen vom Ende: Rückblick und Ausblick auf das amerikanische Jahrhundert." *Osteuropa* 61 (2011): 13-29.

—. "Internal Challenges to the Cold War: Oppositional Movements in East and West." In *Oxford Handbook of the Cold War.* Ed. Richard H. Immermann and Petra Goedde. Oxford: Oxford UP, 2013. 433-50.

—. "Popularität der Apokalypse: Zur Nuklearangst seit 1945", *Aus Politik und Zeitgeschichte* 61.46-47 (2011) https://www.bpb.de/apuz/59696/popularitaet-der-apokalypse-zur-nuklearangst-seit-1945?p=all.

Geiger, Tim. "The NATO Double-Track Decision: Genesis and Implementation." *The Nuclear Crisis*, 52-69.

Gleditsch, Nils Peter, Jonas Nordkvelle and Havard Strand. "Peace Research – Just the Study of War?" *Journal of Peace Research* 51.2 (2014): 145-58.

Greiner, Ulrich. "Apocalypse Now: Über den amerikanischen Film ‚The Day After' und neuere apokalyptische Romane." *Die Zeit*, 2 December 1983, https://www.zeit.de/1983/49/apocalypse-now/komplettansicht (2 December 2019).

Hauswedell, Corinna. *Friedenswissenschaften im Kalten Krieg. Friedensforschung und friedenswissenschaftliche Initiativen in der Bundesrepublik Deutschland in den achtziger Jahren.* Baden-Baden: Nomos, 1997.

Kalic, Sean N. "Reagan's SDI announcement and the European Reaction: Diplomacy in the Last Decade of the Cold War." *The Crisis of Détente in Europe. From Helsinki to Gorbachev, 1975-1985.* Ed. Leopoldo Nuti. London: Routledge, 2009. 99-110.

Kemper, Claudia. "'The Nuclear Arms Race is Psychological at Its Roots'. Physicians and Their Therapies for the Cold War." *Understanding the Imaginary War. Culture, Thought and Nuclear Conflict, 1945-90.* Ed. Matthew Grant and Benjamin Ziemann. Manchester: Manchester UP, 2016. 213-37.

Kennedy, Paul M. *The Rise and Fall and Fall of the Great Powers: Economic Change and Military Conflict from 1500 to 2000.* New York: Random House, 1987.

Klimke, Martin. *The Other Alliance: Student Protest in West Germany and the United States in the Global Sixties.* Princeton: Princeton University Press, 2010.

Knoblauch, William M. "Selling 'Star Wars' in American Mass Media." *Media and the Cold War in the 1980s: Between Star Wars and Glasnost.* Ed. Henrik G. Bastiansen, Martin Klimke, and Rolf Werenskjold. London: Palgrave Macmillan, 2019. 19-42.

Krah, Hans. *Weltuntergangsszenarien und Zukunftsentwürfe. Narrationen vom ‚Ende' in Literatur und Film 1945-1990.* Kiel: Ludwig, 2004.

Kundera, Milan. "Die Weltliteratur. How we read one another." *The New Yorker*, 8 January 2007.

Lentz, Theo F. *Towards a Science of Peace. Turning Point in Human Destiny.* London: Halycon Press, 1955.

Lifton, Robert Jay, and Richard Falk. *Indefensible Weapons: The Political and Psychological Case Against Nuclearism.* New York: Basic Books, 1983.

Lippmann, Walter. *The Cold War. A Study in U.S. Foreign Policy*. New York: Harper, 1947.

Miscamble, Wilson D. *From Roosevelt to Truman: Potsdam, Hiroshima, and the Cold War*. New York: Cambridge UP, 2007.

Moore, Kelly. *Disrupting Science: Social Movements, American Scientists, and the Politics of the Military, 1945-1975*. Princeton: Princeton UP, 2008.

Nehring, Holger. "Searching for Security: The British and West German Protests Against Nuclear Weapons and 'Respectability', 1958-1963." *Peace Movements in Western Europe, Japan, and the USA during the Cold War*. Ed. Benjamin Ziemann. Essen: Klartext, 2008. 167-87.

Neiberg, Michael. Potsdam. *The End of World War II and the Remaking of Europe*. New York: Basic Books, 2015.

The Nuclear Crisis: The Arms Race, Cold War Anxiety, and the German Peace Movement of the 1980s. Ed. Christoph Becker-Schaum, Philipp Gassert et al. New York: Berghahn, 2016.

Protest and Survive: Stop Nuclear War. Ed. Edward P. Thompson and Dan Smith. Introduction Daniel Ellsberg. New York: NYU Press, 1981.

Roberts, Geoffrey. "Antipodes or Twins? The Myths of Yalta and Potsdam." *Das Potsdamer Abkommen 1945-2015: Rechtliche Bedeutung und historische Auswirkungen*. Ed. Christopher Koch. Frankfurt/Main: Peter Lang, 2017. 215-33.

Rotblat, Joseph. *Scientists and the Quest for Peace: A History of the Pugwash Conferences*. Cambridge, MA: MIT Press, 1972.

Rubinson, Paul. "'Crucified on a Cross of Atoms': Scientists, Politics, and the Test Ban Treaty." *Diplomatic History* 35.2 (April 2011): 283-319.

"The Russell Einstein Manifesto", 9 July 1955, Pugwash Conferences on Science and World Affairs, https://pugwash.org/1955/07/09/statement-manifesto/ (18 November 2019).

Sagan, Carl. *Atomkrieg und Klimakatastrophe*. Munich: Droemer Knaur, 1984.

Scholtyseck, Joachim. "The United States, Europe, and the NATO Dual-Track Decision." *The Strained Alliance: U.S.-European Relations from Nixon to Carter*. Ed. Matthias Schultz and Thomas A. Schwartz. New York: Cambridge UP, 2010. 333-52.

Schrafstetter, Susanna, and Stephen Twigge. *Avoiding Armageddon: Europe, the United States, and the Struggle for Nuclear Proliferation, 1945-1970*. Westport, CT: Praeger, 2004.

Senghaas, Dieter. *Abschreckung und Frieden. Studien zur Kritik organisierter Friedlosigkeit*. Frankfurt/Main: Suhrkamp, 1969.

Shapiro, Jerome. *Atomic Bomb Cinema: The Apocalyptic Imagination on Film*. London: Routledge, 2002.

Shimamoto, Mayako. *Henry A. Wallace's Criticism of America's Atomic Monopoly, 1945-1948*. Newcastle upon Tyne: Cambridge Scholars Publishing, 2016.

Singer, David J. "Peace research, Peace action." *Bulletin of Atomic Scientists* 19.1 (1963): 13–7.

Sontag, Susan. "The Imagination of Disaster" [1965]. *Against Interpretation and Other Essays*. New York: Farrar, Straus and Giroux, 1990. 209-25.

Spohr, Kristina. "Conflict and Cooperation in Intra-Alliance Nuclear Politics: Western Europe, America, and the Genesis of Nato's Dual-Track Decision, 1977-1979." *Journal of Cold War Studies* 13.2 (2011): 39-89.

Steel, Ronald. *Walter Lippmann and the American Century*. London: The Bodley Head, 1981.

Stölken-Fitschen, Ilona. *Atombombe und Geistesgeschichte: Eine Studie der fünfziger Jahre aus deutscher Sicht*. Baden-Baden: Nomos, 1995.

The Euromissile Crisis and the End of the Cold War. Ed. Leopoldo Nuti, Frédéric Bozo, Marie-Pierre Rey, and Bernd Rother. Stanford: Stanford UP, 2015.

Reinhoudt, Jurgen, and Serge Audier, eds. *The Walter Lippmann Colloquium: The Birth of Neo-Liberalism*. London: Palgrave Macmillan, 2018.

Walker, J. Samuel. *Henry A. Wallace and American Foreign Policy*. Westport, CT: Greenwood Publishers, 1976.

Wallace, Henry A. *Toward World Peace*. New York: Reynal & Hitchcok, 1948.

Walton, Richard J. *Henry Wallace, Harry Truman, and the Cold War*. New York: The Viking Press, 1976.

Wasmuht, Ulrike C. *Geschichte der deutschen Friedensforschung. Entwicklung, Selbstverständnis, politischer Kontext*. Münster: Agenda, 1998.

Weart, Spencer R. *Nuclear Fear: A History of Images*. Cambridge, MA: Harvard UP, 1988.

Weller, Christoph, and Stefan Böschen. "Friedensforschung und Gewalt. Zwischen entgrenzter Gewaltanalyse und epistemischer Gewaltblindheit." *Zeithistorische Forschungen* 15.2 (2018): https://zeithistorische-forschungen.de/2-2018/5597.

Wittner, Lawrence S. *Resisting the Bomb: A History of the World Nuclear Disarmament Movement 1954-1970*. Stanford: Stanford UP, 1998.

Wittner, Lawrence S. *The Struggle Against the Bomb*, 3 vols. Stanford: Stanford UP, 1993-2003.

Wittner, Lawrence. "The Nuclear Threat Ignored: How and Why the Campaign Against the Bomb Disintegrated in the Late 1960s." *1968: The World*

Transformed. Ed. Carole Fink, Philipp Gassert, and Detlef Junker. New York: Cambridge UP, 1998. 439-58.

X, "The Sources of Soviet Conduct," [1947], reprinted in: *Foreign Affairs* 65.4 (Spring 1987): 852-68.

Zepp, Marianne. "Rationality of Fear: The Intellectual Foundations of the Peace Movement." *The Nuclear Crisis,* 138-53.

PART III

Transatlantic Exchanges between Philosophy, Literature and Film Theory since the 1970s

GERTRUDE POSTL

Continental Postmodernisms in the USA and Canada: The Mediating Role of the International Association for Philosophy and Literature (IAPL)

SOME FACTS

The International Association for Philosophy and Literature (IAPL) was an Academic Society in the USA, founded in 1976 by Hugh J. Silverman, Professor of Philosophy and Comparative Literature at the State University of New York at Stony Brook (now Stony Brook University). The first IAPL conference was held at Harvard Divinity School in 1976 with about thirty people in attendance. The society quickly grew in membership numbers as well as in popularity, and annual meetings were held, some of them resulting in independent book publications. From 1976 to 1990, IAPL conferences were held at various US universities; after that, the society also had meetings outside the US with the first non-US based conference organized in 1991 at the Université de Montréal, Canada. Two more conferences in Canada followed (1994 at the University of Alberta in Edmonton, 2010 at the University of Regina in Regina), but IAPL also convened in locations in Europe, Australia, and Asia. The last IAPL conference took place in Singapore in 2013, the year of Hugh J. Silverman's death.

The society is currently being relaunched as the Association for Philosophy and Literature (APL) with the first conference under its new name held in Klagenfurt, Austria, in 2019.[1]

CONTINENTAL PHILOSOPHY AND POSTMODERNISM

While casually and often used interchangeably, continental philosophy is not to be equated with postmodernism, and postmodernism is not limited to philosophy. However, both terms are central to the history of the IAPL. While continental philosophy was the focus of a number of North American academic societies, the unique feature of IAPL, from the

[1] For the revival of the IAPL as APL see: www.philosophyliterature.com.

beginning, was its interdisciplinary approach, which was a result of its attempt to connect continental philosophy with postmodernism. This is not to say that an academic society such as the IAPL was the cause or reason for an intensified exchange of ideas between Europe and North America. But with its focus on continental philosophy as well as its interdisciplinary appeal, IAPL contributed significantly to promoting an opening of what it means to do philosophy by "importing" European thinkers and theories into the mainstream academic discourse of North America, and – during its later phase – taking continental philosophy to Europe.

But first, what is meant by continental philosophy? Commonly, continental philosophy refers to a philosophical trajectory that focuses on distinctly European schools of thought, such as phenomenology, hermeneutics, existentialism, psychoanalytic theory, structuralism and post-structuralism, deconstruction, French feminism, Frankfurt school, and critical theory. In the words of Hugh J. Silverman:

> While analytic philosophy – comprising the inheritors of logical positivism, ordinary language philosophy, and linguistic analysis – draws primarily on models established in Britain and arising out of eighteenth-century empiricism, continental philosophy appeals to the modes of articulation operative in Western Europe since Descartes and the rationalists. More commonly, continental philosophy in America is understood to mean those types of thinking which are consistent with work on the continent from the appearance of Husserlian phenomenology at the beginning of the twentieth century. (Silverman 1987, 1)

The term "continental philosophy" has to be located within the philosophical climate of post-World War II North America, which was marked by the dominance of what is called analytic philosophy, or the Anglo-American tradition of thought. While there have always been academic philosophers in North America who worked within the context of a continental European tradition, during the 1960s and 1970s philosophers started to address and counter more forcefully their institutional isolation and being sidelined. Academic societies devoted to the continental way of thinking were established and started to hold regular conferences, for example the Society for Phenomenology and Existential Philosophy (SPEP, 1962) the Heidegger Circle (1967), the Husserl Circle

(1969), or the Merleau-Ponty Circle (1976);[2] German and French landmark texts became available in English (e.g. Heidegger's *Being and Time* and Merleau-Ponty's *Phenomenology of Perception*, both in 1962); leading universities started offering programs that specialized in continental philosophy (e.g. Boston College, Loyola University, De Paul University, SUNY Stony Brook; see Brogan, Risser 2000, 5); and European philosophers from France and Germany started to teach and work at US universities (e.g. Ricoeur at the University of Chicago, Gadamer at Boston College, or Derrida at Johns Hopkins University, Yale University, and the University of California, Irvine; see Brogan, Risser 2000, 6). A similar trend was also noticeable in Canada, where the pressure to position continental philosophy against the institutional dominance of analytic philosophy was even more severely felt because of the British influence in the country. With some delay, as compared to the US, in 1984 the Canadian Society for Hermeneutics and Postmodern Thought was founded, and later, in 2004, renamed the Canadian Society for Continental Philosophy. All these developments contributed to the greater public and institutional presence continental philosophy had in North America and helped to establish it as an independent school of thought associated with a diverse range of philosophical activities. The founding of the IAPL in 1976, with its first meeting at Harvard Divinity School in the same year, was part of this shift.

Soon continental philosophy established itself as a distinctly US – and Canadian – enterprise:

> There would be no point designating a German, French, Italian, Dutch, or Belgian philosopher as a continental philosopher. Continental philosophy has come to describe quite precisely what we do here in America. (Silverman 1987, 1)

But, as Walter Brogan and James Risser point out, continental European philosophy underwent a transformation in the process of its transition from Europe to North America.

> [C]ontinental philosophy … is itself a kind of transformational thinking … American continental philosophers do not merely re-present what has been created in Europe. Rather, they engage in the philosophical practices of such philosophizing and thereby

---

[2] Mention should also be made of the founding of the Collegium Phenomenologicum in Perugia, Italy, in 1976, with the deliberate goal of bringing together North American and European philosophers.

> release the fundamentally transformative character of this way of thinking. (Brogen, Risser 2000, 7)

It was in this already transformed version that European philosophies were re-introduced to Europe as continental philosophy.

As to the actual philosophical distinctions between continental and analytic philosophy, most scholars agree that these concern questions of style as much as subject matter. Many locate the beginning of the divide in a different reading of Kant (see Cutrofello 2005, Critchley 2001, 17-19), while others consider Husserl's phenomenology as the starting point (see Silverman 1987, 1; May 1997, 2) with Hegel, Marx, and Nietzsche commonly accepted as predecessors. The distinguishing characteristics between analytic and continental philosophy – however schematic or superficial they might be – are usually drawn along the lines of science and truth versus consciousness and experience, positivism versus Romanticism, science versus humanities (Cutrofello 2005, 2-3),[3] or non-contextual versus context, namely the distinction between analytic philosophy's focus on sentence structure versus continental thinkers' reflection on the status of the writing subject/investigator and the inclusion of a text's historical, cultural, or linguistic context (see Silverman 1987, 5). Richard Kearney describes "the most persistent feature of continental philosophy" as "a commitment to the *questioning of foundations*," whereby "[m]eaning is not some metaphysical essence or substance" but, rather, "a task of intersubjective and intertextual relations" (Kearney 1994, 2). Hugh J. Silverman broadly characterizes continental philosophy in terms of "how to 'think the between' ... by juxtaposing alternative philosophical methods and ... by examining various philosophical texts," so as to create textualities along the lines of the "places between" theories and texts, a strategy he calls "juxtapositional deconstruction" (Silverman 1994, 1 and 3).

Unlike the term "continental philosophy," the term "postmodernism" has never been limited to a strictly philosophical discourse. Rather, it refers to a variety of very different phenomena, and it is much more fluid than "continental philosophy." While clearly demonstrating affinities and overlaps with post-structuralism and deconstruction, the use of the term "postmodernism" started during the 1960s within architecture, and, from

---

[3] Cutrofello's account of the distinction is in reference to Richard Rorty and Michael Friedman.

then on, was used to refer to a variety of cultural developments, to certain trends within the arts, and to a specific brand of theory found mostly within the humanities and social sciences – hence the use of the plural "postmodernisms" in the title of the present text.

According to Joseph Natoli and Linda Hutcheon, the editors of the influential essay collection *A Postmodern Reader*, the term "postmodern"

> has been used to talk about architecture, literature, dance, film, video, theater, television, music, and the visual arts, but also political thought, philosophy, aesthetic criticism and theory, anthropology, geography, historiography, theology, pedagogy, etc. (Natoli, Hutcheon 1993, vii)

Or, as described by Ihab Hassan: "Pop and silence, or mass culture and deconstruction, or Superman and Godot – or as I shall … argue, immanence and indeterminacy – may all be aspects of the postmodern universe" (Hassan 1993, 275).

Many describe postmodernism predominantly in terms of certain cultural developments – mostly resulting from the rise of electronic technology and digital media – that make it difficult to apply traditional categories of analysis and that escape binary value judgements, such as true/false, right/wrong, nature/culture, reality/fiction, authentic/artificial, depth/surface, original/copy, etc. Theories associated with postmodernism are no longer concerned with employing the central concepts and categories of traditional philosophy (e.g. reality, truth, self, identity, unity) but instead point out the limitations of these very concepts and categories, deconstructing them in the process. In the words of Steven Best and Douglas Kellner: "(P)ostmodern theory provides a critique of representation and the modern belief that theory mirrors reality" in that "all cognitive representations of the world are historically and linguistically mediated." Postmodern theory, furthermore

> rejects modern assumptions of social coherence and notions of causality in favor of multiplicity, plurality, fragmentation, and indeterminacy. In addition, postmodern theory abandons the rational and unified subject … in favor of a socially and linguistically decentered and fragmented subject. (Best, Kellner 1991, 4-5)

In the popular view, postmodernism has also been conceived of in a periodical sense as that which comes after the modern. This simplified chronological account has been challenged by a number of theorists and philosophers, starting with Jean-François Lyotard, who famously claimed that “[p]ostmodernism … is not modernism at its end but in the nascent state, and this state is constant” (Lyotard 1984, 79). According to this view, the postmodern is already always inscribed in the modern and thus the task at hand became to explore the interconnections between the modern and the postmodern.

> Postmodernism does not open up a new field of artistic, philosophical, cultural, or even institutional activities. Its very significance is to marginalize, delimit, disseminate, and decenter the primary … works of modernist and premodernist cultural inscriptions. (Silverman 1990, 1)

For Charles Jencks, postmodernism is simply both, “the continuation of Modernism and its transcendence” (Jencks 1986, 15).

Postmodernism has also been defined in terms of style – a form of writing or artistic expression which makes use of irony, parody, playfulness, subversion, paradoxes, contingencies, and indeterminacies. A further stylistic marker frequently referred to as postmodern, especially for architecture, the arts, music, and literature, is a co-existence and blending of styles, a “next-to-each-other” of different historical periods or genres, or “a mixing of the conventions of popular and ‘high art’” (Natoli, Hutcheon 1993, vii).[4]

As to postmodernism’s connection to continental philosophy, Hugh J. Silverman describes “this array from the problem of desire and language, the limits of representation as a philosophical preference, the ends of metaphysics as a traditional philosophical commitment, the rewriting of patriarchal discourse as gender dominance, and the assessment of deconstruction” as the sites “where postmodernism links up with continental philosophy” (Silverman, Welton 1988, 9). As stated, continental philosophy and postmodernism are by no means equivalent, but it was continental philosophy, as developed in North America, which welcomed postmodern theories (including their questions, issues, and their style) and which devoted a substantial amount of effort to “translating” the meaning of theories generated in Europe for a North American readership and audience.

This being said, it is important to note that for postmodernisms, contrary to the situation of continental philosophy, the type of exchange between North America and Europe takes a somewhat different form. By

---

[4] For a strictly philosophical analysis of Postmodernism, see Aylesworth.

the 1970s North America was at the forefront of exhibiting the typical signs of a postmodern culture, while the theories reflecting on these developments were being written in Europe, most significantly in France. As such, was Europe responding to developments in North America before North America was ready to do so? How else could one interpret the following lines from Jean Baudrillard's text *America* than as an indicator for a gap between postmodernism "in action" and the theoretical response to it?

> America is neither dream nor reality. It is a hyperreality … It may be that the truth of America can only be seen by a European, since he alone will discover here the perfect simulacrum – that of the immanence and material description of all values. The Americans, for their part, have no sense of simulation. They are themselves simulation in its most developed state, but they have no language in which to describe it, since they themselves are the model. (Baudrillard 1988, 28-9)

Although he exaggerates, Baudrillard detects something that has to be taken seriously. Irrespective of the fact that European countries lagged behind in developments later to be labelled "postmodern," all the most influential postmodern theorists (Baudrillard himself, Lyotard, Foucault, Derrida and others, whether they considered themselves as postmodernists or not) originated in Europe and were "exported" to North America with the assistance of continental philosophy. Baudrillard seems to suggest that developments in the USA and Canada were first appropriately reflected upon in Europe ("they have no language in which to describe it"). Could this indicate that with the evolvement of postmodernisms the patterns of exchange of theories and ideas between North America and Europe were advanced to a different level?

IAPL'S TWO AXES OF MEDIATION – TRANS-CONTINENTAL AND INTERDISCIPLINARY

The influence and impact of the International Association for Philosophy and Literature during its thirty-seven years of existence closely intersects with the development of continental philosophy and of the various manifestations of postmodernism. To be more specific, IAPL's mediating function played out on two interconnected levels, one trans-continental, and the other, its interdisciplinary foundation, concerned itself with the exchange between disciplines and genres.

The trans-continental axis: IAPL's goal from the beginning was to go beyond the US (originally with respect to its theoretical outreach, later in a literal sense), and – considering the involvement of Canadian scholars in the society – beyond North America. Given its geographical proximity, as well as similar problems and developments within the field of philosophy, the role of Canada for the development of the IAPL has always been unique. Many Canadian scholars were involved in the society from its earliest years, and personal connections and cooperations between IAPL members from the US and Canada flourished. The first conference outside the US was held in Montréal in 1991, followed by Edmonton in 1994, and Regina in 2010, making Canada the only country outside the US where three IAPL conferences have been held. Thus it seems justified to think of the IAPL as a North American, and not just US, project.

The attempt to go beyond North America, or, what I call here the trans-continental axis, played out on the practical level as deliberate efforts were made by the IAPL to involve European scholars and their work, and, from 2000 on, and also by holding its annual conferences at various European universities. On the philosophical level, the task at hand was more complex. The trans-continental agenda meant that theories and ideas that originated in Europe (the defined research area of Continental Philosophy) were "brought back" to Europe, so to speak, now in an often transformed account because of the particular ways North American philosophers engaged with and appropriated those theories and ideas. Continental philosophy, a term mostly unknown within the European philosophical scene, had to be (re)introduced to Europe as a typically North American way of responding to and working with the European tradition. As stated by Hugh J. Silverman in the Introduction to *Was heißt Kontinentalphilosophie in den USA?* – a publication resulting from a conference organized in Vienna in 2001 on the same topic:

> Ziel des vorliegenden Bandes ist es, die Kontinentalphilosophie in den USA einem mitteleuropäischen Publikum vorzustellen … unbestritten ist, daß die Kontinentalphilosophie … zu einer der führenden Denktraditionen geworden ist und daß sie als eigener Denkansatz immer stärker in andere Bereiche und Disziplinen … eindringt. (Vogt 2003, 7)

It is difficult to pinpoint the many different ways North American philosophers transformed the European traditions in question but the institutional setting certainly played a part in this "appropriation." The context for philosophy departments in the US and Canada was quite different from the situation in Europe. Being a minority in the midst of an analytically dominated philosophical landscape left its marks – circumstances that European philosophers did not need to concern themselves with.[5] And these marks manifested themselves in many different ways. Thus the range of continental philosophy is refreshingly diverse: from faithful readings of, for example, Husserl, Heidegger, Sartre, or Merleau-Ponty all the way to making connections with other disciplines, trying to build bridges to the analytic side, or engaging in often creative philosophical speculations. If anything had to be re-introduced to Europe then it was this diversity in responding to an established tradition. The significant role the IAPL played for this transfer of philosophical ideas unfolded on a number of levels: first by expanding the presence and visibility of continental European theories in the US and Canada; later, by introducing a European audience and readership to the transformations these theories had undergone within the North American context, and by bringing – via the annual IAPL conferences – philosophers from Europe to North America and, in the opposite direction, North American philosophers to Europe. One could say the IAPL engaged in a transfer across the Atlantic – of theories and ideas as well as of people.

The interdisciplinary axis: IAPL's goal was to go not only beyond North America, but also beyond philosophy itself, thereby clearly distinguishing itself from other societies established in the US and Canada which promoted continental European thought (e.g. the Society for Phenomenology and Existential Philosophy, or the Canadian Society for Continental Philosophy). One of the founding premises of IAPL was that literature is philosophical and that, conversely, philosophy always has literary qualities. "In the early years, our task seemed straightforward: to show how philosophical ideas appear in literary works or how literary works raise important philosophical questions …" (Silverman 2010, 5). This original focus soon began to expand, partly in response to the new (so-called postmodern) theories that were developed in Europe (mostly France) during the 1960s and 1970s. "As time went by, the IAPL welcomed and encouraged developments in post-structuralism, feminist theory, critical theory, deconstruction, post-colonial, and globalization

[5] At least not until the beginning of the new millennium, which marks a shift in favor of analytic philosophy also on the European philosophy scene.

theory" (*Ibid.* 5-6). Philosophers such as Jacques Derrida, Michel Foucault, Jean-Francois Lyotard, Jean Baudrillard, Julia Kristeva, Luce Irigaray, Hélène Cixous, and many others, now became household names at IAPL conferences – in addition to Husserl, Heidegger, Sartre, or Merleau-Ponty. However, the reason for the rapidly growing popularity of French thinkers among IAPL affiliated scholars was not that it became "fashionable" in certain circles to engage in French post-structuralism or French feminism. More important for the original IAPL agenda of going beyond philosophy was that all these theories frequently situated traditional philosophical questions within the context of non-philosophical areas, such as literature, art, music, film, media, politics, history, or culture at large, thereby broadening the meaning of philosophy and setting examples for how to embrace an interdisciplinary approach without losing or watering down the relevancy and urgency of traditional philosophical issues and questions.

Needless to say, philosophers have always talked about art or literature, beginning with Plato and going all the way to the importance of Hölderlin's poetry for Heidegger's philosophy or Merleau-Ponty's observations on Cézanne (to mention just two famous examples from the continental tradition). What is new in the works of this next generation of (mostly French) thinkers is the intrinsic interconnection between philosophy and – by traditional standards – non-philosophical areas. Texts such as Jacques Derrida's *Truth in Painting*, Julia Kristeva's *The Revolution of Poetic Language*, or Michel Foucault's *Madness and Civilization*, all exemplify an approach that makes it impossible to distinguish any longer between philosophy and literature, art, history, or social theory. In this respect, they all contribute to one of the key targets of postmodern theories: the breakdown of traditional categories and the impossibility of maintaining a clear dividing line between established disciplines. Thus by promoting these new types of theories, IAPL paved the way for a truly interdisciplinary approach and for a philosophical practice that clearly stepped outside traditional confinements as to what it means to do philosophy. As such, IAPL became the gathering place for academics and scholars who have all along worked "in between" disciplines – be it in the USA, Canada, or Europe, and what started out as a transfer of ideas and scholars became the very meeting place for researchers, artists, and writers on both sides of the Atlantic who searched for a theoretical place of belonging often not found in their own departments.

> The IAPL has served as a haven and a breath of fresh air for those who see the need and importance of working across disciplines. Indeed, these disciplinary junctures are the places where eyes are opened and alternative perspectives emerge … The IAPL operates at such junctures, or rather, it is one of the places where the event of juncture happens. (Silverman 2010, 6)

The "juncture" Hugh J. Silverman is talking about cannot be fully understood without again turning to the notion of "postmodernism" and its relation to continental philosophy, so typical of the IAPL. The growing popularity of the term "postmodern" during the 1970s contributed to this interdisciplinary ideal of the IAPL in that postmodernism was not limited to one particular academic discipline or one particular artistic genre. As explained above, postmodernism was conceived of as a reference term for cultural phenomena as well as developments in the arts, in literature, music, the media, as well as theories from various academic fields. Given the specific differences between North America (as the site of the most pronounced postmodern cultural phenomena) and Europe (contributing the theoretical underpinnings and analysis of postmodern phenomena), IAPL's function as mediator entered a new phase that went far beyond introducing continental philosophy to a European audience. In fact, it was European and North American scholars alike who met at IAPL conferences to address the diverse manifestations of a rapidly changing (Western) world, marked by a seeming loss of the distinctions between reality and fiction, the authentic and the artificial, high and low culture, depth and surface. This being so, the task at hand was no longer to introduce one to the other, but to offer a meeting place for all – from the USA, Canada, and Europe alike – who wanted to talk about the loss of theoretical certainty, the inappropriateness and failure of traditional categories, and the growing impossibility of making clear-cut either/or-judgements, be they ethical, political, or aesthetical.

As part of the said transfer of ideas across the Atlantic, a special concern of the IAPL from about 2000 on was to highlight the specific historical, geographical, and intellectual circumstances of IAPL host locations. The overall goal still was to have European scholars become more familiar with theories and ideas generated in North America while introducing researchers in the USA and Canada to European theories. Further, and in addition, it became increasingly important to present the local specifics of the hosting university – often in the spirit of moving from the center to the margins by giving prominence to unknown places rather than famous universities or tourist-saturated cities. For example, for the 2010 conference in Regina, Canada ("Cultures of Differences: National, Indigenous, Historical"), a special thematic focus was placed on issues pertaining to the local indigenous populations of the area and the First Nations University, located in Saskatchewan with a campus in Regina. This special section of the program included a panel on "Canadian Indigenous Epistemologies" with presentations from faculty members of the First Nations University; a lecture by Maria Campbell, a Metis author talking about "Michif Narrative and Storytelling;" a session on "Contemporary Indigenous Literature as Applied Tradition;" and the showing of a film by a local film maker. The way Hugh J. Silverman addressed this commitment to the specific local conditions in the 2010 conference program clearly indicates the attempt to connect local concerns with broader philosophical issues, particularly as they have been developed within the continental tradition or postmodern theories:

> And what happens at the borders between these different nations, cultures, identities? What of those places that don't belong to either and yet are shared by both? And how can cultural knowledge understand these borders, edges, limits, and practices between natures, cultures, identities? Can there be cultural knowledge that comes from neither one side nor the other, nor views both from some transcendental, high-flying point of view? … Can cultural interpretation situate itself between cultures? (IAPL 2010, 7)

This quote – intended to introduce visitors from the US and Europe to the situation of Saskatchewan – is an attempt to apply aspects of a contemporary theoretical framework to the local specifics of this region in Canada: the question of the "in between," the critique of a transcendental approach, the privileging of difference over identity, and the application of the notion of interpretation also to culture and not just to texts. A brief reference to the 2012 IAPL conference in Tallinn, Estonia ("Archaeologies of the Future: Tracing Memories, Imagining Spaces") offers a comparable example going in the opposite direction (reaching out from Europe to North America). Here as well, an effort was made to address themes specific to Estonia or the Baltic region at large (a little known area for most people from North America), including panels on Estonian composers, or – given the overall theme of the conference – writers addressing the specific history and transformation of Estonia, e.g. a Close Encounter session with the Finnish-Estonian author Sofi Oksanen, who, in her novels, addresses the complicated history of Estonia's relationship with Russia and also Finland. And, as in Regina, these explorations of specific local circumstances – given the overall theme of the conference, in this case accounts of history and projections of a future – were related to how continental philosophy and postmodern theories address issues and questions pertaining to past, present, and future:

> The memories of the past – diaries, memoirs, memorials, monuments, life histories, epitaphs, documentaries, painted scenes of past events, critical readings of aesthetic productions, etc. – are juxtaposed with imagined futures, science fictions, literary reconstructions, filmic inquisitions, plastic potentialities, musical interludes, and philosophical hermeneutics. (IAPL 2012, 7)

IAPL's move away from the academic centers to places less well-known resonates, of course, basic premises of postmodernism, and, in particular, one of the central notions of Derrida's theory of deconstruction: the notion of *différance*. Exploring areas considered to be marginal was never meant to replace the one with the other, the center with the margin. Rather, it is one of the many possible manifestations of Derrida's *différance* – an attempt to mark a difference as well as a deferral, opening up a space of difference, a space of the "in-between," where the continuous movement back and forth between the two sides unhinges the fixed parameters of each and makes an ongoing deferral possible. The history of the IAPL is a history of the "in-between" – in between academic centers and marginalized locations, in between philosophy and literature, in between philosophy and non-philosophy, in between continental philosophy and postmodernism, in between Canada, the USA, and Europe.

I would like to end these observations with a quote yet again from Hugh J. Silverman, a quote from the volume he edited together with Ludwig Nagl for the *Wiener Reihe*, entitled *Textualität der Philosophie. Philosophie und Literatur*. In the *Nachwort* to this volume, which refers to the role of IAPL, to the relationship between philosophy and literature in general, but also to the exchange of theories and ideas between North America and Europe, Silverman states:

> In diesem Buch der *Wiener Reihe* kehrt die *Continental Philosophy* als Gast, als wohlwollender Besuch, nach Europa zurück, ausgestattet mit … dem Wissen eines von außerhalb kommenden Denkens und Theoretisierens: als eine Einschreibung von Alterität und Diskontinuität in die europäischen philosophischen Systeme … denen es darum zu tun ist, sich für das 21. Jahrhundert im Kontext einer postmodernen Gesellschaft neu einzurichten. (Nagl, Silverman 257)

WORKS CITED

Aylesworth, Gary. Postmodernism. Stanford Encyclopedia of Philosophy. https://plato.stanford.edu/entries/postmodernism/.

Baudrillard, Jean. America, trans. Chris Turner. London, New York: Verso, 1988 (French 1986).

Best, Steven, and Douglas Kellner, eds. *Postmodern Theory. Critical Interrogations*. New York: The Guilford Press, 1991.

Brogan, Walter, and James Risser, eds. *American Continental Philosophy. A Reader*. Bloomington, Indianapolis: Indiana UP, 2000.

Critchley, Simon. *Continental Philosophy. A Very Short Introduction*. Oxford: Oxford UP, 2001.

Cutrofello, Andrew. Continental Philosophy. A Contemporary Introduction. New York, London: Routledge, 2005.

Hassan, Ihab. "Toward a Concept of Postmodernism." *A Postmodern Reader*. Ed. Joseph Natoli and Linda Hutcheon. Albany: State U of New York P, 1993. 273-86.

The International Association for Philosophy and Literature. *Cultures of Differences. National, Indigenous, Historical*. Conference Program 2010, U of Regina, Saskatchewan, Canada.

The International Association for Philosophy and Literature. *Archeologies of the Future. Tracing Memories, Imagining Spaces*. Conference Program 2012, Tallinn U, Tallinn, Estonia.

Jencks, Charles. *What is Post-Modernism?* London, New York: St. Martin's Press, 1986.

Kearney, Richard, ed. *Twentieth-Century Continental Philosophy*. Routledge History of Philosophy, Volume VIII. London, New York: Routledge, 1994.

Lyotard, Jean-François. *The Postmodern Condition: A Report on Knowledge*. Trans. Geoff Bennington and Brian Massumi. Minneapolis: U of Minnesota P, 1984 (French 1979).

May, Todd, ed. *Twentieth Century Continental Philosophy*. Upper Sadle River, NJ: Prentice Hall, 1997.

Nagl, Ludwig, and Hugh J. Silverman, eds. *Textualität der Philosophie. Philosophie und Literatur. Wiener Reihe. Themen der Philosophie*. Vienna, Munich: R. Oldenburg Verlag, 1994.

Natoli, Joseph, and Linda Hutcheon, eds. *A Postmodern Reader*. Albany: State U of New York P, 1993.

Silverman, Hugh J. *Inscriptions. After Phenomenology and Structuralism.* New York, London: Routledge & Kegan Paul, 1987.

— and Donn Welton, eds. *Postmodernism and Continental Philosophy.* Albany: State U of New York P, 1988.

—, ed. *Postmodernism – Philosophy and the Arts.* Continental Philosophy III. New York, London: Routledge, 1990.

—. *Textualities. Between Hermeneutics and Deconstruction.* New York, London: Routledge, 1994.

— and Kathleen Hulley, eds. *The International Association for Philosophy and Literature.* IAPL Members Bibliography, Seventh Edition, 2010.

Vogt, Erik M., ed. *Was heißt Kontinentalphilosophie in den USA? Eine internationale Debatte über Hermeneutik, Dekonstruktion, Feminismus.* Vienna: Turia+Kant, 2003.

LUDWIG NAGL

Philosophy, Psychoanalysis and Melodrama: Stanley Cavell on Max Ophuls' Screen Version of Stefan Zweig's Short Story *Brief einer Unbekannten*

0. INTRODUCTION

Stanley Cavell, "Professor of Aesthetics and the General Theory of Value" at Harvard's Department of Philosophy, was one of the most influential philosophers of the late twentieth century. His writings are, in deep ways, related to American intellectual life, and, at the same time, significantly influenced by European discourses. Cavell's studies of Emerson[1] and Thoreau[2] prove his extensive interest in Kant's discourse on Enlightenment, in Wittgenstein's *Philosophical Investigations*, and in the work of Sigmund Freud: in thoughts, that is, that have their intellectual origin in Europe. This *double structure* – Cavell's multipolar, transatlantic approach – is constitutive not only for his elaborate studies on skepticism and epistemology[3], but also for his philosophy of film. In his book *Contesting Tears. The Melodrama of the Unknown Woman,*[4] for instance, Cavell gains his core category, "unknownness," via his analysis of the Hollywood film *Letter from an Unknown Woman* by the German director

[1] Stanley Cavell, *Conditions Handsome and Unhandsome. The Constitution of Emersonian Perfectionism*, 1990.

[2] Staney Cavell, *The Senses of Walden. An Expanded Edition*, 1981.

[3] Stanley Cavell, *The Claim of Reason. Wittgenstein, Skepticism, Morality, and Tragedy*, 1979.

[4] Stanley Cavell, *Contesting Tears. The Hollywood Melodrama of the Unknown Woman*, 1996.

Max Ophuls,[5] which is based on the short story *Brief einer Unbekannten* by the Austrian writer Stefan Zweig.[6]

Cavell's American-European double perspective is a significant trait of his entire work. His writings are, however, also characterized by another important motif. All of Cavell's philosophical analyses attempt to re-read critically and re-work the deep split which continues to plague (in spite of many disclaimers) the international philosophical discourse up to now, namely the antagonism between a science-focused "Analytic Philosophy" dominant in the US, and the (so-called) "Continental" philosophy (i.e.: the post-Hegelian philosophical scene in Europe). "The stature of Stanley Cavell is increasingly considered unique among living American philosophers," Michael Payne pointed out in 1995, "because of the

[5] For the history of Ophuls' screen version of Zweig's story (*Letter from an Unknown Woman*, USA 1948) see Helmut G. Asper, *Max Ophüls. Deutscher – Jude – Franzose*, 2011, 91-4. [Please note that there are two ways of spelling this name: Ophuls (English) and Ophüls (German).] Asper points out "dass Ophüls sein Möglichstes [tat], Zweigs Novelle getreu den Intentionen des Autors zu verfilmen," but that he was forced by the production code of the American film industry to alter some aspects of Zweig's novel. (*Ibid.* 92-3). [A list of these alterations can be found in the Wikipedia article "Brief einer Unbekannten (Film)," segment "Hintergrund": see https://de.wikipedia.org/wiki/Brief_einer_Unbekannten_ (Film).] The most significant of these alterations – a modification of Zweig's narrative which is important for Cavell's reading of the category "unknownness" – concerns the final passage of Zweig's novella: "Dass die Liebesunfähigkeit Brands [wie der männliche Protagonist in Ophüls's Zweig Verfilmung genannt wird] zur Selbstzerstörung und zum Versagen als Künstler führt, geht weit über Zweig hinaus und spiegelt eigene Auffassungen und Ängste von Ophüls wieder" (Asper, *Max Ophüls* 93).
Ophuls' movie based on Zweig's story is its most prominent cinematic adaptation. However, in 2001, the French director Jacques Deray produced another film adaptation of Zweig's novella (*Lettre d'une inconnue*); in 2001 a Chinese screen version of Zweig's novella was directed by Xu Jingei; and in 2011 Zweig's short story was turned into a film by the Mongolian film director Naranbaatar.

[6] See Stefan Zweig, *Meistererzählungen*, 2017, 151-97. (The short story *Brief einer Unbekannten* was first published in Vienna in *Neue Freie Presse*, 1 January 1922, 31-8).

potential of his work to provide a means of exchange among Anglo-American and Continental European philosophers."[7]

In the following essay, Cavell's multifaceted *Wirkungsgeschichte* will, *first*, be elucidated *biographically,* i.e. through a short review of Cavell's numerous stays in (and contacts with) Austria. It will then be analyzed — with regard to one of the core themes of Cavell's philosophical work, his "*readings of films:*" parts *two*, *three* and *four* of this essay are dedicated to aspects of Cavell's analyses of the cinematic genre which he called "the melodrama of the unknown woman."[8]

1. BIOGRAPHICAL ANNOTATIONS

First a quick look at Cavell's numerous visits to Austria. As early as 1952, young Cavell – at that time still a graduate student at Harvard University – spent a summer at Schloss Leopoldskron in Salzburg as a participant in the Salzburg Seminar in American Studies. He thus got to know an Austrian city that was of great importance for Stefan Zweig's literary work.[9] After becoming Professor at the Department of Philosophy at Harvard University, Cavell traveled to Vienna five times between 1979 and the turn of the century. Many of these journeys were a result of Cavell's lifelong friendship with his former Austrian student Kurt Rudolf Fischer, who had had to leave Vienna as a young man during the Nazi era, survived in Shanghai, studied after World War II in the United States, became a professor of philosophy there, and returned in the late 1970s to

---

[7] Michael Payne, "Introduction," Stanley Cavell, *Philosophical Passages: Wittgenstein, Emerson, Austin, Derrida*, 1995, 1.

[8] This genre, which Cavell "constitutes" as the inversion of another film genre that he had named "remarriage comedies" (see Cavell, *Pursuits of Happiness. The Hollywood Comedy of Remarriage*, 1981), includes four melodramatic narratives that are characterized by a thematic "family resemblance": the films *Gaslight* (George Cukor 1944), *Now, Voyager* (Irving Rapper 1942), *Stella Dallas* (King Vidor 1937), and the movie that gave Cavell's analyses of the "melodrama" its name, Ophuls' *Letter from an Unknown Woman* (1948).

[9] For Zweig's period of life in Salzburg see Oliver Matuschek, *Stefan Zweig. Drei Leben – Eine Biographie*, 2006, part II, 173-268; and *Stefan Zweig. Bilder, Texte, Dokumente*, eds. Klemens Renoldner, Hildemar Holl, Peter Karlhuber, 1993, Chapter III, 1919-1934, and Chapter IV, 1934-1940.

Austria, where he taught as *Honorar- und Gastprofessor* at the Department of Philosophy of the University of Vienna.[10]

In 1979 Cavell accepted an invitation from the Department of Psychoanalysis at the University of Vienna to "lecture on film comedies of remarriage."[11] On this occasion he established his first contacts with Vienna's Department of Philosophy, where K.R. Fischer introduced some of the younger lecturers to Cavell. When, a few years later, the new generation of Vienna's philosophers started a series of publications under the title *Wiener Reihe. Themen der Philosophie*[12] whose first volume was devoted to the question *Wo steht die analytische Philosophie heute?*, Cavell contributed a paper.[13] For the presentation of volume one of *Wiener Reihe*, which took place at the Wittgenstein House in Vienna, Cavell

[10] Cavell tells about his lifelong friendship with K.R. Fischer in his essay "An Indiscreet Ambassador," *Weltanschauungen des Wiener Fin de Siècle 1900/2000, Festgabe für Kurt Rudof Fischer zum achtzigsten Geburtstag*, Gertraud Diem-Wille, Ludwig Nagl and Friedrich Stadler, eds., 2002, 43-6. (See also Cavell, *Little Did I Know. Excerpts from Memory*, 2010, 334-52 – another of Cavell's texts on Kurt R. Fischer which contains, *inter alia*, passages of the above mentioned Cavellian "Festschrift" – Essay from 2002.) Before K.R. Fischer returned to Austria in the late 1970s, he – as Chairperson of the Department of Philosophy, Millersville University, Lancaster, Pennsylvania, invited three Austrian philosophers (Kurt Buchinger, Michael Benedikt und Ludwig Nagl) to teach courses on European philosophy there. See Ludwig Nagl, "Some Reflections on how the Remigrant K.R. Fischer influenced Vienna's Academic Discourses," *Return from Exile – Rückkehr aus dem Exil. Exiles, Returnees and Their Impact in the Humanities and Social Sciences in Austria and Central Europe*, eds. Waldemar Zacharasiewicz and Manfred Prisching, 2017, 347-62.

[11] Stanley Cavell, *Little Did I Know* 349.

[12] In the early years of its publication, *Wiener Reihe. Themen der Philosophie* was edited by Richard Heinrich, Ludwig Nagl, Herta Nagl-Docekal, and Helmuth Vetter; the current editors are Cornelia Klinger, Ludwig Nagl, Herta Nagl-Docekal, and Alexander Somek. As volume 19 of this series, *Ein Filmphilosophie-Symposium mit Robert B. Pippin*, eds. Ludwig Nagl and Waldemar Zacharasiewicz, 2017, shows, Cavell's film philosophy remains of significant influence on contemporary media discourse. See, in this volume, for example, Ludwig Nagl, "Filmphilosophie in Wien," 7-10.

[13] Stanley Cavell, "Danebenstehen, Gleichziehen: Bedrohungen der Individualität," *Wo steht die Analytische Philosophie heute?*, Ludwig Nagl and Richard Heinrich, eds., *Wiener Reihe. Themen der Philosophie*, Volume 1, 1986, 116-49.

traveled, in 1986, as "Invited Speaker" from Harvard to Austria. In the lecture which he delivered on this occasion, "The Fantastic of Philosophy," Cavell said: "It is wonderful to be here – here in the house that Wittgenstein designed, and in this city that fashioned Wittgenstein. It is almost seven years since I began visiting the Philosophical Institute at the University of Vienna and first met the young philosophers whose conceptions and publication we are celebrating today. Our intellectual companionship over the years has been an inspiration to me. It cheers me to think that our exchanges have played some part in the story that leads to today's event, and I take the event as a promise of continued and growing exchanges between Austrian and American philosophers."[14] And, indeed, Cavell did further develop these contacts between Harvard and Vienna, *inter alia* by inviting two young lecturers from the Department of Philosophy at the University of Vienna to be "Visiting Scholars" in the Department of Philosophy of Harvard University,[15] and by continuing his visits to Austrian institutions during the decades to come. In 2000, Stanley Cavell spoke – after a screening of George Cukor's "remarriage comedy" *The Philadelphia Story* at the Votiv-Kino, a cinema in Vienna – extensively about his philosophical approach to film. In the same year, he traveled to Austria a second time, in order to lecture – at an event held at the Theatre Museum in Vienna and organized by the Friends of the Vienna State Opera – on the topic "Opera in [and as] Film"[16] (on a subject, that is, which plays a central role in his analyses of the melodrama).[17] In 2001, Cavell participated in the Wittgenstein Symposium at Kirchberg am Wechsel in Lower Austria, where he presented his post-analytic approach to Wittgenstein's late philosophy.

---

[14] Quoted from the reprint of this lecture (Stanley Cavell, "The Fantastic of Philosophy") *Cavell on Film*, ed. William Rothman, 2005, 145. Stanley Cavell's book launch address, presented on 26 May 1986 in the Wittgenstein House in Vienna, is published in German translation in: Stanley Cavell, *Nach der Philosophie. Essays*, eds. Ludwig Nagl und K.R. Fischer, *Deutsche Zeitschrift für Philosophie, Sonderband 1*, 2001, 231-8.

[15] Herbert Hrachovec and Ludwig Nagl.

[16] See Stanley Cavell, "Opera in [and as] Film [presented in Vienna]," Rothman, *Cavell on Film*, 205-19. (A German version of this paper, "Oper im Film, Oper als Film," was published in *Deutsche Zeitschrift für Philosophie*, Jahrgang 50, Heft 1, 2002, 3-16.)

[17] See Cavell, "Oper im Film" 13-15.

2. CAVELL'S ANALYSIS OF "THE MELODRAMA OF THE UNKNOWN WOMAN": THE PHILOSOPHICAL BACKGROUND

After these short biographical annotations we turn now to the main theme of this essay, to Cavell's film philosophical reading of Ophuls' screen version of Stefan Zweig's *Brief einer Unbekannten*. This film, Cavell writes, was often dismissed as a "so-called woman's film, or tearjerker," but it is actually a very complex cinematic work of art.[18] Ophuls' movie is characterized – as Helmut Aspen writes – (in spite of the fact that it was produced in Hollywood) by a very "Viennese atmosphere," which is created by the "zahlreichen emigrierten deutschen und österreichischen Schauspielerinnen und Schauspieler ..., die [in Ophüls' Film] den [durch Filmkulissen rekonstruierten] Prater, die Oper, den Bahnhof, Häuser, Restaurants und Plätze Wiens bevölkerten."[19] Zweig's short story revolves, as Aspen writes "um die Unbekannte, die die männliche Hauptfigur ihr ganzes Leben lang liebt, während sie für ihn ein flüchtiges Abenteuer ist, an das er sich nicht einmal erinnern kann."[20] Ophuls' film (which explores, as Cavell writes, "an avoidance of – terror of, disappointment with – acknowledgment"[21]), culminates in a complex sequence that Cavell interprets as the central scene of the movie. In this scene, close to the end of the film, the male protagonist (after he has read the farewell letter which the "unknown woman" – the mother of his child, whom has loved him dearly – had written before her death) faces in a long sequence of images situations that he has forgotten and repressed: here "the man [who] reaches the final words of the letter addressed to him ... by some unknown woman, is shown to be assaulted by a sequence of images from earlier moments of film ... and his response to [this] assault ... is to cover his eyes with the outspread fingers of both hands in a melodramatic gesture of horror and exhaustion."[22] Cavell explores the deep structure of this gesture, which indicates a mode of non-remembering

---

[18] Stanley Cavell, "Psychoanalysis and Cinema: The Melodrama of the Unknown Woman," *Die Philosophen und Freud. Eine offene Debatte*, eds. Helmuth Vetter and Ludwig Nagl, 1988 (*Wiener Reihe. Themen der Philosophie*, vol. 3), 200.

[19] Asper, *Max Ophüls* 93.

[20] Asper, *Max Ophüls* 91-2.

[21] Stanley Cavell, *Contesting Tears* 13.

[22] Stanley Cavell, "Psychoanalysis and Cinema: Moments of Letter from an Unknown Woman," Cavell, *Contesting Tears* 81.

as well as a mode of faint recalling – "a man's hands over his eyes, perhaps to ward off a woman's returning images"[23] – via a net of references which, roughly speaking, involves two strands of thought: one action-theoretical, the other psychoanalytical.

With regard to the first of these strands, Cavell's primary interest – not only in his extensive reading of Wittgenstein in *The Claim of Reason*, but also in his film philosophy – is focused on an analysis of the acting (i.e. communicatively inter-acting, as well as communication-avoiding) *self*. His analyses explore those links between language and action which are deeply connected – as Wittgenstein pointed out in *Philosophical Investigations* – to the plurality of our "ordinary," everyday uses of language (to those dimensions of language which enable, and can destroy[24], our "life forms"). The diverse structure of these (freedom-implying) "language games" (which tends to remain unexplored in science-focused language concepts that focus on the use of the term "description") was a fascinating topic not only for late Wittgenstein: the praxis-related aspect of language was also of interest for many post-Hegelian and phenomenological philosophers. Cavell's analyses of the complex interrelations between language and action only reach their full depth, however, when he starts to read language use within the frame of reference which he calls "Emersonian moral perfectionism."

What is the core idea of this "Emersonianism"? Every human action (Emerson and Cavell claim) is (potentially) free: it is neither fully tied to convention, nor the causal product of coercion. The acting self is able to alter, and to better, itself. Cavell thus focuses on the inner dialectics of the self – on the tension between convention and autonomous action – which is explored in Emerson's essay "Self-Reliance." [25] This text shows – in an indirect reference to Kant's thesis thesis that the human being is "a citizen of two worlds": the empirically given one, and the one he anticipates *idealiter*[26] – that the acting self must decide between "the attained" and

[23] Cavell, *Contesting Tears* 107. See also *Letter from an Unknown Woman. Rutgers Film in Print*, 1986, 132, takes 328 to 340.

[24] For the inscrutable nature of the way language is used see Niklas Forsberg, "Carver, Cavell, and the Uncanniness of the Ordinary," *New Literary History* (Johns Hopkins University), vol. 49.1 (Winter 2018): 1-22.

[25] Ralph Waldo Emerson, "Self-Reliance," *Emerson's Essays*, 1951, 31-66.

[26] See Stanley Cavell, *Cities of Words. Pedagogical Letters on a Register of Moral Life*, 2004, "Introduction" 1.

"the attainable."[27] This inner tension is actualized in every act, and it is present in processes of communication that either succeed or fail, as well as in "solipsistic" attempts to avoid communication altogether.

The second strand of Cavell's reading of films is Freud's psychoanalysis[28], which is interpreted by Cavell, differently from Freud himself, in a *philosophical* mode.[29] Cavell's "Emersonian" analyses of the succeeding or failing interaction-dynamics of "selves" often use Freudian concepts such as "identification," "projection" and "(counter)transference"; even more importantly, Cavell analyzes the interaction-dynamics of the films which he categorizes as "remarriage comedies" – a direct reference to Freud's *Three Essays on the Theory of Sexuality* – as a process in which "the finding of the object is in fact the re-finding of it"[30]: re-marriage is thus seen as a learning process that is made possible by, and mediated through, the (unavoidable) experience of alienation. Cavell philosophically re-reads psychoanalysis as a discourse which is able to correct and reverse the subject-oblivion in contemporary scientism: it is "the place, perhaps the last place, in which the human psyche as such (the idea that there is a life in the mind, hence a death) receives its proof."[31] This claim is plausible only if it can be demonstrated that Freud's thought – differently from what Freud himself on occasion wrote – does, ultimately, not move away from the center of modern (subject-)philosophy. In order to prove this, Cavell insists on Freud's (often denied) "inheritance … of the … thinking initiated by Kant and then

[27] Stanley Cavell, *Conditions Handsome and Unhandsome. The Constitution of Emersonian Perfectionism*, 1990. See also Ludwig Nagl, "Einleitung: Philosophie als Erziehung von Erwachsenen," Stanley Cavell, *Nach der Philosophie. Essays*, eds. Ludwig Nagl and Kurt R. Fischer, 2001, 28.

[28] Stefan Zweig's literary production is also deeply influenced by Freud, as his intense exchange of letters with the founder of psychoanalysis shows (see "Briefwechsel mit Sigmund Freud," 161-265, Stefan Zweig, *Briefwechsel mit Hermann Bahr, Sigmund Freud, Rainer Maria Rilke und Arthur Schnitzler*, 2007). There are no comments by Freud on Zweig's *Brief einer Unbekannten* in this exchange of letters; see, however, note 169, 233, as well as Freud's postcard to Zweig dated 27 October 1922, *Briefwechsel* 169.

[29] See Cavell, "Psychoanalysis and Cinema: The Melodrama of the Unknown Woman," *Die Philosophen und Freud*, eds. H. Vetter and L. Nagl, 209.

[30] *Ibid.* 200.

[31] *Ibid.* 208.

developed continuously by Fichte, Schelling, Hegel, Schopenhauer and Nietzsche."[32]

3. MELODRAMA AND COMEDY – AN INVERSION

In extensive recourse to a set of categories constituted by this multipolar, "transatlantic" approach to philosophy, Cavell analyzes *en detail* two film genres: the genre of "Hollywood Remarriage Comedies" (in which the abyss of intersubjective communication is overcome in a happy ending) and "the Melodrama of the Unknown Woman" (where the inter-gender communication definitively founders).[33]

The "Hollywood Comedies of Remarriage" comprise, in Cavell's definition, the movies *The Lady Eve*; *It Happened One Night*; *Bringing Up Baby*; *The Philadelphia Story*; *His Girl Friday*, and *The Awful Truth*)[34] – a group of films focused on the (possibility of) marriage as a core mode of friendship[35], that is to say based on successful intersubjective acknowledgement. "Remarriage comedies begin with … the threat of divorce; the drive of the narrative is to get the original pair together again."[36] The "working through," and overcoming, of alienation which takes place in these comedies happens by means of quarrels and talks: "The conversation of what I call the genre of remarriage is … of a sort that leads to acknowledgment; to the reconciliation of a genuine forgiveness."[37] In the other genre, the melodrama, such "loving quarrels" no longer occur. Cavell describes the core difference between these two groups of films as follows: "I discuss the amatory wars of the *comedies* as struggles for acknowledgment; in the *melodramas* this is avoided or

[32] *Ibid.* 209.

[33] See *Contesting Tears* 5, where Cavell points out that the genre of the melodrama is "derived" from the "remarriage comedies": "The mechanism of 'derivation' is what I think of as the negation of the features of the comedies by the melodramas."

[34] Stanley Cavell, *Pursuits of Happiness. The Hollywood Comedy of Remarriage*, 1981.

[35] See Cavell's answer to objections raised by some feminists concerning Cavell's focus on "marriage": any marriage that turns out well, Cavell argues, is – from the philosophical point of view – a (sub-)genre of the general category "friendship" – a core ethical category since Aristoteles.

[36] Cavell, *Contesting Tears* 4.

[37] Cavell, *Pursuits of Happiness* 19.

renounced; the man's struggle is there, on the contrary, a struggle against recognition. The woman's struggle is to understand why recognition by the man has not happened or has been denied or has become irrelevant."[38] In the melodramas, the reciprocal acknowledgment of the sexes – marriage – founders once and for all.

This tends to result in despair and accusation. But it can also lead to new expressions: it can become the *locus* of articulations of finitude that are aesthetically configured, as well as of "searches for transcendence" connected to religious imagology. The collapse of intersubjective communication is serious in ways that defy all marginalization, since "there is no human desire without the imagination of one to whom one may be intelligible."[39] This (inner-human, intersubjectivity-oriented) desire – which is re-accentuated through the experience of faltering and finiteness – tends, however, to change: "The woman's isolation," Cavell writes, "is associated in the films of unknownness with some register of her relation to the transcendent."[40] This is the case in all of the melodramas analyzed by Cavell. With regard to Ophuls' screen version of Zweig's novella Cavell notes: "I think … of Joan Fontaine, throughout *Letter from an Unknown Woman*, speaking beyond the grave from a letter countersigned by a nun"[41]; in *Stella Dallas*, this "relation to the transcendent" becomes obvious when the film audience sees "Barbara Stanwyck [the "unknown woman" of this movie] silent at the end walking to and from an ecstatic vision of another world."[42]

Film endings of this kind are significantly different from the way in which Cavell's comedies of remarriage end: "firmly, studiously, turning their couple back into their unsponsored, risky reality, picking up the secular thread."[43]

How is this "longing gaze for a transcendent"[44] to be understood, if it is compared with the "robust secularism" of the "remarriage comedies,"

---

[38] Cavell, *Contesting Tears* 30.

[39] *Ibid.* 37.

[40] *Ibid.*

[41] *Ibid.* 37-8. See also *Letter from an Unknown Woman. Rutgers Film in Print*, 1986, 131, take 327.

[42] Cavell, *Contesting Tears* 38.

[43] *Ibid.*

[44] For an extended analysis of this "longing gaze for a transcendent" see: Ludger H. Viefhues-Bailey, *Beyond the Philosopher's Fear. A Cavellian Reading of*

Cavell asks.[45] Can we interpret the final scenes of the melodramas, without much hesitation, as mere manifestations of those modes of religious *illusion building* of which Feuerbach and Freud, in their criticism of religion, spoke? Does the melodrama re-invoke "das alte Entsagungslied, das Eiapopeia vom Himmel," as Heinrich Heine put it in *Deutschland. Ein Wintermärchen* (when he was still young and – differently from in his late days – saw the world through the lens of a convinced *left-wing Hegelian*).[46] Or is "the longing gaze" of the melodrama structured in a

Gender, Origin and Religion in Modern Skepticism, 2007, 7. To explore, in a non-reductive manner, what this "longing gaze" implies, makes necessary – "in a secular age" – a complex re-reading of the relation between "gender, religion, and philosophy." One way to do this, according to Viefhues, is opened up by Julia Kristeva: "Bringing Cavell into dialogue with a particular woman's voice, namely Julia Kristeva as a critically and attentive reader of Freud, will help to discern the entanglement of gender, religion and philosophy." Kristeva's analyses show that the search for the "attainable" – for a new image of the human – entails, at any time, images and concepts which border on religion: "We can learn from Kristeva's 'Stabat Mater'," Viefhues writes, "how the emergence of a new vision of human subjectivity is involved in probing for a new religious imagination that supports human becoming through the process of bordering."

[45] In addition to this question one might ask what the relationship is between Cavell's analyses of the melodrama and Hegel's explorations of the "unhappy consciousness" in *Phenomenology of Spirit*?

[46] Heine portrays, at the beginning of *Germany. A Winter Tale,* a melodramatic scene: "A little maiden sang to the harp; / Real feeling her song was conveying, / Though false was her voice, and yet I felt / Deep moved at hearing her playing. / She sang of love, and she sang of love's woes, / Of sacrifices, and meeting / Again on high, in yon better world / Where vanish our sorrows so fleeting. / She sang of this earthly valley of tears, / Of joys which so soon have vanish'd, / Of yonder, where revels the glorified soul / In eternal bliss, grief being banish'd. / The song of renunciation she sang, / the heavenly eiapopeia, / Wherewith the people, the booby throng, / Are hush'd when they something require. / I know the tune, and I know the text, / I know the people who wrote it; / I know that in secret they drink wine, / And in public a wickedness vote it. / A song, friends, that's new, and a better one, too, / Shall now for your benefit given! / Our object is, that here on earth / We may mount to the realms of heaven" (Heinrich Heine, *Germany. A Winter Tale,* 2007, "Caput 1," 3; translation by Edgar Alfred Bowring).

A few years later, however, Heine revised his early Feuerbach-inspired hope that mankind, after criticizing and rejecting religion, will be able to establish

much more complex manner?[47] Is what has to be explored here not illusion building, but a full picture of "the human" that avoids ignoring, or denying, the final nature of all (individual as well as social) human action? Does the "longing gaze" re-route us toward a philosophical reflection that, within modern "system philosophy," still informed Hegel's investigations of "the *modi* of the Absolute": towards a re-reading, that is, of mankind's attempts to explore – in art, religion and philosophy – its own bounds, as well as its capacity to focus on the non-finite?

4. THE "ROBUST SECULARISM" OF THE COMEDIES AND ITS CONFINES: CRITICISM OF RELIGION, AND PHILOSOPHY OF RELIGION, IN CAVELL'S ANALYSES OF THE MELODRAMA

Cavell analyzes the foundered modes of acknowledgment in reference to a multi-layered phenomenology of "unknownness." The melodramatic crisis of acknowledgment, firstly, invites "choosing solitude." But it also makes possible the opening up of a new aesthetic space: the space of describing oneself in a melodramatic "aria" (a mode of expression close to the opera, which, as Cavell shows, is latently present in the overall structure of *Letter from an Unknown Woman*). In both these contexts, different ways of focusing on "transcendence" start to surface: on the one hand, reflectively induced *practical* modes that seek to leave behind conventional ways of (gender-) interaction; on the other, experiences that are interlaced with religious imagology and are triggered by the desire to transcend finitude altogether.

In the first (inner-human) sense of "transcendence," "unknownness" is seen as a new mode of action – a mode that does not exist in conventional intersubjectivity and is not present in the happy acknowledgment that

---

"heaven on earth." For this "Umwandlung, welche in Bezug auf göttliche Dinge in meinem Geist stattgefunden," see Heinrich Heine, *Zur Geschichte der Religion und Philosophie in Deutschland*, 2015, Vorrede zur zweiten Auflage (1852), 150-3.

[47] See in this context Peter Dula, *Cavell, Companionship and Christian Theology*, 2011, chapter 6, "'Can we Believe All This?' Cavell's Annexation of Theology," 155-70; and Ludwig Nagl, "Moralische Reflexion und Film: Cavell's Emersonian perfectionism – 'a part of philosophy's quarrel with religion'?," *Besser geht's nur in der Komödie. Cavell über die moralischen Register von Literatur und Film*, eds. E. Brock und M.S. Lotter, 2019, 170-205.

characterizes the comedies of remarriage. Out of the experience of foundering, a "knowing unknownness" – i.e. a radical mode of privacy – is able to develop. Cavell describes this new mode, where the "unknown woman" transposes her search for authenticity into an *identity "beyond marriage,"* as follows[48]: "The route to this alternative integrity is ... some radical, astonishing, one may say melodramatic change of the woman .... [T]his change must take place outside the process of a mode of conversation with a man ... It is as if the women of the melodramas are saying to their sisters in the comedies ...: 'You may call yourselves lucky to have found a man with whom you can overcome the humiliation of marriage by marriage itself. For us, with our talents and tastes, there is no further or happy education to be found there.'"[49]

"Choosing solitude," Cavell writes, is not a freezing of the "dialectics of the self," not an abandonment of the wish for "metamorphosis."[50] The transformation which, in the comedies, was induced by mutual recognition, re-appears, in an altered mode – as "self-theatricalization"[51] – in the melodrama. This alteration is expressed, for instance, by Greta Garbo, "the greatest, or the most fascinating, cinematic image on film of the unknown woman. [...] In Garbo's most famous postures in conjunction with a man she looks away or beyond or through him, as if in an absence

---

[48] In both genres – the comedies as well as in the melodramas – the search for authenticity is (in quite different ways, though) the central pursuit. Both explore (what Emerson has called) the journey from conformity to self-reliance: they enter a learning process which is avoided in bad conventional marriages where the asymmetry of the sexes remains unaddressed. Neither in the genre of the "remarriage comedies" nor in the melodramas "is a marriage of irritation, silent condescension, and questionlessness found more desirable than solitude, or, say, unknownness" (Stanley Cavell, *Contesting Tears* 11).

[49] Stanley Cavell, *Contesting Tears* 6.

[50] *Ibid.* 47-8.

[51] Stephen Mulhall, in his book *Stanley Cavell: Philosophy's Recounting of the Ordinary*, 1994, characterizes "unknownness" as follows: The "unknown women" in Cavell's melodramas "are unknown to those around them ...; their existence as independent autonomous beings is systematically denied or missed, particularly by the men with whom they are paired" (*Ibid.* 241). This situation invites an "enacted unknownness" – an "enactment of human existence, a theatricalization of the self, which constitutes an attempted proof of its reality and freedom" (*Ibid.* 240).

…, hence as if to declare that this man, while the occasion of her passion, is surely not its cause."[52]

Such a "theatricalized" affirmation of the (privatized) self entails, on the on hand, a pointed accusation[53]: "[T]he self-reliance [of the unknown woman] functions as a standing rebuke to the present world, … to the people whose existence takes the form of conformity to that world, people who do not attempt to enact their own existence."[54] The unknown woman in Zweig's novella laments such a mode of inauthenticity – the thoughtlessness of the male protagonist who altogether disrespects her individuality: "Ich habe es bald erfahren, dass Du [Deinen] umfangenden, an Dich ziehenden Blick …, diesen Blick des geborenen Verführers, jeder Frau hingibst, die an Dich streift."[55]

The suffering from non-recognition which the melodramatic movie depicts can be articulated in various, quite different ways. It may be expressed through an "enacted unknownness," that is to say by means of a new form of *expressivity located at the fringe of inexpressivity*. It might also be depicted in an aesthetical mode that turns an entire movie (as Cavell points out in his analyses of *Letter from an Unknown Woman*) into a kind of cinematic (opera) aria. And it can manifest itself in *religious references*: in Ophuls' film, Cavell writes, the letter, in which the unknown woman tells her story "contains a signature, on the letterhead, of the religious order in whose hospital the unknown woman died, of someone styled 'Sister-in-charge'."[56] References of this kind are also present in the film sequence "[where the unknown woman] leaves the train platform after rushing to see the man off for a hastily remembered concert tour. Walking away from us, she gradually disappears into blackness at the center of the vacant scene, upon which, at what we might project as her

---

[52] Stanley Cavell, *Contesting Tears* 106.

[53] Tania Modleski quotes in this context Hélène Cixous, who writes "[that] the experience of loss is at the heart of melodrama." A full exploration of this loss makes necessary "to go beyond the traditional psychoanalytic model[,]" where the experience of loss is, uncritically, reduced to an analysis of "hysteria." (Tania Modleski, "Time and Desire in the Woman's Film," *Letter from an Unknown Woman. Rutgers Film in Print*, 1986, 261.)

[54] Stephen Mulhall, *Stanley Cavell* 244-5.

[55] Stefan Zweig, "Brief einer Unbekannten," in Zweig, *Meistererzählungen* 159.

[56] Cavell, "Psychoanalysis and Cinema: The Melodrama of the Unknown Woman," in *Die Philosophen und Freud*, eds. H. Vetter and L. Nagl, 223; see also *Letter from an Unknown Woman. Rutgers Film in Print* 131, take 327.

vanishing point, there is a re-materialization, and the figure of the woman is replaced by, or transformed into, walking at the same pace toward us, what turns out coming into readable view to be a nun. So the woman is part of the world of religion."[57]

As an artist Ophuls assigns himself, at least indirectly, to this "transforming," religious world, Cavell writes, insofar as he "signs," that is to say cinematically presents, the letter of the "unknown woman."[58] His film shows the manifold experiences of alienation which the "unknown woman" lives through, which include those episodes that contain religious references. Cavell interprets, at that point, Jacques Lacan's thesis on female "self-reliance" ("I believe in the *jouissance* of the woman insofar as it is something more") as follows: "[Lacan] may be taken as saying: What there is (any longer) of God, or of the concept of the beyond, takes place in relation to the woman."[59] The awareness that experiences of finiteness (in complicated, often inexplicit ways) imply modes of reference to infinity (a dialectics which, routinely, is ignored in scientific world-views) does not, however, disappear completely. "[T]he surmise has crossed my mind" – Cavell writes (in unexpected closeness to Charles S. Peirce[60]) – "that philosophical skepticism ... is a male business."[61] This does not mean, Cavell instantly adds, however, "that women do not get into the way of skepticism, but only that the passion of doubt may not express a woman's sense of separation from others."[62] The core dogmas of a scientific "unmasking" of "the subject" – the over-privileging of object-reference, and the physico-causalistic debunking of "the self" (as

---

[57] See *Letter from an Unknown Woman. Rutgers Film in Print*, 1986, 97, takes 196 and 197.

[58] "The world of religion [is] a world Ophuls ... assigns himself, I mean his art, in signing the woman's letter." (Cavell, "Psychoanalysis and Cinema: The Melodrama of the Unknown Woman," in *Die Philosophen und Freud*, eds. H. Vetter and L. Nagl, 223.

[59] *Ibid.* 216.

[60] See Ludwig Nagl, "Charles Sanders Peirce, 'Ein vernachlässigtes Argument für die Realität Gottes,' in *Religionsphilosophie und Religionskritik. Ein Handbuch*, ed. Michael Kühnlein, 2018, 445-57.

[61] Cavell, "Psychoanalysis and Cinema: The Melodrama of the Unknown Woman," in *Die Philosophen und Freud*, eds. H. Vetter and L. Nagl, 214.

[62] *Ibid.* 215.

well as "the other") – tend to harden to a *lived skepticism* most often in men.[63]

The (complexly coded) references to "transcendence" which flash up in the melodramas are read, by Cavell, primarily *modo aesthetico*: as indicators, that is, of a significant interrelation between the cinematic melodrama and the opera.[64] In the cinematic melodrama two paradoxically intertwined modes of expression do meet: an experience of finitude, which tends to terminate "in the terror of absolute inexpressiveness, suffocation,"[65] and a "metamorphosis" of the self, "the possibility and the necessity of, 'the desire to express all'." The melodrama thus organizes an alternative to the "happy" and "robust" secularism of the comedies: it displays the open wound of failing intersubjective relations – the "crisis of expression," Cavell writes, "[which] is for me a characterization of what has become of human exchange as such."[66]

Do these melodramatic questions – insofar as they are intertwined with "the world of religion" – re-articulate anything else (or something more) than the paradoxical (near-melodramatic) desire that Nietzsche's "Toller Mensch," in *Die Fröhliche Wissenschaft*, shouts out, who, in broad daylight, seeks with his lantern the God "that we have killed ourselves"?[67]

Cavell's allusions to the long history of philosophical re-readings of religion after Hegel (to a multi-faceted discourse, that is to say one which, on the one hand, with Feuerbach, assumes that religion can be dissolved and transformed into humanistic energies,[68] and, on the other, seeks to explore the reductionisms contained in today's self-assured "exclusive

---

[63] See in this context Stanley Cavell's essay, "Othello and the Stake of the Other," in Cavell, *Disowning Knowledge: In Six Plays of Shakespeare*, 1987, 125-42.

[64] "In *Letter from an Unknown Woman* it is as if the entire letter (the film) is the aria." (Cavell, *Contesting Tears* 146.)

[65] *Ibid.* 43.

[66] *Ibid.*

[67] See Friedrich Nietzsche, *Die Fröhliche Wissenschaft*, Par. 125, where "der tolle Mensch shouts out: "Wohin ist Gott …: ich will es euch sagen. Wir haben ihn getötet, – ihr und ich. Wir Alle sind seine Mörder! Aber wie haben wir dies gemacht. Wie vermochten wir das Meer auszutrinken? Wer gab uns den Schwamm, um den ganzen Horizont wegzuwischen?" See in this context Cavell, *Contesting Tears* 43-5.

[68] This Feuerbachian project motivates, for instance, the humanism of John Dewey and Richard Rorty.

humanism"[69]) avoid an in-depth exploration of these questions.[70] His reflections on the two film genres remain focused, primarily, on the hope that the excessive paradoxes of expression which characterize the melodrama might, one day, terminate in a positive humanism: "Suppose the secularity of remarriage comedy shows that its moral perfectionism really can survive, can retain itself within, the unknown woman melodrama and its Manichean, demonic lights. Then, in all fragility, we have it attested, that our intelligibility to one another is so far a match for the heydays of chaos reaching our ear."[71] That this hope does not seem implausible from the start implies that a learning process can take place where severe deficits of acknowledgment (like the "carelessness" which the male protagonist of *Letter from an Unknown Woman* displays) can be reflected on and altered. Ophuls' film, it seems, envisions such a learning process. In doing so it follows an idea that – as Cavell notes – cannot be found with the same explicitness in the final passages of Zweig's *Brief einer Unbekannten.*[72]

At the end of Zweig's novella, the male protagonist (to whom the letter, which begins with the words "Du, der mich nie gekannt hat,"[73] is addressed) recalls the identity of the letter writer, after reading her message, only "undeutlich und verworren.[74].... Er dachte an die Unsichtbare körperlos und leidenschaftlich wie an eine ferne Musik."[75] Although he is puzzled and confused, his self-reflection remains very limited, and the "Unbekannte" does not become a real person for him. There is melancholy, and not an insight able to alter *praxis*, at the end of Zweig's novel. Ophuls' film opens up a different learning horizon. Cavell shows this in his analysis of the scene, shortly before the film ends, in which the forgotten and repressed becomes visible to the male protagonist in a sequence of images: "[T]he man [who] reaches the final words of the

[69] See Charles Taylor, *A Secular Age*, 2007; and Charles Taylor, "Shapes of Faith Today," in *Reviewing the Church in a Secular Age*, eds. Charles Taylor, José Casanova, George F. McLean, J. Vila-Chã, 2016, 269-81.

[70] See Ludwig Nagl, "Moralische Reflexion und Film: Cavell's Emersonian perfectionism – 'a part of philosophy´s quarrel with religion'?" 185-205.

[71] Cavell, *Contesting Tears* 45.

[72] Cavell, "Psychoanalysis and Cinema: The Melodrama of the Unknown Woman," in *Die Philosophen und Freud*, eds. H. Vetter and L. Nagl, 225.

[73] Zweig, "Brief einer Unbekannten" 151.

[74] *Ibid.* 196.

[75] *Ibid.* 197.

letter addressed to him … by some unknown woman, is shown to be assaulted by a sequence of images from earlier moments of film … and his response to [this] assault … is to cover his eyes with the outspread fingers of both hands in a melodramatic gesture of horror and exhaustion."[76] This gesture, Cavell writes, has a variety of implications: "[W]hen the man covers his eyes – an ambiguous gesture between avoiding the horror of knowing the existence of others and avoiding the horror of not knowing it … – he is … both warding off his seeing something and warding off at the same time his being seen … by the woman of the letter … and by us, which accordingly identifies us, the audience of the film, as assigning ourselves the position, in its passiveness and its activeness, of the source of the letter and of the film; which is to say, the position of the feminine."[77]

The *audience* of Ophuls' film (not being burdened with any real-life pressure because of the action-distance induced by the "receptive" mode of cinema watching,) identifies itself easily – *regardless of whether it is male or female* – with the victimization experienced by the "unknown woman." The reflection, as well as the learning process, which is started in this way, is made possible by "the revelation … of ourselves in a certain way of being feminine."[78] More generally speaking, it rests on the insight that we all, as moral beings, understand the suffering brought about by the experience of victimization presented in the movie. This experience transgresses all fixed gender limits.[79] Its inner structure can be further explored via a philosophical analysis of "practical reason," the centerpiece of Kant's Enlightenment philosophy, which Cavell re-interprets in the light of Emerson's "perfectionism."

---

[76] Cavell, eds. Vetter and Nagl, 224.

[77] *Ibid.*

[78] *Ibid.* See in this context Tania Modleski, who writes "[that] one of the appeals of [*Letter from an Unknown Woman*] is … its tendency to feminize the man, to complicate and destabilize his identity" (Modleski, *Time and Desire in the Women's Film* 257).

[79] Stephen Mulhall points out that "Cavell's view is that male and female perspectives, the identification, interrogation, and revision of which is the business of any feminist thought, are not the exclusive prerogative of men and women respectively, … but are rather modes or inflections of thought and practice to which any individual may be subject" (Stephen Mulhall, *Stanley Cavell* 314).

What makes itself felt on the *fringes* of experiences of alienation that the melodramas depict – the *unsurpassable bounds* constituted by the *finite quality of all our actions* (bounds which Kant carefully began to explore in *Religion within the Limits of Practical Reason*) – start to come into sight in the allusions to "transcendence" that pervade the melodramas.

Concerning these open questions, which – in Cavell's texts – are posed but remain unanswered, a complex discourse developed in the Anglo-American reception of Cavell in recent decades. This debate, which can here, at the end of this essay, be only mentioned but not analyzed, focuses on the problem whether Cavell's "Emersonian perfectionism" is able "fully to acknowledge the uttermost depths of the self's finitude."[80]

---

[80] Mulhall, *Stanley Cavell* 311. In this extended discourse the question is raised whether Cavell's analyses (which predominantly focus on the learning processes that concern "self-reliance") tend, indirectly, to (co-)transport thought figures that are derived from those post-Hegelian criticisms of religion that avoid a *radical* investigation of the finiteness of the human subject. Such a strategy of avoidance, it is argued, has (at least) two dimensions: it concerns, *firstly*, all questions that focus on a problem which was of core relevance for philosophy since its origin: why there is something at all, and not nothing? And it, *secondly*, leaves unanalyzed a thought figure which is central to most religions: that the individual's self-realization – important as it is – is, at the same time, *not at all* the *ultimate* goal of ethical action, since human action, in its full sense, includes (as, for example, Søren Kierkegaard and Simone Weil insisted) the praxis of "dying to the self." Stephen Mulhall summarizes these critical considerations (Cavell 311) as follows: Cavell's critics insist that he "fails fully to interrogate the ego's maddened and maddening desire to believe itself at the centre of things, and so fails fully to acknowledge … the uttermost depths of the self's finitude." For a more detailed overview of this debate see Ludwig Nagl, "Moralische Reflexion und Film: Cavell's Emersonian perfectionism – 'a part of philosophy´s quarrel with religion'"? (in particular segment 4, "Der rezente Diskurs über die religionkritisch-religionsphilosophischen Implikationen von Cavells Begriff des 'Selbst'"), *Besser geht's nur in der Komödie. Cavell über die moralischen Register von Literatur und Film*, 2019, 185-205.

WORKS CITED

Asper, Helmut G. *Max Ophüls. Deutscher – Jude – Franzose.* Berlin: Hentrich und Hentrich, 2011.

"Brief einer Unbekannten (Film)." *Wikipedia.* https://de.wikipedia.org/wiki/Brief_einer_Unbekannten_(Film). Accessed 5 February 2020.

Cavell, Stanley. "An Indiscreet Ambassador." *Weltanschauungen des Wiener Fin de Siècle 1900/2000, Festgabe für Kurt Rudof Fischer zum achtzigsten Geburtstag.* Ed. Gertraud Diem-Wille, Ludwig Nagl, and Friedrich Stadler. Frankfurt a. M.: Peter Lang, 2002. 43-6.

—. *Nach der Philosophie. Essays.* Ed. Ludwig Nagl and K.R. Fischer. *Deutsche Zeitschrift für Philosophie,* Sonderband 1. Berlin: Akademie Verlag, 2001. 231-8.

—. *Cities of Words. Pedagogical Letters on a Register of Moral Life.* Cambridge: Harvard UP, 2004.

—. *Conditions Handsome and Unhandsome. The Constitution of Emersonian Perfectionism.* Chicago & London: U of Chicago P, 1990.

—. *Contesting Tears. The Hollywood Melodrama of the Unknown Woman.* Chicago & London: U of Chicago P, 1996.

—. "Danebenstehen, Gleichziehen: Bedrohungen der Individualität." *Wo steht die Analytische Philosophie heute?.* Eds. Ludwig Nagl and Richard Heinrich. *Wiener Reihe. Themen der Philosophie*, volume 1. Vienna: Oldenbourg, 1986. 116-49.

—. *Disowning Knowledge: In six Plays of Shakespeare.* Cambridge: Cambridge UP, 1987.

—. *Little Did I Know. Excerpts from Memory.* Stanford: Stanford UP, 2010.

—. "Opera in [and as] Film [presented at the Vienna State Opera]." *Cavell on Film.* Ed. William Rothman. Albany: State University of New York P, 2005. 205-19.

—. "Oper im Film, Oper als Film." *Deutsche Zeitschrift für Philosophie* 50.1 (2002): 3-16.

—. "Psychoanalysis and Cinema: Moments of Letter from an Unknown Woman." *Contesting Tears. The Hollywood Melodrama of the Unknown Woman.* Chicago & London: U of Chicago P, 1996. 199-226.

—. "Psychoanalysis and Cinema: The Melodrama of the Unknown Woman." *Die Philosophen und Freud. Eine offene Debatte.* Ed. Helmuth Vetter and Ludwig Nagl. *Wiener Reihe. Themen der Philosophie*, volume 3. Vienna: Oldenbourg, 1988. 199-226.

—. *Pursuits of Happiness. The Hollywood Comedy of Remarriage.* Cambridge: Harvard UP, 1981.

—. *The Claim of Reason. Wittgenstein, Skepticism, Morality, and Tragedy.* New York & Oxford: Oxford UP, 1979.

—. "The Fantastic of Philosophy." *Cavell on Film.* Ed. William Rothman. Albany: State U of New York P, 2005. 145-52.

—. *The Senses of Walden. An Expanded Edition.* San Francisco: North Point P, 1981.

Dula, Peter. *Cavell, Companionship and Christian Theology.* Oxford: Oxford UP, 2011.

Emerson, Ralph Waldo. "Self-Reliance." *Emerson's Essays.* New York: Harper & Row, 1951. 31-66.

Forsberg, Niklas. "Carver, Cavell, and the Uncanniness of the Ordinary." *New Literary History* 49.1 (Winter 2018): 1-22.

Gaslight. Directed by George Cukor, Metro-Goldwyn-Mayer, 1944.

Heine, Heinrich. *Germany. A Winter Tale.* New York: Mondial, 2007.

—. *Zur Geschichte der Religion und Philosophie in Deutschland.* Stuttgart: Reclam, 2015.

Letter from an Unknown Woman. Directed by Max Ophüls, Rampant Productions & Universal Pictures, 1948.

Lettre d'une inconnue. Directed by Jacques Deray, 2001.

Matuschek, Oliver. *Stefan Zweig. Drei Leben – Eine Biographie.* Frankfurt a. M.: Fischer, 2006.

Modleski, Tania. "Time and Desire in the Woman's Film." *Letter from an Unknown Woman. Rutgers Film in Print.* New Brunswick: Rutgers UP, 1986.

Mulhall, Stephen. *Stanley Cavell: Philosophy's Recounting of the Ordinary.* Oxford: Claredon P, 1994.

Nagl, Ludwig. "Charles Sanders Peirce, 'Ein vernachlässigtes Argument für die Realität Gottes'." *Religionsphilosophie und Religionskritik. Ein Handbuch.* Ed. Michael Kühnlein. Berlin: Suhrkamp, 2018. 445-57.

—. "Einleitung: Philosophie als Erziehung von Erwachsenen." *Stanley Cavell: Nach der Philosophie. Essays.* Ed. Ludwig Nagl and K.R. Fischer. Berlin: Akademie Verlag, 2001. 7-32.

—. "Filmphilosophie in Wien." *Ein Filmphilosophie-Symposium mit Robert B. Pippin.* Ed. Ludwig Nagl and Waldemar Zacharasiewicz. *Wiener Reihe. Themen der Philosophie*, Volume 19. Berlin: De Gruyter, 2017. 7-10.

—. "Moralische Reflexion und Film: Cavells Emersonian perfectionism – 'a part of philosophy's quarrel with religion'?" *Besser geht's nur in der Komödie. Cavell über die moralischen Register von Literatur und*

Film. Ed. Eike Brock und Maria-Sibylla Lotter. Freiburg: Alber, 2019. 170-205.

—. "Some Reflections on how the Remigrant K.R. Fischer influenced Vienna´s Academic Discourses." *Return from Exile – Rückkehr aus dem Exil. Exiles, Returnees and Their Impact in the Humanities and Social Sciences in Austria and Central Europe.* Ed. Waldemar Zacharasiewicz and Manfred Prisching. Vienna: Austrian Academy of Sciences, 2017. 347-62.

Nietzsche, Friedrich. *Die Fröhliche Wissenschaft.* Chemnitz: Verlag von Ernst Schmeitzner, 1882.

Now, Voyager. Directed by Irving Rapper, Warner Bros., 1942.

Payne, Michael. Introduction. *Philosophical Passages: Wittgenstein, Emerson, Austin, Derrida,* by Stanley Cavell. Oxford: Blackwell, 1995. 1-11.

Renolder, Klemens, Holl, Hildemar and Peter Karlhuber, editors. *Stefan Zweig. Bilder, Texte, Dokumente.* Residenz Verlag, 1993.

Stella Dallas. Directed by King Vidor, Samuel Goldwyn Productions, 1937.

Taylor, Charles. *A Secular Age.* Cambridge: Harvard UP, 2007.

—. "Shapes of Faith Today." *Reviewing the Church in a Secular Age.* Ed. Charles Taylor, José Casanova, George F. McLean and João J. Vila-Chã. Washington, D.C.: Council for Research in Values and Philosophy, 2016. 269-81.

Viefhues-Bailey, Ludger H. *Beyond the Philosopher´s Fear. A Cavellian Reading of Gender, Origin and Religion in Modern Skepticism.* Aldershot: Ashgate Publishing Limited, 2007.

Wexman, Virginia. *Letter from an Unknown Woman. Rutgers Film in Print.* New Brunswick: Rutgers UP, 1986.

Zweig, Stefan. "Brief einer Unbekannten." *Neue Freie Presse* 1 January 1922: 31-8.

—. *Meistererzählungen.* Frankfurt a. M..: Fischer, 2017.

—. *Briefwechsel mit Hermann Bahr, Sigmund Freud, Rainer Maria Rilke und Arthur Schnitzler.* 2nd ed. Frankfurt a. M.: Fischer, 2007.

STEVEN BURNS

A PHILOSOPHER CROSSES THE ATLANTIC: PETER WINCH ON PHILOSOPHY AND ETHICS

As a contribution to this volume devoted to "transatlantic elective affinities: traveling ideas and their mediators," I propose to discuss a very particular example. The example involves a personal connection, which I shall explain. It also involves some extremely interesting ideas from the mid-twentieth century. I shall attempt to justify this claim, not only that the ideas travelled because of the elective affinities of a particular philosopher, but also that the ideas in question are of a fundamental nature, and that I am thus justified in claiming that they are "extremely interesting."

Peter Winch supervised my doctoral thesis at the University of London (1970). I have maintained a steady admiration for the firm but very helpful guidance which he provided me, and for the continually expanding work which he produced for the rest of his career. In this essay I wish to explore just one of his later papers, "*Einheit: Voraussetzung oder Forderung.*" "Unity: Presupposition or Demand" is not a typical Winch paper. It was written, in German, for an annual meeting of the German Philosophy Congress, held in Giessen in 1987. Moreover, it was written at the invitation of Professor Schnädelbach, as part of a multi-speaker workshop. Winch's contribution questioned the apparent presupposition of the topic chosen for the occasion, and offered several arguments partially drawn from work that he had already published on Wittgenstein and Weil. It was, then, a statement of themes that he was prepared to discuss, even go to battle for, on this particular occasion. But because of that, I think that it is a good introduction to some major themes of his work.

How did Winch's ideas cross the Atlantic? Platonic Ideas, of course, are neither spatial nor temporal, but are universal and eternal. So they do not travel at all. People who grasp them (metaphorically, of course) do travel, and there are thus histories of the spread of ideas. In the present case, Winch gained access to the ideas from his study of Ludwig

Wittgenstein (who was raised in Vienna and worked in Cambridge),[1] and Simone Weil (who was raised in Paris and died near London).[2] His own thought developed in Swansea (1951-64) and London, where he taught until moving to the University of Illinois at Urbana-Champaign in the United States of America in 1985. He taught there until his death in 1997. (He was born in 1926, served in the Royal Navy from 1944-47, then finished a PPE degree at Oxford University.) That he should return to Europe often, while teaching in the USA, is a token of his understanding that he was taking European ideas across the Atlantic, but also returning to bring his later work from the USA back to Europe.

The ideas with which Winch was most concerned on this occasion in 1987 also had their independent trans-Atlantic lives. Wittgenstein sailed to America, living with his former student, Norman Malcolm and his wife, for a few months (1949), holding frequent discussions with Malcolm and some of his colleagues.[3] Simone Weil fled to New York from Nazi-occupied France, before returning to England (where she died in 1943) to write her final works. Her wonderful essay, "The *Iliad* or the Poem of Force," which Winch quotes in his Giessen paper, was translated by the American author, Mary McCarthy, and widely read in the USA. While he was working in the USA, I should add, Winch did not just disappear into the western sunset. He had a profound influence on a new generation of philosophy students, some of whom in various ways continue his work.

I shall claim not only that Winch's paper is an example of the transfer of ideas across the Atlantic Ocean (in both directions), thus illustrating a theme of this volume, but also that the ideas in question are particularly interesting and important. What were the ideas that Winch took from Europe to America and then back again?

They begin with the topic chosen for the whole 1987 congress: "*Einheit und Vielheit.*" This invokes the One and the Many – the great problem of the pre-Socratic philosophers. What is the one prime element from which came all the diversity of the universe? Or, if we translate it more carefully, Unity and Multiplicity. This formulation can suggest the question: can the infinite particularity of the world be explained by simple and universal laws? The conference organizers no doubt expected a *Vielheit* of contributions to this attempt to find *Einheit* among a large number of

---

[1] See, e.g., *Studies in the Philosophy of Wittgenstein*, ed. Peter Winch.

[2] See, e.g., Peter Winch, *Simone Weil: 'the just balance'*.

[3] See Ray Monk, *Ludwig Wittgenstein*, 552-59.

philosophers. I imagine that the conference topic would have suited Winch very well; he would enjoy contributing to the multiplicity of voices, and would argue that unity was a misleading goal. His first move in such a situation was usually to say something like: "Many things can be called 'one', and there are thus many 'ones'. Which one would you like to discuss?" And since his workshop topic, under the general theme of the conference, was to be universalism in ethics, the implied task was to discuss the possibility of universal laws of morality.

Having acknowledged this workshop goal of finding unity in the diversity of moral views, Winch's next move was to expose a misleading presupposition. He phrased his objection this way:

> I do not know exactly how Professor Schnädelbach himself conceives this matter. His way of putting it, however, suggests a certain background presupposition, namely that the correct line of argument would be, *first* to confirm (so-called) "factual" cultural universals in order *subsequently* to base some "normative" demands on them. Something like this is certainly a well-known procedure, in which one strives, e.g., to base a universalist ethic on needs that are thought to stem from a presumed common human nature.[4]

For example, human beings universally need food. So we might imagine that there is a moral demand that people be fed (children, certainly; the very old and the ill, presumably; strangers, perhaps; the indigent; the indolent?) This is in some ways a scientific basis for ethics. The empirical foundations serve as necessary and perhaps as sufficient conditions determining the universal ethical principles. This idea thus frames the paper. Winch concludes with the claim: "I do not know one could justify such an 'ethical unity' of humanity scientifically" (9/100).

By challenging this apparent presupposition of the workshop theme, Winch has focused on a specific problem, narrowing the theme quite dramatically. But this is far from all that he has accomplished. For the problem he has formulated is that of "facts and values," specifically about whether it is possible to derive value claims from a set of facts. David Hume had famously decreed that this move, from facts to values, is

[4] Winch, "Unity" 3/94. (In my text I shall insert page numbers when I quote from my translation of Winch's "Einheit: Voraussetzung oder Forderung?". The translation is now published online, in *Philosophical Investigations*, but it is not yet in print, so I shall include a second number which will refer to the corresponding page in the original German publication.)

illegitimate. From the fact that a son has killed and eaten his father, it does not follow (a) that something wrong has occurred, (b) that we observers should condemn the act, or (c) that we should be motivated to do something about it. If the son were a tree, which grew and stole light from its parent, eventually thriving on the parent's rotting carcass, we should simply say that this was the natural regeneration of a forest. So Hume argued that there was always a step missing when facts were stated and a value judgement ensued that could motivate us to take action. Winch cites two of his own papers, which he calls a "comprehensive critique of this view."[5]

Moral philosophers continue to struggle with this problem, trying to find ways of expressing factual truths which carry with them motivational force; and the entire problem goes back to the Socratic paradoxes: e.g., that no one does evil knowingly. Plato portrays Socrates as maintaining that if a person really understands a situation, s/he will respond by doing good; that evildoing is based on a mistake, on misunderstanding. And that clear understanding of a situation will bring forth its own motivation to do 'the right thing'. It is no accident that Winch's final concern in this paper is to discuss Socrates. Winch's focus, then, first zooms in on a particular aspect of the workshop's topic, and then zooms back out to one of the oldest and most venerable of issues in the philosophy of morality. It may seem at first glance that Winch has cobbled together disparate items for discussion on this occasion: a bit of Wittgenstein, a bit of Weil, a bit of Manichaeism, and a bit of Socrates …. But in fact Winch has his main goal in sight from the very beginning of his paper, and it is never far from view. His main goal is to say what can be said about the role of unity in thinking about ethics, given that a scientific foundation is ruled out.

Let us consider Winch's title: "Unity: Prerequisite or Demand." The terms 'prerequisite' and 'demand' are sometimes used as equivalents. 'Prerequisite or requirement?' could also serve as a translation; this tends to blur the differences. But Winch is thinking of the terms as very different operations. To require a prerequisite is to make a *preliminary* move, one which seeks to establish a foundation, one *from which* one can move on. Winch is thinking of the explicit aspect of the workshop topic: finding some cultural universals, which could then ground a claim that certain

---

[5] Winch, "Unity" 3/94. The papers are "Human Nature," and "Man and Society in Hobbes and Rousseau," from *Ethics and Action*, chapters 4 and 5.

values are universal. In our example, 'People who cannot feed themselves ought to be fed.' Making demands plays a very different role in an ethical form of life, and we shall discuss such demands in due course. But Winch reacts strongly against the idea that there could be such 'merely factual' prerequisites.

PRIMITIVE REACTIONS

Winch begins his positive argument by invoking work by two of his favourite research subjects: Ludwig Wittgenstein and Simone Weil. From Wittgenstein he takes the idea of "the primitive human reactions from which our most fundamental concepts develop" (4/94). He uses the example of the concept of cause, which we come to grasp only because we react naturally to causes. If I feel a blow to my foot, for instance, I look instinctively at my foot. Because I naturally do this, I can develop the idea that some object has hit my foot, causing the pain, and thus the concept of 'cause' can arise, and be developed and refined. Winch notes that we say 'we' react in such a way, as though we were depending on a common human nature. He would be very surprised, he says, to meet someone who would not react with disgust to a heap of rotting meat, "and you would be too" (4/95). Such primitive reactions are widely shared, and shape the natural history of human beings. But it is not clear that these are factual foundations. We might also say, "that in these cases we construct a norm, against which we then measure future experiences" (5/95).

Winch then offers a second example, taken from the essay, "The *Iliad* or the Poem of Force," by Simone Weil. "If we step aside for a passer-by on the road, it is not the same thing as stepping aside to avoid a billboard; alone in our rooms we get up, walk about, sit down again quite differently from the way we do when we have a visitor." This sketches another pattern of primitive reactions. Weil calls it "that interval of hesitation, wherein lies all our consideration for our brothers in humanity" (5/96). This is another candidate for "natural reaction from which our most fundamental concepts develop." This time it is the concept of common humanity, and she suggests that we would have no such concept if our natural reactions did not distinguish between humans and other objects in some such way.

Perhaps to his reader's surprise, Winch now goes on to raise a powerful objection to this way of thinking, but before I turn to the objection I want to explore further this idea of primitive reactions. Both of Winch's examples come from a developed stage of our lives. Looking at the area of a causal event is beyond the capacity of an infant who cannot yet find her feet. And the hesitation in the presence of another person is not merely natural; it is something that we learn about, probably also as children learning to identify and to cope with adults and other children. 'Primitive' means 'first', among other things, and these reactions come before certain kinds of conceptualization, but they too are preceded by earlier stages of development. They are not absolutely 'first.'

Wittgenstein is well known for having investigated much more primitive reactions. He once asked: "Are we perhaps over-hasty in our assumption that the smile of a baby is not pretence?"[6] He is investigating the idea of a private language to describe our own sensations, and has claimed that a child's natural reaction to pain is to cry. "[T]hen adults talk to him and teach him … new pain behaviour …. [T]he verbal expression of pain replaces crying, it does not describe it" (*PI* §244). The most obvious implication of these remarks is that crying is a primitive reaction, part of the natural history of humankind, and that it makes possible the learning of pain-language and more sophisticated concepts. The question about the baby's smile is interesting precisely because it makes us think of priority. It begins very early in an infant's life. Perhaps a baby makes an inadvertent grimace, which is interpreted by its parents as a smile. But the baby soon learns of its effects, and takes delight in smiling and recognizing the smiles of others, and imitating smiles, and so on. But for an infant to pretend to smile? That, we want to say, requires much more learning. The infant must separate the facial gesture from the feeling that it naturally expresses, and from the effects that it evokes, and develop the intent to achieve the effects by means of the gesture, but without the feeling. This is a relatively complicated advance on the primitive reaction, and would be impossible without the reaction having *priority*, coming first.

Wittgenstein goes on immediately to claim that, "Lying is a language-game that needs to be learned like any other one." In the next paragraph he asks whether a dog can pretend to be in pain, and, although we can teach a dog tricks, he argues that "the right surroundings for this behaviour to be real simulation would still be missing" (*PI* §250). Pretending is not as primitive as other behaviour. All of this has interesting ramifications for

[6] See L. Wittgenstein, *Philosophical Investigations* §249. (I shall abbreviate to '*PI*' in the text.)

the familiar question, are infants guileless? Or are they conceived in sin and imbued with evil motives from their very beginning? I hope that most of my readers will prefer the first alternative, and agree that lying is not primitive, but has to be learned. That, however, is a topic for another conversation.

In another ingenious example, Wittgenstein asks why we follow the direction of a pointing finger, and do not instead look from fingertip to wrist.[7] Is this a matter of convention? Or an accident of human development? A contingency? I think that the answer to these questions is clearly that pointing is an activity rooted in primitive reactions. Again, think of an infant: it will learn gradually to co-ordinate its eyes to focus on, say a foot. And on its hands and their ability to touch and eventually to grasp things, like a foot. It is out of these primitive gestures, I should say, that the idea emerges that a grasping gesture might be seen as pointing, as a short-hand for reaching and grasping. We would have to be quite differently constructed for over the-shoulder-pointing to have been a natural development for human beings. So I have given some illustrations of the 'firstness' of primitive reactions, of their being early stages in the natural development of concepts like pointing and smiling and pretending. And Winch has argued also for the priority of relatively primitive reactions as being prerequisites for our development of concepts like cause, and humanity.

A FUNDAMENTAL OBJECTION: MANICHAEISM

I think that Winch begins his paper thinking of primitive reactions as a source of moral concepts ('humanity', 'insincerity'), as well as non-moral ones ('cause'). So he seems to begin with the idea that there might be common foundations to moral concepts after all. They just are not where the anthropologist might have looked for them. Consider what he writes on p. 4/95 of "Unity":

> When I say in this regard, "we" behave in this way, I obviously mean that such reactions are characteristically human .... It is also most important that I, as well as any one of you, be in a position to assert that with such confidence .... That hangs together with the fact that each of us expects similar reactions from people whom we meet for

[7] See L. Wittgenstein, *Philosophical Investigations* §185, and cf. §85.

> the first time. I would, for example, be very surprised if I were to meet someone who did *not* react with gestures of disgust to a heap of rotting meat; and you would be too!

This idea, that human beings in general should have similar primitive reactions, sounds suspiciously like the very cultural universals that Prof. Schnädelbach proposed as starting points for ethics. They are not found among human needs, although they do seem to be empirically observable. They are, however, not mere generalizations from empirical observations, but seem to be known ahead of time (in a way, *a priori*) by all of us. They seem to be foundations of our concept acquisition, and to be needed for our moral judgement. Now Winch raises his objection. It is one that had been in the air in the 1980s. D. Z. Phillips had proposed the objection to him, and an ingenious, recent discussion of it can be found in a paper by David Cockburn.[8]

The objection is raised with the Manichaeism introduced on p. 7/97. The third-century religion founded by the Persian, Mani, was widespread, and notably adhered to by Augustine until he converted to Christianity. The Manichaean faith held what was considered a heresy by Christians, namely that the powers of Good and Evil are equal, independent and opposite forces. It is offered by Winch as an objection to the claim that primitive reactions are the foundation of our concept-acquisition, and that they are the foundation especially of ethical concepts, like 'sincerity', and 'humanity', and of our hesitation in the presence of other humans as a form of recognizing their power to refuse our moral demands. The objection is that what we might think of as evil reactions, insincerity, inhumanity, and having no regard for the view-points of others, are reactions just as primitive as the good ones that Winch has proffered as fundamental. Evil is as foundational as Good. Primitive reactions, it seems, cannot be the foundation of ethics, for they give rise to wrongdoing as much as to doing good.

Winch seems to dismiss Manichaeism as a merely theological doctrine. He does accept, however, that there are natural reactions which contradict the idea that universal ethical norms can be derived from them. Here he offers a remarkable phrase, "the question of the ethical equivalence of the Good and the Evil" (7/97). The Manichaeans believed in the equivalence of the Good and the Evil as metaphysical forces, but the ethical was all on the side of the Good. Why does Winch speak of their *ethical* equivalence?

[8] David Cockburn, "In the Beginning was the Deed."

He wants "to look at this matter in the light of a remarkable passage in Plato's *Gorgias*" (7/98).

SOCRATIC PARADOX

This passage is one of Plato's key presentations of the Socratic paradox, that all people, regardless of what they claim to believe about themselves, will be motivated by what they understand to be good; the particular form of the idea, in this debate with Polus and Callicles, is that everyone believes that to do wrong is worse than to be wronged. We may think that Winch endorses this as a reassertion of the primacy of primitive reactions in the development of morality. Our primitive reaction is to do what we understand to be good. At least some primitive reactions do have precedence; they make it possible to have a concept, and that is a prerequisite for negating it. Kant understood this, when he argued that unless promise-keeping is the norm, the practice of promising would be unintelligible. And only when promise-keeping is established can the breaking of promises become a possibility. Thus, for other instances, speaking with meaning precedes scepticism, and benign smiling precedes hypocrisy. And the Socrates example seems to insist that our natural inclination is to do what our understanding of a situation shows to be good.

Perhaps to our surprise, Winch does not fully embrace this conclusion. Instead of treating Socrates as the moral model, and Callicles as a model of immorality, he treats the two of them as having a moral debate. He accepts the objection that primitive human reactions range widely over the moral spectrum. Both Callicles and Socrates appeal to primitive reactions, though to different ones, "and the conflict between the two also belongs to the natural history of human beings" (9/100). I think that we should not be surprised that what Socrates maintains, that everyone really believes his doctrine, even though they claim that they do not, resembles in certain key ways Winch's insistence that 'we' need to have the confidence to maintain (even though we do not know much about "those people with whom each of you is confronted") that we all react in common ways when confronted by a blow to the foot, or another human in our space, or by a heap of rotting meat. But now Winch insists that common primitive reactions do not necessitate common value judgements. "[I]t is Polus who must decide," so that Socrates cannot simply have brought into the light what Polus (and everyone else!) always already believed" (8/98).

This is dialectically complex territory. It is not just that what is right is whatever Polus prefers or chooses. Even less is it merely the will of the stronger. For Polus's choosing involves working with certain common concepts, and acknowledging the shape of his conversational interaction with Socrates. But when Callicles protests that Socrates has simply duped Polus, Winch insists that the "inclinations to which Callicles appeals certainly belong to the natural history of humans; but so do the inclinations to which Socrates appeals;" and so does the conflict between them (9/100).

At this point we are in Winch's final paragraph, and a little abruptly he makes what I take to be his most indelible move. "[T]o the same natural history belongs the fact that we do not simply confront other human beings as observers. Sometimes we also make demands on one another" (9/100). These are the "demands" of Winch's title question. Sometimes the demands we make on others are not met. Sometimes we are not surprised by this. Sometimes we nonetheless insist that the demands ought to be met. "It is in this that, for someone who makes such demands, that is what constitutes the 'ethical unity' of humanity" (9/100). Here, then, is Winch's conclusion. It is not the 'factual / scientific' foundations which give unity to ethics. Not the "prerequisite" of his title. Rather, it is a natural tendency to make "demands" on others which gives the ethical 'form of life' its unity. We need to recognize that people make different, even incompatible demands of this sort. So, instead of it being a presupposition – that there must be a reason why we call all this ethics, or that there must be a common answer to the 'what is good?' question, – Winch just notes that we make moral demands on one another. That is also a primitive reaction, and it makes the development of a moral form of life possible – and it supports both agreement and disagreement in judgements within it. But we agree in form of life. That is the unity we can (must) allow; and it does not provide universality of moral judgements or principles. So the answer to the title's question is "demand."

Winch closes his essay by insisting that we should not expect to find a "scientific" foundation for ethics. Rather, "In my opinion it is sufficient to lay out the possibility of such an attitude" (9/100). What can we make of these claims? This should not simply be left to the reader. First of all, his claim that empirical sciences will not provide a foundation for morality does not suggest that empirical discoveries are irrelevant. It does suggest that they are not foundational, they will not *determine* our ethical demands, resolutions or conclusions. Our reactions and our choices will always make our ethical lives somewhat open-ended.

Second, the claim about laying out the possibilities is a claim about the limits of philosophy. One might be reminded of Winch's inaugural lecture in the Chair of Philosophy at King's College, London, in 1968. Two decades before the conference in Giessen, Winch wrote about the connection between a person and his or her actions. He criticises a standard view of that connection: the person is "a spectator of a world which includes his own body," and who needs guidance in the exercise of his will to initiate one action rather than another. "Morality is thought of by many philosophers as one such guide," he writes.[9] A person is not, however, connected to her actions as a spectator and manipulator. In Winch's own words (written before the wide-spread adoption of gender-neutral language):

> what a man makes of the possibilities he can comprehend is a matter of what man he is. This is revealed in the way he lives; it is revealed to him in his understanding of what he can and what he cannot attach importance to. But philosophy can no more show a man what he should attach importance to than geometry can show a man where he should stand.[10]

Philosophy, that is, has its limits. It can "make clear the distinction between corrupt and non-corrupt forms of the thought that something is worthy of admiration. But neither it, nor any other form of enquiry, can show what *is* worthy of admiration.[11]

Winch's leaving Britain for the United States has, of course, its deeper causes. The then Prime Minister of Britain's Conservative government, Margaret Thatcher, was intent on higher education reforms. Those reforms were intended to diminish the role of the humanities in higher education, and to strengthen the role of science and technology. This was, of course, an indirect insult to Winch's own work, which tried to show that the methods of the natural sciences could be counter-productive in the human sciences, and in the case of our present essay, that ethics could not be founded on empirical science. But the Thatcher reforms were also a direct threat to the livelihoods of the colleagues whom Winch had supported and recruited at King's. He resolved to strengthen the job security of his

---

[9] "Moral Integrity," in Winch, *Ethics and Action*, 171-72.

[10] "Moral Integrity," 191.

[11] *Ibid.*

colleagues by resigning his own chair, and moving to another country. He had that option; most of his colleagues did not. This was one of the important reasons for his decision to cross the Atlantic.

I claimed earlier that students whom Winch influenced have continued to pursue some of his themes, and to carry on his work into the new century. Perhaps I may mention as examples my Dalhousie colleague, Lynette Reid, who was the last doctoral student to complete her work with Winch, and Michael Campbell, who was supervised by Winch's close colleague at King's College London, Raymond Gaita. Campbell and Reid are working on Winch's *Nachlass*, and have just published a collection of papers on Winch's continued legacy, *Ethics, Society and Politics: Themes from the Philosophy of Peter Winch*. Winch's occupation with ideas as fundamental as the origin of concepts in primitive reactions, and the unity of ethics, thus exemplifies the great tradition in the realm of ideas of trans-Atlantic elective affinities.

WORKS CITED

Burns, Steven. "Something from Nothing: Peter Winch on philosophy and religion." *Religion nach der Religionskritik*. Ed. Ludwig Nagl. Vienna: Oldenbourg Verlag / Berlin: Akademie Verlag, 2003. 195-217.

—. "Peter Winch: 'Unity: Presupposition or Demand?'". [Translation of Winch, "Einheit".] *Philosophical Investigations* (online) (2020): 1-10.

Campbell, Michael, and Lynette Reid, eds. *Ethics, Society and Politics: Themes from the Philosophy of Peter Winch*. Heidelberg & New York: Springer, 2020.

Cockburn, David. "In the Beginning was the Deed." *Philosophical Investigations* 36.4 (October 2013): 303-319.

Monk, Ray. *Ludwig Wittgenstein: The Duty of Genius*. London: Vintage, 1990.

Weil, Simone. "The *Iliad* or the Poem of Force." *Simone Weil: an anthology*. Ed. Siân Miles. New York: Weidenfeld & Nicolson, 1986. 162-95.

Winch, Peter. *Studies in the Philosophy of Wittgenstein*. London: Routledge & Kegan Paul, 1969.

—. *Ethics and Action*. London: Routledge & Kegan Paul, 1972.

—. *Trying to Make Sense*. Oxford: Basil Blackwell, 1987.

—. "*Einheit: Voraussetzung oder Forderung?*" *Einheit und Vielheit:* Proceedings of the XIV German Congress of Philosophy – Giessen, 21-26 September,

1987. Ed. Odo Marquard. Hamburg: Felix Meiner Verlag, 1990. 94-100. ["Unity: Prerequisite or Demand?" Tr. Steven Burns. Unpublished, 2019.]

—. *Simone Weil: The Just Balance.* Cambridge: Cambridge UP, 1989.

Wittgenstein, Ludwig. *Philosophical Investigations.* Tr. G. E. M. Anscombe, P. M. S. Hacker and Joachim Schulte. Revised fourth edition. Oxford: Blackwell Publishing, 2009.

—. "Cause and Effect: Intuitive Awareness." *Ludwig Wittgenstein: Philosophical Occasions 1912-1951.* Translation Peter Winch. Eds. James Klagge and Alfred Nordmann. Indianapolis: Hackett Publishing, 1993. 371-426.

LIST OF CONTRIBUTORS

Carmen Birkle has taught at the universities of Mainz, Vienna, Bergen, Dijon, and at Columbia University in New York City. She has been full professor of North American Literary and Cultural Studies at Philipps-Universität Marburg. She was president, vice president, and executive director of the German Association for American Studies and currently is the association's international delegate. She is Dean of the Faculty of Foreign Languages, Literatures, and Cultures at Philipps-Universität (2017-20) and co-editor of the *American Studies Journal* (2017-). She is the author of two monographs, *Women's Stories of the Looking Glass* (1996) and *Migration—Miscegenation—Transculturation* (2004), and of numerous articles and (co-)editor of 14 volumes of essays and special issues of journals, among them *Literature and Medicine* (2009), *Communicating Disease* (2013), and *Waging Health* (2015). Her research focuses on gender, ethnicity, and popular culture. She is currently working on a monograph at the intersection of American literature, culture, and medicine, above all in the nineteenth and early twentieth centuries.

Stephen Burns studied philosophy in Canada, Australia, and London, England (D.Phil., 1970). He was Professor of Philosophy at Dalhousie University and cross-appointed as Professor of Contemporary Studies at the University of King's College (Halifax, Canada). He is now retired.
In 2001 he published a translation of *On Last Things,* a posthumous book by the 23-year-old Otto Weininger which Wittgenstein much admired. Other publications include: "Something from Nothing: Peter Winch on philosophy and religion," in *Religion nach der Religionskritik*, ed. L. Nagl, 2003; "The World Hued: Jarman and Wittgenstein on colour," in *Wittgenstein at the Movies: film and philosophy*, eds. B. Szabados and C. Stojanova, 2011; and "Politics in *Beautiful Losers*," in *Leonard Cohen and Philosophy*, ed. J. Holt, 2014.

Tibor Frank is professor emeritus of history at the Department of American Studies, director of the Ph.D. program in American Studies, and a former director of the School of English and American Studies at Eötvös Loránd University, Budapest, Hungary (1994-2001, 2006-2014). A Fulbright visiting professor at the University of California, Santa Barbara and UCLA (1988-1990), an NEH Distinguished Visiting Professor at the

University of Nevada-Reno (1990-1991), and a recurrent visiting professor at Columbia University, N.Y. (2001, 2007, 2010), he was recipient of the Humboldt Award (Humboldt Forschungspreis, Bonn, Germany, 2002). Fellow of the Royal Historical Society, London (2006), elected to the Hungarian Academy of Sciences (2013). Editor of *Századok*, journal of the Hungarian Historical Society (2015-) and President of the History Commission of the Hungarian Academy of Sciences (2017-), Chairman of the Board of the Hungarian-American Fulbright Commission (2010-11, 2017-). Co-teamleader of the Research Project of the *European Science Foundation* "Representations of the Past: The Writing of National Histories in Europe," published as *Disputed Territories and Shared Pasts: Overlapping National Histories in Modern Europe* (Tibor Frank and Frank Hadler, eds.) by Palgrave Macmillan in 2011, as part of the series *Writing the Nation*. Author of *Ethnicity, Propaganda, Myth-Making: Studies on Hungarian Connections to Britain and America 1848-1945* (Budapest: Akadémiai Kiadó, 1999); *From Habsburg Agent to Victorian Scholar: G. G. Zerffi 1820-1892* (New York: Columbia UP, 2000); *Picturing Austria-Hungary: The British Perception of the Habsburg Monarchy 1865—1870* (New York: Columbia UP, 2005); *Double Exile: Migrations of Jewish-Hungarian Professionals through Germany to the United States 1919–1945* (Oxford: Peter Lang, 2009).

Philipp Gassert has been teaching Contemporary and Transatlantic History at the University of Mannheim, Germany, since 2014. Previously he taught at the German Historical Institute in Washington, D.C., the University of Heidelberg, the University of Pennsylvania in Philadelphia, and the University of Augsburg. He has been Visiting Professor of History at the University of Haifa and Sir Peter Ustinov Visiting Professor at the University of Vienna. From 2011 onwards he served as Executive Director of the German Association for American Studies (GAAS) and is currently its President. He specializes in twentieth century transatlantic and international history, with Anti-Americanism, issues of Americanization and mutual perceptions of Europe, Germany, and the United States as one of the major themes of his research. Currently he is working on a global history of protest marches and street demonstrations. Most recent book publication: *Amerikas Kriege* [America's Wars] (Darmstadt: Theiss, 2014).

Christoph Irmscher is Provost Professor of English at Indiana University Bloomington and the George F. Getz Jr. Professor in the Wells Scholars Program, which he also directs. Among his many books are *The Poetics of Natural History* (1999), *Longfellow Redux* (2006), and *Louis Agassiz: Creator of American Science* (Houghton Miffllin Harcourt, 2013). His biography of the writer and activist Max Eastman was published by Yale University Press in 2017. His edition of Stephen Spender's juvenilia was published by Indiana University Press in 2019. He frequently writes book reviews for national publications, among them the *Wall Street Journal*. His homepage can be found at www.christophirmscher.com.

Ludwig Nagl is Ao. University Professor i. R. at the Department of Philosophy, University of Vienna. From 1970-71, in 1978 and 1980 he was Assistant Professor at Millersville University, Lancaster, Pennsylvania, USA. In 1987 and 1996 he was Visiting Scholar at Harvard University, USA. He was also Visiting Professor at the University of Jena, Germany, and at the University of St. Petersburg, Russian Federation. His research interests are focused on American Pragmatism, Philosophy of Religion, Philosophy and Psychoanalysis and Film Philosophy. His homepage can be found at http://homepage.univie.ac.at/ludwig.nagl/.

Gertrude Postl, Professor of Philosophy and Women's and Gender Studies at Suffolk County Community College, Selden, NY, USA. Research focus: feminist philosophy, especially the intersection between body, language, and representation (Luce Irigaray, Julia Kristeva, Hélène Cixous), and the political implications of the notions of reading/writing, author, and text (Roland Barthes and Jacques Derrida). Recent publications include: *Hélène Cixous. Das Lachen der Medusa zusammen mit aktuellen Beiträgen* (co-editor with Esther Hutfless and Elisabeth Schäfer, Vienna: Passagen, 2013); "Kristeva's Revolt, Illusion, and the Feminine," in: Maria Margaroni et al. (eds.), *Textual Layering: Contact, Historicity, Critique* (London: Lexington Books, 2017); entry on "Language, Writing, and Difference," *The Routledge Companion to Feminist Philosophy* (London, New York: Routledge: 2017); "The Origin That Never Was: The Loss of *Heimat* and New Beginnings," in: Kelly Oliver et al. (eds.), *Refugees Now. Rethinking Borders, Hospitality, and Citizenship* (London, New York: Rowman & Littlefield, 2019); "'Life as a Narrative.' Julia Kristeva and Hannah Arendt," in: Brigitte Buchhammer (ed.), *Freiheit — Gerechtigkeit — Liebe; Freedom — Justice — Love. Festschrift zum 75. Geburtstag von Herta Nagl-Docekal* (Vienna: LIT Verlag, 2019).

Waldemar Zacharasiewicz is Emeritus Professor of American Studies at the University of Vienna. He chairs the commission "The North Atlantic Triangle" of the Austrian Academy of Sciences. He is also a member of Academia Europaea and a Foreign Fellow of the Royal Society of Canada. His main research interests have been travel literature and imagology, the study of transatlantic migration, and the literatures of the American South and of Canada. He served as director of the Canadian Studies Center of the University of Vienna from 1998 to 2014. Among his publications are a monograph on the theory of climate in English literature and literary criticism (1977), two book-long studies on *Images of Germany in American Literature* (1998 and 2007), a collection of his essays entitled *Imagology Revisited* (2010), and a monograph on *Transatlantic Networks and the Perception and Representation of Vienna and Austria between the 1920s and 1950s* (2018). He has also edited or co-edited more than twenty collections of essays.

INDEX